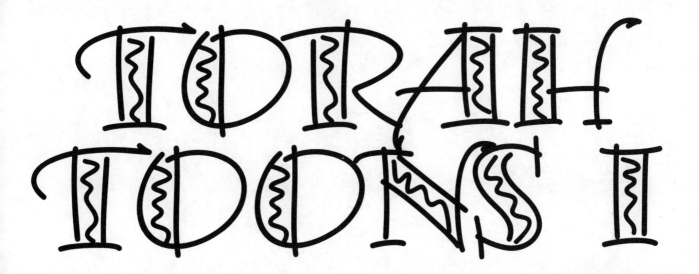

TORAH TOONS II

Joel Lurie Grishaver with C.J. Glass

Biblical Translations by Everett Fox

Torah Aura Productions

ISBN 0-933873-95-6

Published by Torah Aura Productions

TORAH AURA PRODUCTIONS · 4423 FRUITLAND AVENUE, LOS ANGELES, CA 90058
(800) 238-6724 · (323) 585-7312 · (323) 585-0327 FAX
Visit our web site at http://www.torahaura.com

MANUFACTURED IN THE UNITED STATES OF AMERICA

FROM JOEL

What's Up?

When I was a kid, I spent a lot of time doodling on the back of the handouts they always want you to take home from Hebrew School, and in the margins of old homework assignments. I did it often, because I just wanted to figure out how something might look, or because I wanted to create my version of something I read. Since then, I've done a reasonable job of growing up and the doodling has turned into a way of earning a living—drawing cartoons to go with the books I write.

A bunch of years ago, when I was teaching for the Los Angeles Hebrew High School, I began doing a thing called "Torah Toons." I'd draw these huge poster-sized drawings of some verses from the weekly Torah portion. We hung them on clotheslines during Shabbat morning services—so we could study Torah as a mob. The cartoons were a lot of fun and worked well. When we started TORAH AURA PRODUCTIONS, we turned *Torah Toons* into a filmstrip and a book. Now, more than ten years later, *Torah Toons* is on video and C.J. and I are redoing the book. Just like the first doodles I used to do in class, *Torah Toons* is my way of figuring out how things in the Torah might look, and a way of working out my own version of what the portions mean.

Have the same fun with it we did in producing it—draw your own doodles and figure out your own versions.

HAZAK, HAZAK V'NIT-HAZEIK

GRIS

P.S. I was at a CAJE Conference in Massachusetts. This hat (with glasses somewhere underneath the visor) walked up asked, "How come you made so many mistakes when you wrote *Torah Toons*?" I said, "Like what?" The hat reeled off a list. I said, "You're hired." Under the hat and behind the glasses was then (and still is) the inimitable (and then 12-year-old) C.J. Glass. For the past year, C.J. has "DJ-ed" *The Torah Toons Gazette* (a listserve devoted to talking Torah) and worked on this book. He is still finding lots of mistakes I have made—and pushing me to do some great learning to answer his irrepressible questions. He also makes me smile a lot.

We've added a whole layer to this new *Torah Toons*, which is questions from C.J. and others—and answers from C.J., me, and others, too. We did this because (1) there is a lot of interesting Torah stuff in these dialogues, and (2) we hope it gives you permission to ask you own Torah questions and find your own Torah truths. Real Torah study is not open your mouth and swallow. Real Torah study is open your heart and wonder.

DEDICATION

For C.J,. whose interest and dedication renewed the life of this book.

FROM C.J.

Attending the 1995 CAJE conference with my parents and cousin, I knew exactly what was on my agenda of things to do. First, I went to Joel Lurie Grishaver's lecture on Bar Mitzvah. Later, eager to ask about things in his book *Torah Toons*, I confronted the man who looks like the cartoons he draws (except he's much taller). Although my father always says he shooed me off (in the manner of W.C. Fields), I always took it that Joel was a nice but busy businessman. This is why he gave me his e-mail address. I wrote him and after we had "spoken" the whole deal started a week or two later. Great story of modern technology, huh?

Reading and interpreting the text is a lot like playing the role of detective. I have to look at everything carefully for a number of reasons (I also like listing things, as you'll later see). The first reason has to do with originality. The Torah was written long ago, but we read the same things each year. The purpose of doing this is to find more meaning in the text and to learn from it. Since there have been a WHOLE LOT of people interpreting the Torah before I came along, I have to try to find topics people haven't looked at yet. While trying to get ideas, one thought leads to another and I eventually get the "big picture."

It is a lot of fun writing sidebars. I feel like Rashi or the guys who comment for ArtScroll. I hope the readers have fun with them; I think they will. These sidebars are the building blocks and the chronicles of our writing and conversation.

I sent my comments to Joel (or his alter-ego Gris, sometimes) normally telling how one idea led to another. He responded, getting the conversation going, and putting it in the book. Of course, not ALL of the conversations we have go into the book. For obvious reasons certain things need to be edited out. All the good and important stuff is left in. New (and in my opinion, better) cartoons, midrashim on the text, Everett Fox translations, Hebrew text, and summaries of each *parashah* are also included in this new book as well. It is very exciting that when the secular new year comes around, a book I both contributed to and had fun working on will come out with it.

C.J.

DEDICATION

This book is dedicated to my parents and family. It is also dedicated to Jonathan Levine: teacher, hazzan, friend, and all around great guy.

INTRODUCTION

It is a Jewish thing to study part of the Torah every week.

The Torah has been broken into *parshiot* (a.k.a. *sidrot*) and by studying all these Torah portions you can go through the entire Torah in a year.

It is another Jewish thing to do Torah study as a social event. It is done by getting together with a good friend or a small group. Torah study is a combination of reading, discussing, guessing, remembering and finding your own understandings. Torah study is a combination of uncovering answers that other people who've studied the Torah have found, and finding your own meaning in the text. Torah study is a way of making friends, forming community and doing Jewish learning.

The Torah is like a library. It is made up of all kinds of Jewish literature. It is filled with stories, poems, pieces of history, collections of laws and other kinds of writings. It has everything from farming tips to blueprints for buildings. When we go through the Torah, we can learn about the history of the Jewish people, the stories which have been important to our people, Jewish laws and customs, and almost every important Jewish idea and value. Going through the Torah takes us on a guided tour of almost everything Jewish, because most Jewish things either have their origin in the Torah, or something in the Torah will remind us of them anyway.

The Torah has been studied by Jews in every age and in every Jewish community. Jews all over the world are exploring the same *sidrah* during the same week. When we study Torah, we not only look at our own opinions, but match them with the questions and answers of the generations who have gone through the text before us.

The study of *parshat ha-shavua* (the portion of the week) doesn't only teach us something about the Torah. It also introduces us to other Jews in different places and times, who have also looked for meaning in the same words.

The Rabbis were a group of Jewish scholars who lived in *Eretz Yisrael* and in Babylon between 200 B.C.E. and 500 C.E. They were the ones who wrote the Talmud, the Siddur, the Haggadah for Pesah and much of what is important to us as basic Jewish source material.

One of the ways they studied the Torah was through a way of learning called midrash. Midrash was a way of reading the Torah and fitting pieces together from all over the text—sort of weaving one story into another. Midrash was a way of writing down new stories between the lines of the stories found in the Torah. These stories still kept all the facts of the original Torah stories, but gave new answers and understandings. And, midrash was a way of inventing new stories, parables about kings and princes, stories which by comparison help us to understand the points the Torah is making.

This book is based on midrash. Every week, you will find a piece of Torah with some questions. First you'll work out your answers to these questions, and then you'll see how the midrash answered them. You'll learn—not only about the Torah, but about a whole new way of thinking called midrash.

1. Bereshit

Genesis 1:1-6:8

At the beginning of God's creating of the heavens and the earth (Genesis 1:1).

[1] BERESHIT starts things. **God creates the world**. This is done in seven days. On the first day, light is created. On the second day, there is a division of the waters. On the third day, dry land appears and plants begin to grow. On the fourth day, God creates the things which give light—the sun, moon and stars. On the fifth day, birds and fish are created. And, on the sixth day, God creates animals and people. On the seventh day, God rests.

[2] Next, the *sidrah* tells the story of what happens in **the Garden of Eden**. The garden is described, and Adam then Havva are created. The garden has two trees in its center—the Tree of Life and the Tree of Knowing Good from Evil. Havva and Adam are told not to eat from the trees in the center, but do so at the urging of the snake. God then sends Adam and Havva from the garden. Two angels guard the entrance.

[3] Once outside the garden, Adam and Havva have two sons: **Kayin and Hevel.** Kayin is a farmer and Hevel is a shepherd. Both offer sacrifices to God, but God accepts only Hevel's offering. The two then fight and Kayin kills Hevel. God then marks Kayin, who heads off into the sunset.

[4] The *sidrah* ends with a list of the **ten generations from Adam to Noah.** At the end of the list the Torah gives us a preview of COMING ATTRACTIONS: Tune in next week for the Flood.

C.J.'S COMMENTS:

[1]: In the introduction to this sidrah Gris says that, in *Parashat* Bereshit **"God creates the world. This is done in seven days."** He goes on to state what happened on each day. There is a contradiction: If on the seventh day God rested—God created the world in only six days? **[C.J.]**

I think that "the resting" is part of the creation. I think that Shabbat is part of the creation. The Torah says God does *"va-Yinafash"* on Shabbat. *Va-Yinafash* means re-souling—making the soul new. That means that Shabbat creates something new—a new soul—and therefore is part of the creation. **[GRIS]**

[2]: Gris says, **"The garden has a tree in the center—…"** shouldn't it be **"The garden has two trees in the center—…"** seeing as the Tree of Life and the Tree of Knowledge are two different trees. **[C.J.]**

I originally wrote the text the way C.J. criticized. I changed the book because of C.J.'s comment. He is right about the *p'shat* (literal meaning) of the text, but I think I am right about the *drash* (interpretation): In the midrash, "life" and "knowledge" are two sides of the same tree—not two trees. **[GRIS]**

[3]: I wonder how long it took before they ate the fruit. How did they know they had nothing to accomplish or no job to do? How did they know what they were missing ? **[Linda Kirsch]**

According to Pirke Avot and a bunch of midrashim, it was less than an hour. Adam and Hawa were created during the twilight of the first Shabbat. The fruit eating took place before Shabbat actually began. And the exile from the garden happened Saturday night

CONTINUED ON PAGE 180

YHWH	=	Yhwh, the Lord, ha-Shem (God's Name)
Adam	=	Human
Havva	=	Eve
Kayin	=	Cain
Hevel	=	Abel

THE BIBLICAL TEXT

Here is the way the Torah tells the story of Kayin and Hevel. As you read it, see if you can figure out these two things:

[a] Why did God rejected Kayin's offering?

[b] Why didn't God stop the fight between the two brothers?

Genesis 4:1-12

4.1 The human knew <u>H</u>avva his wife;
   she became pregnant and bore Kayin.
   She said:
   Kaniti/I have gotten
   a man, as has Y<small>HWH</small>!

2. She continued bearing—his brother, Hevel.
   Now Hevel became a shepherd of flocks, and Kayin became a worker of the soil.

3. It was, after the passing of days,
   that Kayin brought from the fruit of the soil, a gift to Y<small>HWH</small>,

4. and as for Hevel, he too brought—from the firstborn of his flock, from their fat-parts.
   Y<small>HWH</small> had regard for Hevel and his gift,

5. for Kayin and his gift he had no regard.
   Kayin became exceedingly upset and his face fell.

6. Y<small>HWH</small> said to Kayin:
   Why are you so upset? Why has your face fallen?

7. Is it not thus:
   If you intend good, bear-it-aloft,
   but if you do not intend good,
   at the entrance is sin, a crouching-demon,
   toward you his lust—
   but you can rule over him.

8. Kayin said to Hevel his brother...
   But then it was, when they were out in the field
   that Kayin rose up against Hevel his brother
   and killed him.

9. Y<small>HWH</small> said to Kayin:
   Where is Hevel your brother?
   He said:
   I do not know. Am I the watcher of my brother?

10. Now He said:
    What have you done! A sound—your brother's blood cries out to me from the soil!

11. And now,
    damned be you from the soil,
    which opened up its mouth to receive your brother's blood from your hand.

12. When you wish to work the soil
    it will not henceforth give its strength to you;
    wavering and wandering must you be on earth!

1 וְהָאָדָם יָדַע אֶת־חַוָּה אִשְׁתּוֹ וַתַּהַר וַתֵּלֶד אֶת־קַיִן וַתֹּאמֶר קָנִיתִי אִישׁ אֶת־יְהוָה:

2 וַתֹּסֶף לָלֶדֶת אֶת־אָחִיו אֶת־הָבֶל וַיְהִי־הֶבֶל רֹעֵה צֹאן וְקַיִן הָיָה עֹבֵד אֲדָמָה:

3 וַיְהִי מִקֵּץ יָמִים וַיָּבֵא קַיִן מִפְּרִי הָאֲדָמָה מִנְחָה לַיהוָה:

4 וְהֶבֶל הֵבִיא גַם־הוּא מִבְּכֹרוֹת צֹאנוֹ וּמֵחֶלְבֵהֶן וַיִּשַׁע יְהוָה אֶל־הֶבֶל וְאֶל־מִנְחָתוֹ:

5 וְאֶל־קַיִן וְאֶל־מִנְחָתוֹ לֹא שָׁעָה וַיִּחַר לְקַיִן מְאֹד וַיִּפְּלוּ פָּנָיו:

6 וַיֹּאמֶר יְהוָה אֶל־קָיִן לָמָּה חָרָה לָךְ וְלָמָּה נָפְלוּ פָנֶיךָ:

7 הֲלוֹא אִם־תֵּיטִיב שְׂאֵת וְאִם לֹא תֵיטִיב לַפֶּתַח חַטָּאת רֹבֵץ וְאֵלֶיךָ תְּשׁוּקָתוֹ וְאַתָּה תִּמְשָׁל־בּוֹ:

8 וַיֹּאמֶר קַיִן אֶל־הֶבֶל אָחִיו וַיְהִי בִּהְיוֹתָם בַּשָּׂדֶה וַיָּקָם קַיִן אֶל־הֶבֶל אָחִיו וַיַּהַרְגֵהוּ:

9 וַיֹּאמֶר יְהוָה אֶל־קַיִן אֵי הֶבֶל אָחִיךָ וַיֹּאמֶר לֹא יָדַעְתִּי הֲשֹׁמֵר אָחִי אָנֹכִי:

10 וַיֹּאמֶר מֶה עָשִׂיתָ קוֹל דְּמֵי אָחִיךָ צֹעֲקִים אֵלַי מִן־הָאֲדָמָה:

11 וְעַתָּה אָרוּר אָתָּה מִן־הָאֲדָמָה אֲשֶׁר פָּצְתָה אֶת־פִּיהָ לָקַחַת אֶת־דְּמֵי אָחִיךָ מִיָּדֶךָ:

12 כִּי תַעֲבֹד אֶת־הָאֲדָמָה לֹא־תֹסֵף תֵּת־כֹּחָהּ לָךְ נָע וָנָד תִּהְיֶה בָאָרֶץ:

QUESTIONS ABOUT THE BIBLICAL TEXT

a. The trouble seems to start when God accepted Hevel's offering and did not accept Kayin's offering. Why do you think that God accepted one and not the other?

b. Why do you think God started the fight between Kayin and Hevel and then didn't stop it?

_____

_____

_____

_____

_____

_____

THE MIDRASH ANSWERS THESE SAME QUESTIONS

MIDRASH 1.
[Bereshit Rabbah 22.8ff]

The slaying of Hevel by Kayin wasn't a total surprise. There had been warnings. The two brothers had been fighting since they were children. This is why Adam, their father, gave them different jobs. He made Kayin a farmer and Hevel a shepherd to keep them apart.

This fight started with their sacrifices. Adam told his sons that they had to offer the first of their new crops and herds to God. Hevel selected the best of his flocks, but Kayin just offered the vegetables which were left over after his own meal. That is why God rejected Kayin's offering.

Kayin blamed his brother and told him: "Let's separate and divide our possessions." He told Hevel: "Take the sheep and cattle and I will take the land." Hevel agreed. The next day Kayin told Hevel: "Get yourself and your herd off my land—I own the earth." Hevel answered: "Your clothing is made of wool—take it off—I own it." This is the way the fight began.

Separating the P'shat from the Drash

1. Underline/Highlight the parts of this midrash which are not told to us in the Torah.

2. What facts from the Torah does this midrash use?

Separating the Answers from the Messages

3. According to this midrash, what is the reason that *God rejected Kayin's offering?*

4. What other questions about the Torah text does this midrash answer?

5. If you were going to base a *D'var Torah* (sermon) on this midrash, what would be your major lesson?

_____

_____

_____

_____

_____

MIDRASH 2. [Ibid]

God in this story seems to be acting like a king who is watching two gladiators fight it out. If one of the gladiators is killed, it would be the king's fault, because he didn't stop the contest.

Kayin asked God: "Isn't it Your fault, because You did not command me to stop?" God answered: "I made you in My image with a brain and a soul. Were I to direct your every action—you would be just like a puppet. You have a will of your own and you are responsible for your own actions."

Separating the P'shat from the Drash

6. Underline/Highlight the parts of this midrash which can be found in the Torah. *Hint: It may not come from this story. Midrashim often use pieces of Torah from other places.*

Separating the Answers from the Messages

7. According to the midrash—Why didn't God stop Kayin?

8. If you were going to base a *D'var Torah* (sermon) on this midrash, what would be your major lesson?

_____

_____

_____

_____

_____

BEYOND THIS LESSON:

[1] Think about writing your own "Kayin and Hevel" midrash about one of these questions: (a) What arguments did Kayin use in his own defense at his trial? (b) What happened to Kayin's sacrifice, the one that God rejected? (c) Whom did Kayin marry? (d) Was the end of his life happy or sad? (e) The story ends "AT THAT TIME THEY FIRST CALLED OUT THE NAME OF YHWH." What is the story behind that verse? What happened?

[2] Some other midrashim on BERESHIT which might be fun to write: (a) Where did the light which God created on the first day come from—when the sun, moon, and stars don't make an appearance until day four? What happens to that light? (b) What did God do on the eighth day? (c) Where was Adam, when Havva and the snake were having their little meeting? Where was Mrs. Snake when her husband was hanging out with Havva?

[3] List some other questions about parashat BERESHIT that would be triggers for midrashim. Find your own question and then write your own midrashic answer.

2. Noah

Genesis 6:9-11:32

These are the begettings of Noah. Noah was a righteous, wholehearted man in his generation, in accord with God did Noah walk (Genesis 6:9).

[1] NOAH brings us to the flood. The world has been filled with violence. God decides to flush the world clean and save only one family. God picks Noah, the one righteous man, and orders him to **build an ark** to save himself, his family, and animal life from the coming flood. Noah follows the instructions.

The group spends **7 days** in the ark before the rain.
It then rains for **40 days and 40 nights**.
For **150 days** the water rises.

For **150 days** the water then goes down—
enough for the mountain tops to be seen.
Then Noah waits **40 more days** and sends out a raven to look for dry land.
7 days later Noah sends a dove to look for dry land and it returns with an olive branch. And **7 days** later the dove flies off for good.

[2] **Noah and company leave the ark.** They offer sacrifices to God and a rainbow appears as the sign of a covenant that God will never again destroy the earth. Noah also ferments the first grapes and gets drunk. This leads to some family problems.

[3] A group of people gather in the Shinar valley and try to **build a tower** up to the heavens. God stops them by making them speak many different languages. The place is called Bavel.

[4] At the end of the *sidrah*, we are given the **10 generations from Noa_h to Avram**.

The *sidrah* ends with a preview of COMING ATTRACTIONS: Tune in next week for the saga of Avram & Family.

C.J.'S COMMENTS:

[1]: Gris says that **God makes a rainbow appear as a sign that never again will the earth be destroyed** (not in those exact words). It is never mentioned that God will never wipe out humans again. Does not destroying the earth include not destroying people? Or can God get people and leave the land? **[C.J.]**

Maybe, to go along with the "God will never destroy earth/humans again", a twist about environmental stuff can go in (i.e., although God won't, humans can destroy the earth, as well as ourselves). **[Josh Barkin]**

[2]: Noa_h also ferments the first grapes and gets drunk. Yet, in a total flood, all plants would drown, except the ones that live on the ocean floor, maybe. Where did the grapes come from? **[C.J.]**

In the midrash according to Dr. Doolittle (I don't remember in which of his books you'll find it), a giant turtle saves some extra people and plants. Maybe they had the grapes. In the real midrash (*Genesis Rabbah* 36.4) we learn that Noa_h had grape plants on the ark (as well as other seed-bearing trees so that he could both feed the animals and start over). I have a vision of the vine strapped onto the back of the boat like the palm tree in *Mister Roberts* (an old black-and-white World War II movie). The "real" midrash also teaches that Satan was more than happy to help Noa_h plant the vines. Satan (God's inspector general angel) knew that wine is always a test. You add some wine and then see if you get holiness or addiction. In a really powerful midrash written by my friend Peter Pitzele, Noa_h gets drunk on purpose to numb out the pain of having to be the grave digger for the world. **[GRIS]**

NOTE: Do you know if Bavel is where we get the word babble from? **[C.J.]**

CONTINUED ON PAGE 181

Noa_h	= Noah
Bavel	= Babel
Avram	= Abram (to become Avraham/Abraham)
Nimrod	= Nimrod

THE BIBLICAL TEXT

Here is the way the Torah tells the story of the Tower of Bavel. As you read it, see if you can figure out:

[a] Why did God want to stop people from building a tower?

[b] What is wrong with a tower?

Genesis 11:1-9

11:1 Now all the earth was of one language and one set-of-words.

2. And it was when they migrated to the east that they found a valley in the land of Shinar and settled there.

3. They said, each man to his neighbor:
Come-now! Let us bake bricks and let us burn them well-burnt!
So for them brick-stone was like building-stone, and raw-bitumen was for them like red-mortar.

4. Now they said:
Come-now! Let us build ourselves a city and a tower, its top in the heavens,
and let us make ourselves a name,
lest we be scattered over the face of all the earth!

5. But Yhwh came down to look over the city and the tower that the humans were building.

6. Yhwh said:
Here, (they are) one people with one language for them all, and this is merely the first of their doings—
now there will be no barrier for them in all that they scheme to do!

7. Come-now! Let us go down and there let us baffle their language,
so that no man will understand the language of his neighbor.

8. So Yhwh scattered them from there over the face of all the earth,
and they had to stop building the city.

9. Therefore its name was called Bavel/Babble,
for there Yhwh baffled the language of all the earth-folk,
and from there, Yhwh scattered them over the face of all the earth.

1 וַיְהִי כָל־הָאָרֶץ שָׂפָה אֶחָת וּדְבָרִים אֲחָדִים:

2 וַיְהִי בְּנָסְעָם מִקֶּדֶם וַיִּמְצְאוּ בִקְעָה בְּאֶרֶץ שִׁנְעָר וַיֵּשְׁבוּ שָׁם:

3 וַיֹּאמְרוּ אִישׁ אֶל־רֵעֵהוּ הָבָה נִלְבְּנָה לְבֵנִים וְנִשְׂרְפָה לִשְׂרֵפָה וַתְּהִי לָהֶם הַלְּבֵנָה לְאָבֶן וְהַחֵמָר הָיָה לָהֶם לַחֹמֶר:

4 וַיֹּאמְרוּ הָבָה נִבְנֶה־לָּנוּ עִיר וּמִגְדָּל וְרֹאשׁוֹ בַשָּׁמַיִם וְנַעֲשֶׂה־לָּנוּ שֵׁם פֶּן־נָפוּץ עַל־פְּנֵי כָל־הָאָרֶץ:

5 וַיֵּרֶד יְהוָה לִרְאֹת אֶת־הָעִיר וְאֶת־הַמִּגְדָּל אֲשֶׁר בָּנוּ בְּנֵי הָאָדָם:

6 וַיֹּאמֶר יְהוָה הֵן עַם אֶחָד וְשָׂפָה אַחַת לְכֻלָּם וְזֶה הַחִלָּם לַעֲשׂוֹת וְעַתָּה לֹא־יִבָּצֵר מֵהֶם כֹּל אֲשֶׁר יָזְמוּ לַעֲשׂוֹת:

7 הָבָה נֵרְדָה וְנָבְלָה שָׁם שְׂפָתָם אֲשֶׁר לֹא יִשְׁמְעוּ אִישׁ שְׂפַת רֵעֵהוּ:

8 וַיָּפֶץ יְהוָה אֹתָם מִשָּׁם עַל־פְּנֵי כָל־הָאָרֶץ וַיַּחְדְּלוּ לִבְנֹת הָעִיר:

9 עַל־כֵּן קָרָא שְׁמָהּ בָּבֶל כִּי־שָׁם בָּלַל יְהוָה שְׂפַת כָּל־הָאָרֶץ וּמִשָּׁם הֱפִיצָם יְהוָה עַל־פְּנֵי כָל־הָאָרֶץ:

QUESTIONS ABOUT THE BIBLICAL TEXT

a. Why was God angry that the people were building a tower and a city? (Find a verse which serves as "proof" for your theory.)

b. Do you think that God was really afraid of what the people were doing?

c. Is the ending of this story "good" or "bad" for humanity? Why?

_____

_____

_____

_____

_____

THE MIDRASH ANSWERS THE SAME QUESTIONS:

MIDRASH 1
[Pirke D'Rabbi Eliezer 24]

The tower was built with careful planning. On the east side were steps which were used to go up and on the west side was a down staircase. The tower got to be so high that it took a year to reach the top. People cared more about the bricks than they did about other people. If a person fell—no one cried. But if a brick were dropped, the workmen cried and tore out their hair—because it would take a year to replace it.

People lived all their lives on the tower. They married, had children and raised them without setting foot on the ground. Nimrod, the leader of the group, cared only about finishing the tower. Often he would send up bricks but no food. Only when the workers refused to continue would the food be sent. If a worker fell off the tower, no one cared. But, if a brick fell, there was much wailing and mourning.

MIDRASH 2
[Talmud, Sanhedrin 109a]

Once the rabbis of the Talmud were studying this story: Rabbi Shila said, "The people after the flood said to each other, 'Come-now! Let us build ourselves a city and a tower, its top in the heavens.' (Genesis 11.7) They said, 'We can reach the sky and use axes to cut holes in the heavens. Then the waters will pour down. We can start our own flood, just the way that God did.'" Later, when the rabbis of the the Judean academies heard this explanation they broke out laughing, saying, "If this was their plan, it would have made much more sense to build the tower on a mountain and not in a valley."

Rabbi Jeremiah ben Elazar said: "The generation after the flood broke into three parties. All three wanted to build the tower. The first wanted to build a tower and then live at the top—in heaven. The second wanted to build a siege tower, and use it to fight a war with God and then take over heaven. The third wanted to build a tower and use it as the platform for their idols. God punished each group differently. God punished those who wanted to live in heaven by "SCATTERING THEM." (Genesis 11.9). God punished those who wanted to fight a war against heaven by turning them into apes, spirits, devils, and night-demons. God punished those who wanted to worship idols by "BAFFLING THE LANGUAGE OF ALL EARTH-FOLK." (Genesis 11.9). In each case the punishment fit the sin.

MIDRASH 3
[Umberto Cassuto, A Commentary on the Book of Genesis]

At the end of the No<u>a</u>h story, God tells people: "Bear fruit and be many and fill the earth and subdue it." (Genesis 1.28). This story begins with all humanity traveling together. It says: "And it was when they migrated to the east that they found a valley in the Land of Shinar and settled there." (Genesis 11.2). God wasn't punishing them for the city or the tower, but for violating the directions given in the post-flood blessing. They didn't "fill the earth."

MIDRASH 4
[Bereshit Rabbah 38.6]

Somehow, people thought that every 1,656 years the sky fell and the world was flooded. People said, "Come-now! Let us build ourselves a city and a tower, its top in the heavens." (Genesis 11.4). The tower will serve as a brace and keep the sky from falling and world from flooding. (*Hint: The first flood was 1,656 years after creation.*) After it, God has said: "Never again shall there be a Deluge, to bring the earth to ruin!" (Genesis 9:11).

Answer these three questions for all four midrashim.

Separating the P'shat from the Drash

1. What facts from the Torah does this midrash use? Overline/Underline the parts which come from other parts of the Bible.

Separating the Answers from the Messages

2. Each of these midrashim has its own answer to the question "What did the people do wrong in building the tower?" State each answer.

3. Each of these midrashim also conveys a message. Each midrash teaches its own way in which we are not supposed to be like the people who built the Tower. What is the lesson of each of these midrashim?

_____

_____

_____

BEYOND THIS LESSON:

[1] Think about writing your own "Tower of Bavel" midrash about one of these: (a) How did Nimrod (the midrashic leader of the Tower Gang) became the boss over all of humanity? (b) What it was like to be a worker on the Tower? (c) What it was it like to be a worker at the moment the languages were baffled? (d) What happened to the Tower?

[2] Some other NO<u>A</u>H midrashim which need writing: (a) What lesson did each color in the rainbow teach? (b) Where did No<u>a</u>h get the grapes to make the wine to become the first drunk? (c) How did each language group become a country?

[3] List some other questions about parashat NO<u>A</u>H that would be good triggers for midrashim. Find your own question and then write your own midrashic answer.

3. Lekh Lekha

Genesis 12:1-17:27

YHWH said to Avram: Go-you-forth from your land, from your kindred, from your father's house, to the land that I will let you see (Genesis 12:1).

[1] LEKH LEKHA begins Avram and Sarai's story. **Avram is called by God** and moves to the land of Canaan. He moves there with his wife Sarai/Sara, and with Lot, his brother's son.

[2] Shortly after their arrival in Canaan, a famine breaks out and **the family moves to Egypt**. There, Pharaoh falls in love with Sarai, and Avram tells him "She is my sister." When Pharaoh finds out the truth, he gives Avram a great deal of wealth. (This is the first "WIFE-SISTER" story.) The family then returns to Canaan. Hagar, Sarah's handmaid is one of the gifts of Pharaoh.

[3] There, **Avram and Lot split up**, with Lot moving near the city of Sedom. Next, **the war of the kings** breaks out; Lot is taken as a hostage. Avram enters the campaign, and rescues Lot. Melki-Tzedek, a local king, praises Avram and his God.

[4] God and Avram enter into an agreement—called **"The Covenant between the Pieces"**—and God promises to make

Avram's offspring as numerous as the stars in the sky. Meanwhile, Sarai gives her servant Hagar to Avram, and then regrets it. Hagar runs away from home and then returns with an angel's help. Then **Hagar gives birth to** Avram's first son, **Yishmael**.

[5] God and Avram then enter into a second covenant. This **covenant** involves **circumcision**. As part of the process Avram becomes Avraham and Sarai becomes Sara. The circumcision and the name change pave the way for next week's *sidrah*.

TUNE IN NEXT WEEK to find out if Avraham and Sara can do what Avram and Sarai could not—have a son.

C.J.'S COMMENTS

[1]: I don't understand the first WIFE-SISTER story. Then again, maybe I'm not supposed to. Why did Avram tell Pharaoh that Sarai was his sister? Was it to protect himself from a fight over Sarai? Why did Pharaoh pay Avram when he heard the news? Was it to pay for the trouble he had caused between Avram and Sarai's relationship? **[C.J.]**

I have some of my own personal answers for your questions… (midrashim, if you will)… Regarding the whole WIFE-SISTER controversy: I have two (count 'em) ideas on why Avram said Sarai was his sister and why Pharaoh gave Avram cash… [1] The money Pharaoh paid Avram was for some sort of prostitution. Perhaps it was the custom to pay off relatives of women (being that at the time they were merely considered objects) for the woman to (ya know…) with him. That would explain Avram saying he was the brother and not the husband (then Pharaoh would not be sleeping with a married woman)… It all kinda makes sense. [2] Perhaps Pharaoh wanted to do (ya know) with Sarai, but when Avram said that she was his sister, Pharaoh chose not to because it would be some kind of insult to him. Therefore Avram was protecting Sarai. I don't have any explanation for the whole payment thing in this one. I plan on looking at Rashi today or tomorrow to find out if he said anything… If so, I'll report back to you. **[Josh Barkin]**

DEAR JOSH, At least one of us is getting just

CONTINUED ON PAGE 182

Avram	= Abram
Avraham	= Abraham
Sarai	= Sarai
Sara	= Sarah
Lot	= Lot
Sedom	= Sedom
Negev	= South
Bet-El	= Beth El
Melki-Tzedek	= Melchizedek (King of Salem)
Hagar	= Hagar
Yishmael	= Ishmael

THE BIBLICAL TEXT

This is the way the Torah tells the story of the split between Avram and Lot. See if you can figure out the real reason for this split.

Genesis 13:1-12

13:1 Avram traveled up from Egypt, he and his wife and all that was his, and Lot with him, to the Negev.

2. And Avram was exceedingly heavily laden with livestock, with silver and with gold.

3. He went on his journeys from the Negev as far as Bet-El, as far as the place where his tent had been at the first, between Bet-El and Ai,

4. to the place of the slaughter-site that he had made there at the beginning.
   There Avram called out the name of YHWH.

5. Now also Lot, who had gone with Avram, had sheep and oxen and tents.

6. And the land could not support them, to settle together,
   for their property was so great that they were not able to settle together.

7. So there was a quarrel between the herdsman of Avram's livestock and the herdsmen of Lot's livestock.
   Now the Canaanite and the Perizzite were then settled in the land.

8. Avram said to Lot:
   Pray there be no quarreling between me and you, between my herdsmen and your herdsmen,
   for we are brother men!

9. Is not all the land before you?
   Pray part from me!
   If to the left, then I to the right,
   if to the right, then I to the left.

10. Lot lifted up his eyes and saw all the plain of the Jordan—
    how well-watered was it all, before YHWH brought ruin upon Sedom and Amora,
    like YHWH's garden, like the land of Egypt, as you come toward Tzo'ar.

11. So Lot chose for himself all the plain of the Jordan.
    Lot journeyed eastward, and they parted, each man from the other:

12. Avram settled in the land of Canaan, while Lot settled in the cities of the plain, pitching-his-tent near Sedom.

1 וַיַּעַל אַבְרָם מִמִּצְרַיִם הוּא וְאִשְׁתּוֹ וְכָל־אֲשֶׁר־לוֹ וְלוֹט עִמּוֹ הַנֶּגְבָּה:

2 וְאַבְרָם כָּבֵד מְאֹד בַּמִּקְנֶה בַּכֶּסֶף וּבַזָּהָב:

3 וַיֵּלֶךְ לְמַסָּעָיו מִנֶּגֶב וְעַד־בֵּית־אֵל עַד־הַמָּקוֹם אֲשֶׁר־הָיָה שָׁם אָהֳלֹה בַּתְּחִלָּה בֵּין בֵּית־אֵל וּבֵין הָעָי:

4 אֶל־מְקוֹם הַמִּזְבֵּחַ אֲשֶׁר־עָשָׂה שָׁם בָּרִאשֹׁנָה וַיִּקְרָא שָׁם אַבְרָם בְּשֵׁם יְהוָה:

5 וְגַם־לְלוֹט הַהֹלֵךְ אֶת־אַבְרָם הָיָה צֹאן־וּבָקָר וְאֹהָלִים:

6 וְלֹא־נָשָׂא אֹתָם הָאָרֶץ לָשֶׁבֶת יַחְדָּו כִּי־הָיָה רְכוּשָׁם רָב וְלֹא יָכְלוּ לָשֶׁבֶת יַחְדָּו:

7 וַיְהִי־רִיב בֵּין רֹעֵי מִקְנֵה־אַבְרָם וּבֵין רֹעֵי מִקְנֵה־לוֹט וְהַכְּנַעֲנִי וְהַפְּרִזִּי אָז יֹשֵׁב בָּאָרֶץ:

8 וַיֹּאמֶר אַבְרָם אֶל־לוֹט אַל־נָא תְהִי מְרִיבָה בֵּינִי וּבֵינֶיךָ וּבֵין רֹעַי וּבֵין רֹעֶיךָ כִּי־אֲנָשִׁים אַחִים אֲנָחְנוּ:

9 הֲלֹא כָל־הָאָרֶץ לְפָנֶיךָ הִפָּרֶד נָא מֵעָלָי אִם־הַשְּׂמֹאל וְאֵימִנָה וְאִם־הַיָּמִין וְאַשְׂמְאִילָה:

10 וַיִּשָּׂא־לוֹט אֶת־עֵינָיו וַיַּרְא אֶת־כָּל־כִּכַּר הַיַּרְדֵּן כִּי כֻלָּהּ מַשְׁקֶה לִפְנֵי שַׁחֵת יְהוָה אֶת־סְדֹם וְאֶת־עֲמֹרָה כְּגַן־יְהוָה כְּאֶרֶץ מִצְרַיִם בֹּאֲכָה צֹעַר:

11 וַיִּבְחַר־לוֹ לוֹט אֵת כָּל־כִּכַּר הַיַּרְדֵּן וַיִּסַּע לוֹט מִקֶּדֶם וַיִּפָּרְדוּ אִישׁ מֵעַל אָחִיו:

12 אַבְרָם יָשַׁב בְּאֶרֶץ־כְּנָעַן וְלוֹט יָשַׁב בְּעָרֵי הַכִּכָּר וַיֶּאֱהַל עַד־סְדֹם:

QUESTIONS ABOUT THE BIBLICAL TEXT

a. Why is there a quarrel between Avram's and Lot's shepherds?

b. When you read this story in the Torah, what is strange about the line: "NOW THE CANAANITE AND THE PERIZZITE WERE THEN SETTLED IN THE LAND."

_____

_____

_____

_____

_____

THE MIDRASH ANSWERS THE SAME QUESTION:

MIDRASH 1 [Genesis Rabbah 41.6]

When Avram and Lot returned from Egypt, both of them had lots of sheep and cattle. Avram was very careful about his sheep and cattle, so he had them muzzled so that they would not eat from fields where they weren't welcome. Avram knew that allowing his flocks and herds to graze on someone else's fields was a kind of robbery. Lot didn't muzzle his cattle and sheep. He felt that it was too much bother, and he didn't really worry about what his animals ate. Avram told Lot: "It is wrong not to muzzle your flocks and herds—it is the same thing as stealing. This land belongs to the Canaanites and the Perizzites. These fields are theirs." Lot said to Avram: "If it is stealing—we are stealing from ourselves. God has already promised this land to us—there is no problem in our using it now."

Avram decided not to continue the argument. For the sake of *shalom bayit* he let the matter drop. Later the argument was picked up by the herdsmen. Lot's herdsmen said: "You are really stupid—doing all that extra work—putting on and taking off muzzles." Avram's herdsmen answered: "You are no better than thieves." Lot's men answered: If we are stealing, it is only from ourselves. Avram has no son. After he is dead the land will belong to Lot. We are just using some of it now."

When Avram heard this, he decided that it was time to separate.

Separating the P'shat from the Drash

1. Underline/Highlight the parts of this midrash which are taken directly from the Torah?

Separating the Answers from the Messages

2. How does the midrash explain the fight between the herdsmen?

3. What is the message of this midrash? How does it want us to imitate Avram?

_____

_____

_____

_____

_____

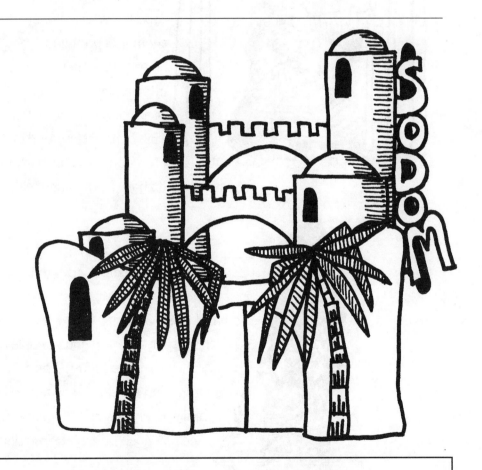

4. Va-Yera

Genesis 18:1-22:24

Now Y_{HWH} was seen by him by the oaks of Mamre as he was sitting at the entrance of his tent at the heat of the day (Genesis 18:1).

[1] VA-YERA brings Yitzhak into the picture. The action opens with **Avraham** sitting in the doorway of his tent and **seeing three strangers** appear. He welcomes them and provides hospitality. They then inform him that Sara will give birth to a son. **Sara laughs** at this conception, God shows up, and the son to be born is pre-named Yitzhak (from "laughter").

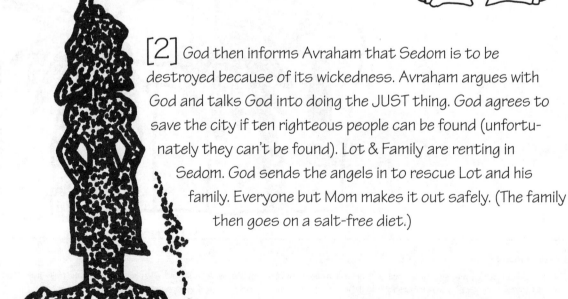

[2] God then informs Avraham that Sedom is to be destroyed because of its wickedness. Avraham argues with God and talks God into doing the JUST thing. God agrees to save the city if ten righteous people can be found (unfortunately they can't be found). Lot & Family are renting in Sedom. God sends the angels in to rescue Lot and his family. Everyone but Mom makes it out safely. (The family then goes on a salt-free diet.)

[3] Again it is time for there to be a famine in the land. This time **Avraham and Sara go to Avimelekh** in Gerar. There they replay the WIFE-SISTER routine. Finally, **Yitzhak is born** and a party is thrown. At this point tensions continue to mount between Sara and Hagar and God tells **Avraham to send Hagar and Yishmael off**. They leave, and are rescued in the wilderness by an angel.

[4] Next we have a little story about Avraham and Avimelekh **arguing over some wells.** The *sidrah* ends with the story of **The Binding of Yitzhak**—a test where God asks Avraham to sacrifice his son Yitzhak. At the last moment an angel stops Avraham from completing the command. And finally, blessing is given.

TUNE in NEXT WEEK to find out how what happens to the family next—after this test.

C.J.'S COMMENTS

[1]: *"Avraham was sitting in the doorway of his tent."* Tents don't have doors, Gris. They have flaps. **[C.J.]** You have that one pegged. **[GRIS]**

[2]: I asked myself, "Is it possible that the same angel that rescued Ishmael rescued Isaac?" Speaking of Ishmael, even though he ended up the father of Islam, he, too had a sort-of Bar Mitzvah. At 13 Ishmael was circumcised (happened last week in Lekh Lekha). **[C.J.]**

There is a midrashic tradition that angels only do one job then go out of business. For the Zohar, an angel is a packet of Divine energy—sort of like a "bot" program that is sent off to do a single task and then return the Divine Presence. (That is why three angels visit Avram and only two make it to Lot's house. The one who announces Isaac's birth has done his job and is gone.) That works against your interpretation. But, if we say that saving the two was one job—it works again. I like your image a lot. It suggests a great midrash. Maybe, if it is two angels, the two of them talk over their work over beers in the angels' bar. **[GRIS]**

I asked myself, why all of a sudden was Ishmael kicked out into the desert? Of course the first answer that came to mind was: What do you think? It's right there in the portion! It says that G-d made a great nation out of Ishmael. But I didn't think that that was the entire story. When I looked over the portion for about the fourth time, I realized that it was probably because Ishmael's leadership skills were not so good. I decided to put that idea aside, and continue on, so I did. Then came time for my speech to be done, and I had nothing. Mr. Finn (my Bar Mitzvah instructor) brought up the point that Ishmael was not a good leader, why didn't I work on that? So I did. Looking at the commentators (who say surprisingly little on my part of the portion) I saw the line "And Sarah

CONTINUED ON PAGE 183

Yitzhak = Isaac
Avimelekh = Abimelekh

THE BIBLICAL TEXT

At the beginning of this *sidrah*, Avraham welcomes three strangers. This is the way the Torah tells that story. As you read it, see if you can figure out why Avraham was sitting in front of his tent—almost looking for visitors.

Genesis 18:1-7

18:1 Now Yʜᴡʜ was seen by him by the oaks of Mamre
    as he was sitting at the entrance of his tent at the heat of the day.

2. He lifted up his eyes and saw:
    here, three men standing over against him.
    When he saw them, he ran to meet them from the entrance to his tent and bowed to the earth

3. and said:
    My lords,
    pray if I have found favor in your eyes,
    pray do not pass by your servant!

4. Pray let a little water be fetched, then wash your feet and recline under the tree;

5. let me fetch (you) a bit of bread, that you may refresh your hearts,
    then afterward you may pass on—
    for you have, after all, passed your servant's way!
    They said:
    Do thus, as you have spoken.

6. Avraham hastened into his tent to Sara and said:
    Make haste! Three measures of choice flour! Knead it, make bread-cakes!

7. Avraham ran to the oxen,
    he fetched a young ox, tender and fine, and gave it to a serving-lad, that he might
    hasten to make it ready;

8. then he fetched cream and milk and the young ox that he had made ready, and placed it before them.
    Now he stood over against them under the tree while they ate.

QUESTION ON THE BIBLICAL TEXT

a. Why was Avraham sitting in front of his tent?

_____

_____

_____

_____

_____

_____

1 וַיֵּרָא אֵלָיו יְהוָה בְּאֵלֹנֵי מַמְרֵא וְהוּא יֹשֵׁב פֶּתַח־הָאֹהֶל כְּחֹם הַיּוֹם:

2 וַיִּשָּׂא עֵינָיו וַיַּרְא וְהִנֵּה שְׁלֹשָׁה אֲנָשִׁים נִצָּבִים עָלָיו וַיַּרְא וַיָּרָץ לִקְרָאתָם

מִפֶּתַח הָאֹהֶל וַיִּשְׁתַּחוּ אָרְצָה:

3 וַיֹּאמַר אֲדֹנָי אִם־נָא מָצָאתִי חֵן בְּעֵינֶיךָ אַל־נָא תַעֲבֹר מֵעַל עַבְדֶּךָ:

4 יֻקַּח־נָא מְעַט־מַיִם וְרַחֲצוּ רַגְלֵיכֶם וְהִשָּׁעֲנוּ תַּחַת הָעֵץ:

5 וְאֶקְחָה פַת־לֶחֶם וְסַעֲדוּ לִבְּכֶם אַחַר תַּעֲבֹרוּ כִּי־עַל־כֵּן עֲבַרְתֶּם עַל־עַבְדְּכֶם וַיֹּאמְרוּ כֵּן תַּעֲשֶׂה

כַּאֲשֶׁר דִּבַּרְתָּ:

6 וַיְמַהֵר אַבְרָהָם הָאֹהֱלָה אֶל־שָׂרָה וַיֹּאמֶר מַהֲרִי שְׁלֹשׁ סְאִים קֶמַח סֹלֶת לוּשִׁי וַעֲשִׂי עֻגוֹת:

7 וְאֶל־הַבָּקָר רָץ אַבְרָהָם וַיִּקַּח בֶּן־בָּקָר רַךְ וָטוֹב וַיִּתֵּן אֶל־הַנַּעַר וַיְמַהֵר לַעֲשׂוֹת אֹתוֹ:

8 וַיִּקַּח חֶמְאָה וְחָלָב וּבֶן־הַבָּקָר אֲשֶׁר עָשָׂה וַיִּתֵּן לִפְנֵיהֶם וְהוּא־עֹמֵד עֲלֵיהֶם תַּחַת הָעֵץ וַיֹּאכֵלוּ:

THE MIDRASH ANSWERS THE SAME QUESTION

MIDRASH 1 [Bereshit Rabbah 54.6]

Avraham lived in Beer-sheva for many years. He planted a garden there—and made it with four gates—facing north, south, east and west—and he planted a vineyard. No matter which direction a visitor would come from, there was always a gate facing him. The visitor would come into the garden, sit in the grove and eat and drink until he was satisfied. The house of Avraham was always open to all—and they came daily to eat and drink there. If one was hungry—Avraham gave him food and drink. If one was naked—Avraham provided a choice of garments and even provided him with silver and gold.

Separating the P'shat from the Drash

1. Underline/Highlight the parts of this midrash which are taken directly from the Torah.

Separating the Answers from the Messages

2. How does this midrash explain why Avraham is sitting in the door of his tent?

3. What is the message of this midrash? (How are we supposed to imitate Avraham?)

_____

_____

_____

_____

_____

_____

MIDRASH 2
[Bereshit Rabbah 48.8-9]

The day after the circumcision of Avraham,* God bored a hole down to the core of the earth so that the heat might fill the earth and so that no strangers would be wandering the roads and so Avraham would be left undisturbed in his pain. But the lack of strangers upset Avraham and he sent Eliezer his servant to look for them. When the servant returned with no results, Avraham, in spite of his weakness and pain, prepared to go out and look for those in need of hospitality.

If you look at the last thing that happened in LEKH LEKHA you will notice that Avraham was circumcised. The rabbis connected it to the beginning of VA-YERA.

Separating the P'shat from the Drash

4. Underline/Highlight the parts of this midrash which are taken directly from the Torah.

Separating the Answers from the Messages

5. How does this midrash explain why Avraham is sitting in the door of his tent?

6. What is the message of this midrash? (Is it the same or different than the previous midrash?)

_____

_____

_____

_____

BEYOND THIS LESSON:

[1] Some other "hospitality" midrashrim that are waiting to be written are: (a) What other things did Avraham and Sara do to make these guests welcome? (b) There is a midrash which connects the calf eaten here to the choice of calves as one of only three animals sacrificed in the Temple. Write a story which explains this connection. (c) Rashi and C.J. are both bothered by the fact that Avraham serves milk and meat to his visitors. Write a midrash which solves the kashrut issue.

[2] Some other midrashim on Va-Yera which might be fun to write are: (a) A "Day in the Life of Lot's Family" in Sodom. (b) What happens to Lot and his daughters after the destruction of Sedom (they fade out of the Torah)? (c) The story of Hagar's childhood. (d) What happened when Ishmael and Isaac played together?

[3] Find your own question and then write your own midrashic answer.

5. <u>H</u>ayyei Sara

Genesis 23:1-25:18

Now Sara's life was one hundred years and twenty years and seven years (thus) the years of Sara's life (Genesis 23:1).

[1] <u>H</u>AYYEI SARA means the life of Sara and this is the *sidrah* in which **Sara dies.** In this *sidrah*, Avraham goes into a long series of business negotiations with Efron the Hittite. He **buys the cave of the Makhpela** which is used for the burial of all of the patriarchs and matriarchs except Ra<u>h</u>el. Sara is buried in the cave.

C.J.'S COMMENTS [BY JOSH BARKIN]

[1]: I thought I'd take a bit of initiative and write a few thoughts about Hayyei Sara… The biggest item that hit me was the way in which the servant (Eliezer) chose a wife for Yitzhak. Can this be applied to a more "modern" situation?

I looked at some *drashim* (or is it *drashot*, or can I just be ignorant and say *drashes*?), i.e. Rashi, Rambam, Ramban, and anything else in the book my school gave me, and I couldn't find anything on the subject; at least not a question like "Is that a suitable way to find a wife?" I just saw things like "It was wise of Eliezer to choose Rivkah as a suitable wife." No "Why?"

So, here's my take on the situation… No, we can't use Eliezer's criteria in choosing Rivkah (in choosing friends, or boy-girl friends/husbands-wives). We can't just walk up to everyone at Starbucks (I guess it's the modern day equivalent of the well) and ask them to do a good deed, choosing the first one who does it. I have to say, that in my own humble (well maybe humble) opinion, the Torah is pretty far off on this one. I think the Torah (or its writer(s)) don't want us to use this as an example. Eliezer acted out of desperation, and got lucky (or at least Yitzhak did). There wasn't a large number of women to choose from… Eliezer chose one he thought was right. [**Josh Barkin**]

I think you are completely WRONG here! It wasn't luck—it was God. The servant asks God "to do the right thing" (*tzedakah*) by his master Avraham—and in return he picks the woman who does *tzedakah*. In other words Rivkah is both chosen by God and God-like. But the truth is, if we are smart, we do pick

CONTINUED ON PAGE 183

[2] Avraham sends his servant back to the land of Aram-of-Two-Rivers, to Nahor's town, to find a wife for Yitzhak. There, at the well **he meets Rivka**, the daughter of Betuel—a distant relative of Avraham. He brings her back to Canaan and she and Yitzhak fall instantly in love. Yitzhak brings her into his mother's tent and the two begin their married life.

[3] Meanwhile Avraham remarries and has a few more children. At the end of the *sidrah* he dies, and is **buried** in the cave of the Makhpela **by Yitzhak and Yishmael.**

Efron	= Ephron
Makhpela	= Makhpela
Nahor	= Nahor
Aram-of-Two-Rivers	= Aram-naharaim
Rivka	= Rebekah
Betuel	= Bethuel
Rahel	= Rahel

THE BIBLICAL TEXT

In this *sidrah* it is made clear that Rivka is the right wife for Yitzhak. As you read these sections from the Torah:

[a] Find the conditions Eliezer sets for finding the right woman.

[b] Decide what makes these conditions the right ones for finding Yitzhak's wife.

[c] See if you can figure out why Yitzhak feels that Rivka is the right woman.

Genesis 24:10-20

10. The servant took ten camels from his lord's camels and went, all kinds of good-things from his lord in his hand.
    He arose and went to Aram-of-Two-Rivers, to Nahor's town.

11. He had the camels kneel outside the town at the water well
    at setting time, at the time when the water-drawers go out,

12. and said:
    YHWH, God of my lord Avraham,
    pray let it happen today for me, and deal faithfully with my lord Avraham!

13. Here, I have stationed myself by the water spring as the women of the town go out to draw water.

14. May it be
    that the maiden to whom I say: Pray lower your pitcher that I may drink,
    and she says: Drink, and I will also give your camels to drink—
    let her be the one that you have decided on for your servant, for Yitzhak,
    by means of her may I know that you have dealt faithfully with my lord.

15. And it was: Not yet had he finished speaking, when here, Rivka came out,
    —she had been born to Betuel, son of Milca, wife of Nahor, brother of Avraham—
    her pitcher on her shoulder.

16. The maiden was exceedingly beautiful to look at,
    a virgin—no man had known her.
    Going down to the spring, she filled her pitcher and came up again.

17. The servant ran to meet her and said:
    Pray let me sip a little water from your pitcher!

18. She said:
    Drink, my lord!
    And in haste she let down her pitcher on her arm and gave him to drink.

19. When she had finished giving him to drink, she said:
    I will also draw water for your camels, until they have finished drinking.

20. In haste she emptied her pitcher into the drinking-trough,
    then she ran to the well again to draw,
    and drew for all his camels.

Genesis 24: 62-67

62. Now Yitzhak had come from where you come to the Well of the Living-One Who-Sees-Me—for he had settled in the Negev.

63. And Yitzhak went out to stroll in the field around the turning of sunset.
    He lifted up his eyes and saw: here, camels coming!

64. Rivka lifted up her eyes and saw Yitzhak;
    she got down from the camel and said to the servant:
    Who is the man over there that is walking in the field to meet us?
    The servant said:
    That is my lord.
    She took a veil and covered herself.
65. Now the servant recounted to Yitzhak all the things that he had done.
66. Yitzhak brought her into the tent of Sara his mother,
    he took Rivka and she became his wife, and he loved her.
    Thus was Yitzhak comforted after his mother.

10 וַיִּקַּח הָעֶבֶד עֲשָׂרָה גְמַלִּים מִגְּמַלֵּי אֲדֹנָיו וַיֵּלֶךְ וְכָל־טוּב אֲדֹנָיו בְּיָדוֹ וַיָּקָם וַיֵּלֶךְ אֶל־אֲרַם נַהֲרַיִם אֶל־עִיר נָחוֹר:

11 וַיַּבְרֵךְ הַגְּמַלִּים מִחוּץ לָעִיר אֶל־בְּאֵר הַמָּיִם לְעֵת עֶרֶב לְעֵת צֵאת הַשֹּׁאֲבֹת:

12 וַיֹּאמַר יְהוָה אֱלֹהֵי אֲדֹנִי אַבְרָהָם הַקְרֵה־נָא לְפָנַי הַיּוֹם וַעֲשֵׂה־חֶסֶד עִם אֲדֹנִי אַבְרָהָם:

13 הִנֵּה אָנֹכִי נִצָּב עַל־עֵין הַמָּיִם וּבְנוֹת אַנְשֵׁי הָעִיר יֹצְאֹת לִשְׁאֹב מָיִם:

14 וְהָיָה הַנַּעֲרָ אֲשֶׁר אֹמַר אֵלֶיהָ הַטִּי־נָא כַדֵּךְ וְאֶשְׁתֶּה וְאָמְרָה שְׁתֵה וְגַם־גְּמַלֶּיךָ אַשְׁקֶה אֹתָהּ הֹכַחְתָּ לְעַבְדְּךָ לְיִצְחָק וּבָהּ אֵדַע כִּי־עָשִׂיתָ חֶסֶד עִם־אֲדֹנִי:

15 וַיְהִי־הוּא טֶרֶם כִּלָּה לְדַבֵּר וְהִנֵּה רִבְקָה יֹצֵאת אֲשֶׁר יֻלְּדָה לִבְתוּאֵל בֶּן־מִלְכָּה אֵשֶׁת נָחוֹר אֲחִי אַבְרָהָם וְכַדָּהּ עַל־שִׁכְמָהּ:

16 וְהַנַּעֲרָ טֹבַת מַרְאֶה מְאֹד בְּתוּלָה וְאִישׁ לֹא יְדָעָהּ וַתֵּרֶד הָעַיְנָה וַתְּמַלֵּא כַדָּהּ וַתָּעַל:

17 וַיָּרָץ הָעֶבֶד לִקְרָאתָהּ וַיֹּאמֶר הַגְמִיאִינִי נָא מְעַט־מַיִם מִכַּדֵּךְ:

18 וַתֹּאמֶר שְׁתֵה אֲדֹנִי וַתְּמַהֵר וַתֹּרֶד כַּדָּהּ עַל־יָדָהּ וַתַּשְׁקֵהוּ:

19 וַתְּכַל לְהַשְׁקֹתוֹ וַתֹּאמֶר גַּם לִגְמַלֶּיךָ אֶשְׁאָב עַד אִם־כִּלּוּ לִשְׁתֹּת:

20 וַתְּמַהֵר וַתְּעַר כַּדָּהּ אֶל־הַשֹּׁקֶת וַתָּרָץ עוֹד אֶל־הַבְּאֵר לִשְׁאֹב וַתִּשְׁאַב לְכָל־גְּמַלָּיו:

QUESTIONS ABOUT THE BIBLICAL TEXT

a. What was Eliezer's test for finding just the right wife?

b. Why was this a good test?

c. How did Yitzhak learn that Rivka was the right woman?

_____

_____

_____

_____

THE MIDRASH ANSWERS THESE SAME QUESTIONS

A MIDRASH
[Bereshit Rabbah 57.1]

When Eliezer saw a beautiful woman coming towards the well with a jug on her shoulder—he saw her stop beside a crying child. The child had cut his foot on a sharp stone. She washed and bound the wound and told the child: "Do not worry—it will soon heal." Then a half-blind woman had come to the well to draw water. Rivka helped her carry the full pitcher of water home. When Rivka returned, Eliezer asked her, "Pray let me sip a little water from your pitcher!"

ANOTHER MIDRASH [Bereshit Rabbah 60.7/Cf Zohar 1.113a]

Yitzhak took Rivka to the tent of his mother Sara, and she showed herself to be worthy to be the second mother of Yisrael, because she was very much like Sara. Rivka entered the tent and made Shabbat. She baked hallah. She kindled the Shabbat candles. She made sure that there was a *Ner Tamid*, an ever-burning light, in the tent. The cloud which was always over the tent during Sara's life was again visible. Again the tent glowed with light. When Sara was alive, she would light Shabbat candles and the glow would last the whole week, this too happened with Rivka. The blessing returned with Rivka and hovered over the tent.

Separating the P'shat from the Drash

1. Underline/Highlight the parts of each of these midrashim which are based on facts or statements in the Torah.

2. Mark the things in the second midrash which foreshadow things yet to come in the Torah.

Separating the Answers from the Messages

3. What does each of these midrashim cite as proof that Rivka was the right woman to be Yitzhak's wife?

4. The first midrash teaches that Rivka was a _____.

   The second midrash teaches that Rivka was like the _____.

5. What is the message of each of these midrashim? How does the first midrash want us to be like Rivka? How does the second midrash want us to be like Rivka?

_____

_____

_____

_____

_____

_____

BEYOND THIS LESSON:

[1] Think about writing your own "Rikva at the Well" midrash. (a) Write a midrash about how Rivka decided to be a kind person (was she like or unlike her parents in this)? (b) Nachmanides writes that the Temple was built to resemble Sarah's tent. Write the story of how this got decided. (c) Write your version of a letter home to her family that Rivka writes the week after the marriage.

[2] Some other midrashim that this *sidrah* invites are: (a) Adam and Havva, Avraham and Sara, Yitzhak and Rivka, Yaakov and Leah are all buried in the cave of Makhpela. What might they all talk about at night? (b) Yishmael and Yitzhak are together for the first time since childhood at their father's funeral. Write the story of their reunion.

[3] What other questions about parashat HAYYEI SARA would be good triggers for midrash? Find your own question and then write your own midrashic answer.

6. Toldot

Genesis 25:19-28:9

Now these are the begettings of Yitzhak, son of Avraham. Avraham begot Yitzhak (Genesis 25:19).

[1] TOLDOT is a *parashah* which is mainly concerned with the struggles between Yaakov and Esav. At the beginning of the *sidrah*, Rivka has a difficult time getting pregnant. Yitzhak prays to God and Rivka becomes pregnant with twins. **The two children struggle in her womb** causing her a great deal of pain. When the two are finally born, Esav is the firstborn, but Yaakov is grabbing at his heel.

[2] When the two children are grown, **Yaakov convinces Esav to sell him the birthright** of the firstborn for a bowl of lentils. Then the focus shifts to Yitzhak.

[3] Again there is a famine in the land, and Yitzhak brings the family down to Gerar to Avimelekh—again we have a WIFE-SISTER story. There is then a series of conflicts over the right to wells which Avraham had dug.

C.J.'S COMMENTS

[1]: In the overall look at the *parashah* you say that Yaakov is holding Esav's heel, but you don't mention that that is how he got the name Yaakov. **[C.J.]**

True. **[GRIS]**

[2]: I must tell you about a conversation my family had over Thanksgiving break. It was Friday night. My cousin Rebecca was rehearsing her *Davar Torah* for the family. She finally finished and my father made some comments. He said that in the Torah itself, it does not mention anywhere that Esav was a bad person. Only in the midrashim is Esav made to look evil. The whole truth is that if you pay attention to the text, you will notice that Yaakov was the one who wasn't such a great guy. He played tons of tricks, favored one son over his others, was not overall the greatest of the forefathers. Yishmael and Esav were made to look bad by the commentators, just to make Yitzhak and Yaakov look better.

Notice that Esav was very obedient. He only wanted to help his parents. He went out to hunt, not as it is said to kill someone, but because his father asked him to go out and hunt for him. When Esav later saw Yaakov hurt from his fight with the angel, he didn't hurt him. Esav was pretty much a good guy, he just became a scapegoat. He thought his parents would be pleased to know he was marrying locals. He might have married anyone else if he was told to do so beforehand. This is what my dad said and I agree. **[C.J.]**

C.J.—There are three things to talk about here in your really good version of the story. (And to deal with your comment.)

[a] Is midrash the real Torah (of which the written Torah is just the "Cliff Notes" for the longer version)—or is it a creative layer added to, but not really part of the "real Torah?" Or is it both? This is important here,

CONTINUED ON PAGE 184

[4] When Yitzhak feels old, he sends for Esav, and tells him to prepare for his blessing. Rivka overhears this and prepares Yaakov to steal the blessing. Yaakov fools his father and receives his brother's blessing. When Esav returns, Yitzhak gives him a blessing too.

[5] At the end of the Torah portion we are given two reasons why Yaakov should leave for the country of Aram. **Reason # 1:** Esav wants to kill him. **Reason # 2:** Rivka doesn't want him to marry a Canaanite woman.

Yehudit	= Judith
Ba'semat	= Basemath
country of Aram	= Paddan Aram

THE BIBLICAL TEXT

Here is the way the Torah tells the story of Yaakov stealing the blessing. Read it carefully. Decide if you think Yitzhak really believed he was blessing Esav.

Genesis 26:34—27:1-30

26:34. When Esav was forty years old, he took to wife Yehudit daughter of B'eri the Hittite and Ba'semat daughter of Elon the Hittite.

35. And they were a bitterness of spirit to Yitzhak and Rivka.

27:1. Now when Yitzhak was old and his eyes had become too dim for seeing,
he called Esav, his elder son, and said to him:
My son!
He said to him:
Here I am.

2. He said:
Now here, I have grown old, and do not know the day of my death.

3. So now, pray pick up your weapons—your hanging-quiver and your bow,
go out into the field and hunt me down some hunted-game,

4. and make me a delicacy, such as I love;
bring it to me, and I will eat it,
that I may give you my own blessing before I die.

5. Now Rivka was listening as Yitzhak spoke to Esav his son,
and so when Esav went off into the fields to hunt down hunted-game to bring (to him),

6. Rivka said to Yaakov her son, saying:
Here, I was listening as your father spoke to Esav your brother, saying:

7. Bring me some hunted-game and make me a delicacy, I will eat it
and give you blessing before Yhwh, before my death.

8. So now, my son, listen to my voice, to what I command you:

9. Pray go to the flock and take me two fine goat kids from there,
I will make them into a delicacy for your father, such as he loves;

10. you bring it to your father, and he will eat, so that he may give you blessing before his death.

11. Yaakov said to Rivka his mother:
Here, Esav my brother is a hairy man, and I am a smooth man,

12. perhaps my father will feel me—then I will be like a trickster in his eyes,
and I will bring a curse and not a blessing on myself!

13. His mother said to him:
Let your curse be on me, my son!
Only: listen to my voice and go, take them for me.

14. He went and took and brought them to his mother, and his mother made a delicacy, such as his father loved.

15. Rivka then took the garments of Esav, her elder son, the choicest ones that were with her in the house,

16. and clothed Yaakov, her younger son;
and with the skins of the goat kids, she clothed his hands and the smooth-parts of his neck.

17. Then she placed the delicacy and the bread she had made in the hand of Yaakov her son.

18. He came to his father and said:
Father!
He said:
Here I am. Which one are you, my son?

19. Yaakov said to his father:
I am Esav, your firstborn.
I have done as you spoke to me:
Pray arise, sit and eat from my hunted-game, that you may give me your own blessing.

20. Yitzhak said to his son:
How did you find it so hastily, my son?
He said: Indeed, Yhwh your God made it happen for me.

21. Yitzhak said to Yaakov:
Pray come closer, that I may feel you, my son,
whether you are really Esav or not.

22. Yaakov moved closer to Yitzhak his father.
He felt him and said:
The voice is Yaakov's voice, the hands are Esav's hands—
but he did not recognize him, for his hands were like the hands of Esav his brother, hairy.
Now he was about to bless him,

24. when he said:
Are you he, my son Esav?
He said:
I am.

25. So he said: Bring it close to me, and I will eat from the hunted-game of my son, in order that I may give you my own blessing.
He put it close to him and he ate,
he brought him wine and he drank.

26. Then Yitzhak his father said to him:
Pray come close and kiss me, my son.

27. He came close and he kissed him.
Now he smelled the smell of his garments and blessed him and said:
See, the smell of my son
is like the smell of a field
that YHWH has blessed.

34 וַיְהִי עֵשָׂו בֶּן־אַרְבָּעִים שָׁנָה וַיִּקַּח אִשָּׁה אֶת־יְהוּדִית בַּת־בְּאֵרִי הַחִתִּי וְאֶת־בָּשְׂמַת בַּת־אֵילֹן הַחִתִּי׃

35 וַתִּהְיֶיןָ מֹרַת רוּחַ לְיִצְחָק וּלְרִבְקָה׃

1 וַיְהִי כִּי־זָקֵן יִצְחָק וַתִּכְהֶיןָ עֵינָיו מֵרְאֹת וַיִּקְרָא אֶת־עֵשָׂו בְּנוֹ הַגָּדֹל וַיֹּאמֶר אֵלָיו בְּנִי וַיֹּאמֶר אֵלָיו הִנֵּנִי׃

2 וַיֹּאמֶר הִנֵּה־נָא זָקַנְתִּי לֹא יָדַעְתִּי יוֹם מוֹתִי׃

3 וְעַתָּה שָׂא־נָא כֵלֶיךָ תֶּלְיְךָ וְקַשְׁתֶּךָ וְצֵא הַשָּׂדֶה וְצוּדָה לִּי צֵידָה צָיִד׃

4 וַעֲשֵׂה־לִי מַטְעַמִּים כַּאֲשֶׁר אָהַבְתִּי וְהָבִיאָה לִּי וְאֹכֵלָה בַּעֲבוּר תְּבָרֶכְךָ נַפְשִׁי בְּטֶרֶם אָמוּת׃

5 וְרִבְקָה שֹׁמַעַת בְּדַבֵּר יִצְחָק אֶל־עֵשָׂו בְּנוֹ וַיֵּלֶךְ עֵשָׂו הַשָּׂדֶה לָצוּד צַיִד לְהָבִיא׃

6 וְרִבְקָה אָמְרָה אֶל־יַעֲקֹב בְּנָהּ לֵאמֹר הִנֵּה שָׁמַעְתִּי אֶת־אָבִיךָ מְדַבֵּר אֶל־עֵשָׂו אָחִיךָ לֵאמֹר׃

7 הָבִיאָה לִּי צַיִד וַעֲשֵׂה־לִי מַטְעַמִּים וְאֹכֵלָה וַאֲבָרֶכְכָה לִפְנֵי יְהוָה לִפְנֵי מוֹתִי׃

8 וְעַתָּה בְנִי שְׁמַע בְּקֹלִי לַאֲשֶׁר אֲנִי מְצַוָּה אֹתָךְ׃

9 לֶךְ־נָא אֶל־הַצֹּאן וְקַח־לִי מִשָּׁם שְׁנֵי גְּדָיֵי עִזִּים טֹבִים וְאֶעֱשֶׂה אֹתָם מַטְעַמִּים לְאָבִיךָ כַּאֲשֶׁר אָהֵב׃

10 וְהֵבֵאתָ לְאָבִיךָ וְאָכָל בַּעֲבֻר אֲשֶׁר יְבָרֶכְךָ לִפְנֵי מוֹתוֹ׃

11 וַיֹּאמֶר יַעֲקֹב אֶל־רִבְקָה אִמּוֹ הֵן עֵשָׂו אָחִי אִישׁ שָׂעִר וְאָנֹכִי אִישׁ חָלָק׃

QUESTIONS ABOUT THE BIBLICAL TEXT

a. Do you think Yaakov really fooled Yitzhak? Bring evidence from the text.

b. Was it okay for Yaakov to try to trick Yitzhak?

_____

_____

_____

THE MIDRASH ANSWERS THESE SAME QUESTIONS

A MIDRASH [Tanḥuma Toldot 8]

Esav's marriage with the daughters of Canaan upset Yitzḥak as much as it did Rivka. In fact he suffered more at the hands of his daughters-in-law. It was their fault that he lost his sight and became old so quickly. His daughters-in-law began to burn incense to their idols both day and night. Rivka was used to the smoke from the incense because she had been raised in a home which worshiped idols. Yitzḥak had never experienced this before. Both the smoke from the incense and the presence of the idols hurt him. It made him blind.

Separating the P'shat from the Drash

1. Highlight/Underline the "facts" and "quotations" from the Torah which this midrash uses.

2. How did the rabbis "learn this midrash" from the Torah? (Look back at the text and read closely.)

Separating the Answers from the Messages

3. According to this midrash, why did Yitzḥak go blind?

4. What does this midrash teach us about (1) Esav, and (2) why it was okay for Yaakov to steal the blessing?

5. This midrash suggests that Yitzḥak might have chosen to be fooled by Yaakov. State the reason for that possibility.

6. What is the moral of this midrash? What does it teach us about idolatry?

_____

_____

_____

_____

_____

_____

ANOTHER MIDRASH [Bereshit Rabbah 65.19-23]

Yaakov entered the tent and called to Yitzhak: "Father." Yitzhak answered: "Hineini (HERE I AM)." When his father asked: "WHICH ONE ARE YOU, MY SON? Yaakov carefully phrased his answer. He said: "IT IS I, ESAV, YOUR FIRST-BORN." This way he didn't lie, even though he did mislead his father. When Yitzhak asked how the work had been completed so quickly, Yaakov said: "INDEED, YHWH YOUR GOD MADE IT HAPPEN FOR ME." Yitzhak realized that this wasn't Esav because Esav would never have mentioned the name of God.

Separating the P'shat from the Drash

7. Highlight/Underline the "facts" and "quotations" from the Torah which this midrash uses.

8. Explain how and why this midrash changed the Torah without changing it.

Separating the Answers from the Messages

9. According to this midrash, did Yaakov fool Yitzhak?

11. According to this midrash, did Yaakov lie?

10. What are some morals (good sermon lessons) you can draw from this midrash?

_____

_____

_____

_____

_____

BEYOND THIS LESSON:

[1] Think about writing your own marriage midrash. (a) Why, when Esav was married, were his clothes still in his mother's tent? (b) What was Rivka doing while Yaakov was in with his father? (c) Did Esav find out that Rivka helped Yaakov? (d) Does their relationship change? Write the conversation between Rivka and Yitzhak when he tells her about his day (this day)? (e) What is the story of the goat chosen to make the arm and neck wig? (And whatever happens to them?)

[2] Other great needed midrashim for this *sidrah* include: (a) What did Esav and Yaakov fight about in the womb? (b) What was Yaakov's secret lentil recipe? (c) What was actually buried in the well that Yitzhak redug? (d) Yaakov knew his father was old and sick—what did he put in his farewell letter?

[3] What other questions about the *parashah* would be good triggers for midrash? Choose one and write it.

7. Va-Yetze

Genesis 28:10-32:3

Yaakov went out from Be'er-Sheva and went toward Haran (Genesis 28:10).

[1] VA-YETZE is the *parashah* where Yaakov comes into his own. It begins with his leaving home and stopping to sleep at Bet El. There he has **a dream of angels going up and down on a ladder.**

[2] When he arrives in Haran **he meets Rahel and falls in love.** He discovers that she is the daughter of Lavan his relative. He works out a deal to work for seven years in order to marry her. At the end of the seven years Lavan substitutes Lea, his older daughter. Yaakov is forced to work another seven years for Rahel.

[3] Then Lea and Ra<u>h</u>el enter into **the battle of the births.** They have a contest to see who could provide Yaakov with the most children. Lea gives birth to Re'uven, Levi and Yehuda. Then Rahel has her maid Bilha mother sons: Dan and Naftali. To stay in the competition, Lea enters her maid Zilpa who gives birth to Gad and Asher. Then Lea mothers Yissakhar, Zevulun and a daughter, Dina. Finally, Ra<u>h</u>el gives birth to Yosef.

[4] Finally Yaakov prepares to leave Lavan. They work out a deal on what part of the flock will be Yaakov's. With all his possessions in hand, he leaves with his family. However, he didn't know that Ra<u>h</u>el had stolen the family idols. **Lavan chases him to retrieve the idols but doesn't find them.** The *sidrah* ends with the family returning to Canaan and being met by angels. Meanwhile we have a cliff-hanger. How will the reunion with Esav go down?

C.J.'S COMMENT:

[1]: Not many comments on this portion. I think you should put the midrashim before the text in this portion (at least). It makes it easier to answer the question, how could Lavan fool Yaakov? **[C.J.]** No way CJ! That would be saying that this midrash is the only right understanding of the text. Besides, a little hard is good for you. **[GRIS]**

[2]: I like the first two intertwining midrashim. The last one is confusing. I don't get a lot of it, but the main problem is, how did Lea know of Yaakov's trickery? **[C.J.]** My assumption: He bragged about it (and often). That is the way of tricksters—to celebrate their successes. **[GRIS]**

Bet El	=	Beth El
Lea	=	Leah
Rahel	=	Rahel
Lavan	=	Laban
Bilhah	=	Bilha
Zilpa	=	Zilpah
Reuben	=	Re'uven
Simeon	=	Shim'on
Judah	=	Yehuda
Naphtali	=	Naftali
Issachar	=	Yissakhar
Zebulun	=	Zevulun

THE BIBLICAL TEXT

Here is the way the Torah describes the wedding in which Yaakov expected to marry Ra<u>h</u>el and wound up with Lea. As you read it, see if you can figure out how he was fooled:

Genesis 29: 15-30

29:15. Lavan said to Yaakov:

Just because you are my brother, should you serve me for nothing?

Tell me, what shall your wages be?

16. Now Lavan had two daugthers: the name of the elder was Lea, the name of the younger was Ra<u>h</u>el.

17. Lea's eyes were delicate, but Ra<u>h</u>el was fair of form and fair to look at.

18. And Yaakov fell in love with Ra<u>h</u>el.

He said:

I will serve you for seven years for Ra<u>h</u>el , your younger daughter.

19. Lavan said:

My giving her to you is better than my giving her to another man;

stay with me.

20. So Yaakov served seven years for Ra<u>h</u>el ,

yet they were in his eyes as but a few days, because of his love for her.

21. Then Yaakov said to Lavan:

Come-now (give me) my wife, for my days-of-labor have been fulfilled,

so that I may come in to her.

22. Lavan gathered all the people of the place together and made a drinking-feast.

23. Now in the evening

he took Lea his daughter and brought her to him,

and he came in to her.

24. Lavan also gave her Zilpa his maid,

for Lea his daughter as a maid.

25. Now in the morning:

here, she was Lea!

He said to Lavan:

What is this that you have done to me!

Was it not for Ra<u>h</u>el that I served you?

Why have you deceived me?

26. Lavan said:

Such is not done in our place, giving away the younger before the firstborn;

27. just fill out the bridal-week for this one, then we shall give you that one also,

for the service of which you will serve me for yet another seven years.

28. Yaakov did so—he fulfilled the bridal-week for this one,

and then he gave him Ra<u>h</u>el his daughter as a wife.

29. Lavan also gave Ra<u>h</u>el his daughter Bilha his maid,

for her as a maid.

30. So he came in to Ra<u>h</u>el also,

and he loved Ra<u>h</u>el also,

more than Lea.

Then he served him for yet another seven years.

15 וַיֹּאמֶר לָבָן לְיַעֲקֹב הֲכִי־אָחִי אַתָּה וַעֲבַדְתַּנִי חִנָּם הַגִּידָה לִּי מַה־מַּשְׂכֻּרְתֶּךָ:

16 וּלְלָבָן שְׁתֵּי בָנוֹת שֵׁם הַגְּדֹלָה לֵאָה וְשֵׁם הַקְּטַנָּה רָחֵל:

17 וְעֵינֵי לֵאָה רַכּוֹת וְרָחֵל הָיְתָה יְפַת־תֹּאַר וִיפַת מַרְאֶה:

18 וַיֶּאֱהַב יַעֲקֹב אֶת־רָחֵל וַיֹּאמֶר אֶעֱבָדְךָ שֶׁבַע שָׁנִים בְּרָחֵל בִּתְּךָ הַקְּטַנָּה:

19 וַיֹּאמֶר לָבָן טוֹב תִּתִּי אֹתָהּ לָךְ מִתִּתִּי אֹתָהּ לְאִישׁ אַחֵר שְׁבָה עִמָּדִי:

20 וַיַּעֲבֹד יַעֲקֹב בְּרָחֵל שֶׁבַע שָׁנִים וַיִּהְיוּ בְעֵינָיו כְּיָמִים אֲחָדִים בְּאַהֲבָתוֹ אֹתָהּ:

21 וַיֹּאמֶר יַעֲקֹב אֶל־לָבָן הָבָה אֶת־אִשְׁתִּי כִּי מָלְאוּ יָמָי וְאָבוֹאָה אֵלֶיהָ:

22 וַיֶּאֱסֹף לָבָן אֶת־כָּל־אַנְשֵׁי הַמָּקוֹם וַיַּעַשׂ מִשְׁתֶּה:

23 וַיְהִי בָעֶרֶב וַיִּקַּח אֶת־לֵאָה בִתּוֹ וַיָּבֵא אֹתָהּ אֵלָיו וַיָּבֹא אֵלֶיהָ:

24 וַיִּתֵּן לָבָן לָהּ אֶת־זִלְפָּה שִׁפְחָתוֹ לְלֵאָה בִתּוֹ שִׁפְחָה:

25 וַיְהִי בַבֹּקֶר וְהִנֵּה־הִוא לֵאָה וַיֹּאמֶר אֶל־לָבָן מַה־זֹּאת עָשִׂיתָ לִּי הֲלֹא בְרָחֵל עָבַדְתִּי עִמָּךְ וְלָמָּה רִמִּיתָנִי:

26 וַיֹּאמֶר לָבָן לֹא־יֵעָשֶׂה כֵן בִּמְקוֹמֵנוּ לָתֵת הַצְּעִירָה לִפְנֵי הַבְּכִירָה:

27 מַלֵּא שְׁבֻעַ זֹאת וְנִתְּנָה לְךָ גַּם־אֶת־זֹאת בַּעֲבֹדָה אֲשֶׁר תַּעֲבֹד עִמָּדִי עוֹד שֶׁבַע־שָׁנִים אֲחֵרוֹת:

28 וַיַּעַשׂ יַעֲקֹב כֵּן וַיְמַלֵּא שְׁבֻעַ זֹאת וַיִּתֶּן־לוֹ אֶת־רָחֵל בִּתּוֹ לוֹ לְאִשָּׁה:

29 וַיִּתֵּן לָבָן לְרָחֵל בִּתּוֹ אֶת־בִּלְהָה שִׁפְחָתוֹ לָהּ לְשִׁפְחָה:

30 וַיָּבֹא גַּם אֶל־רָחֵל וַיֶּאֱהַב גַּם־אֶת־רָחֵל מִלֵּאָה וַיַּעֲבֹד עִמּוֹ עוֹד שֶׁבַע־שָׁנִים אֲחֵרוֹת:

QUESTIONS ABOUT THE BIBLICAL TEXT

a. Why did Lavan want to fool Yaakov? Why was he so mean?

b. Couldn't Yaakov tell that he had the wrong woman?

_____

_____

_____

_____

_____

_____

THE MIDRASH ANSWERS THESE SAME QUESTIONS

A MIDRASH [Megillah 13a/ Gen. R. 70.19/71.18 /Lamentations Rabbah 1.23]

The Talmud records this conversation between Yaakov and Raḥel.

Yaakov: "Do you want to marry me?"

Raḥel: "Yes, but my father is a swindler and he will cheat you."

Yaakov: "Do not worry, I know how to trick him back."

Raḥel: "Is a Tzadik allowed to cheat?"

Yaakov: "If the person with whom he is dealing is a cheat—one is allowed to outwit him. But what fraud does he intend to pull?"

Raḥel: "I have an older sister. He will try to switch me for her."

Yaakov: "If so, let us now work out signs by which I will know that it is really you."

When Lea was about to be presented as the bride, Raḥel thought, "I can't allow my sister to be shamed in public."

She added: "If I have not been found worthy to build up the Jewish people, let my sister do it." She then told her the secret signs. She even hid under the wedding bed where the couple were staying and answered Yaakov's questions so that Lea's voice would not give her away.

The morning after the wedding night, Yaakov said to Lea: "You are the daughter of a deceiver and a cheat. Why did you answer "Hineini" everytime I called Raḥel's name?"

She answered him: "Is there a teacher who doesn't have a student? I learned from you. When your father called you Esav—you answered: 'Hineini.'"

Separating the P'shat from the Drash

1. Overline/Underline the parts of these midrashim which are taken directly from the Torah.

2. Which things are learned from other places in the Torah?

Separating the Answers from the Messages

3. How do these midrashim explain how Yaakov was fooled?

4. How do these midrashim explain why it was fair/just to fool Yaakov?

5. If you had to write a sermon which taught a major lesson from these midrashim, what would your message be?

_____

_____

_____

_____

_____

_____

_____

_____

_____

_____

_____

_____

_____

_____

BEYOND THIS LESSON:

[1] Think about writing your own "Yaakov's marriages" midrashim: (a) What were Lea and Raḥel like as children? What kind of sisters are they? (b) What did Raḥel say to Lavan when he told her about the plan to fool Yaakov? (c) What did Yaakov love about Lea? What did Yaakov love about Raḥel?

[2] Some other VA-YETZE midrashim which need writing are: (a) What happened to the rock that was Yaakov's pillow? (b) How did Yaakov live with four wives? How did the four women get along? (c) Why did Raḥel steal the family idols? (d) What happened to the idols after Raḥel fooled Lavan?

[3] What other questions about parashat VA-YETZE would be good triggers for midrashim? Why not write one?

8. Va-Yishla<u>h</u>

Genesis 32:4-36:43

Now Yaakov sent messengers on ahead of him to Esav his brother in the land of Se'ir, in the territory of Edom (Genesis 32:4).

[1] VA-YISHLA<u>H</u> begins on the eve of Yaakov's reunion with Esav. He sends messengers ahead to greet Esav; then he divides his people and herds into two camps. He also prepares gifts for Esav. On the night before the meeting, Yaakov is left alone, and **he wrestles with a man** (who might be an angel) until dawn is breaking. At the end of the struggle, Yaakov has a hurt leg, but the other wrestler is unable to escape. When he demands to be released, Yaakov demands a blessing. The wrestling partner changes his name from *Yaakov* ("the heel") to *Yisrael* ("the Godwrestler").

[2] In the morning, **Yaakov and Esav meet**, and an understanding of living in peace is worked out between the brothers. After the meeting Yaakov moves to Shekhem.

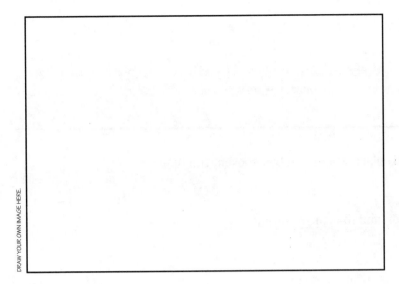

[3] There, **Dina,** his daughter with Lea, **gets involved with a man named Shekhem.** Simon and Levi destroy the city of Shekhem as a way of getting revenge.

[4] Next, Yaakov goes to Bet-El and builds an altar. There, God appears to him and blesses him: again changing his name from Yaakov to Yisrael. After the blessing, **Rahel dies in childbirth. Her son is named Binyamin,** and she is buried on the road.

The *sidrah* ends with an incident between Re'uven and Bilha, a listing of Yaakov's twelve sons, the death of Yitzhak (who is buried in the Cave of the Makhpela by Yaakov and Esav) and a long genealogy of Esav's children.

CJ'S COMMENTS

[1]: Yaakov divided his people and herds into two camps; was this so that if half of them died, the other half would live? **[C.J.]**

That's the logical answer, unless you can see the sheep cavalry surrounding Esav and catching him like Custer at the *Kerin ha-Gadol M'at* (The Little Big Horn). Another possibility is that it is a metaphor—showing how Yaakov is divided against himself (being of two minds how to deal with Esav). It certainly invites commentary. **[GRIS]**

[2]: I thought Yaakov's hip was hurt, not his leg (although: the hip bone's connected to the leg bone). Why all of a sudden, in the middle of the night, would ANY being, angel or man, go into a tent and wrestle with a total stranger? **[C.J.]**

C.J., you are getting picky again. The actual Hebrew *"gid-ha-nashe"* is a mystery. The modern implication (the vein we don't eat in cows) is a thigh vein. But there are midrashic indications that this is a "groin" injury—that the angel grabbed him in "his covenant!" This explanation is parallel to where the servant's hand went (before he took the camels to find the right girl for Yitzhak), and Avraham says, "Put your hand under my leg."

The fight is even more interesting. If this were a Robin Hood movie, it would have been some drunk guy (Will Scarlet or the like) and the two of them would have fought and then become fast friends. If this were a psychological thriller, it would have been some version of his alter-ego who confronted him. If this were a great Shakespearean effort, the angel would have been Esav in a costume who either (a) wanted to assassinate his brother in private to pre-empt the public meeting, or (b) lost on purpose to give

CONTINUED ON PAGE 185

Binyamin	= Benjamin
Bet El	= Beth El
Bet-Lehem	= Bethlehem
Dina	= Dinah
Yisrael	= Yisrael
Shekhem	= Shechem
Shimon	= Simeon

THE BIBLICAL TEXT

This is the way the Torah tells the story of Rahel's death and burial. Read it closely. See if you can figure out why Rahel was the only one of the patriarchs and matriarchs who wasn't buried in the cave of the Makhpela.

Genesis 35:15-20

35:15. And Yaakov called the name of the place where God had spoken with him:
Bet-El/House of God!

16. They departed from Bet-El.
But when there was still a stretch of land to come to Efrat,
Rahel began to give birth,
and she had a very hard birthing.

17. It was, when her birthing was at its hardest,
that the midwife said to her:
Do not be afraid,
for this one too is a son for you!

18. It was, as her life was slipping away
—for she was dying—
that she called his name: Ben-Oni/Son-of-My-Woe.
But his father called him: Binyamin/Son-of-the-Right-Hand.

19. So Rahel died;
she was buried along the way to Efrat—that is now Bet-Lehem.

20. Yaakov set up a standing-pillar over her burial place,
that is Rahel's burial pillar of today.

We find this passage later in the Bible. It speaks of the end of the Babylonian exile.

Jeremiah 31:15

31:15. Thus said YHWH:
"A voice is heard in Ramah,
lamentation and bitter weeping.
Rahel is weeping for her children;
she refuses to be comforted for her children who are gone."

16. Thus said YHWH:
Stop your voice from crying
your eyes from shedding tears.
Your labor is going to be rewarded"—said YHWH
"They shall return from the enemy's land.

17. There is hope in your future"—said YHWH
Your children shall return to their country." *

* This translation by Joel Lurie Grishaver

15 וַיִּקְרָא יַעֲקֹב אֶת־שֵׁם הַמָּקוֹם אֲשֶׁר דִּבֶּר אִתּוֹ שָׁם אֱלֹהִים בֵּית־אֵל:

16 וַיִּסְעוּ מִבֵּית אֵל וַיְהִי־עוֹד כִּבְרַת־הָאָרֶץ לָבוֹא אֶפְרָתָה וַתֵּלֶד רָחֵל וַתְּקַשׁ בְּלִדְתָּהּ:

17 וַיְהִי בְהַקְשֹׁתָהּ בְּלִדְתָּהּ וַתֹּאמֶר לָהּ הַמְיַלֶּדֶת אַל־תִּירְאִי כִּי־גַם־זֶה לָךְ בֵּן:

18 וַיְהִי בְּצֵאת נַפְשָׁהּ כִּי מֵתָה וַתִּקְרָא שְׁמוֹ בֶּן־אוֹנִי וְאָבִיו קָרָא־לוֹ בִנְיָמִין:

19 וַתָּמָת רָחֵל וַתִּקָּבֵר בְּדֶרֶךְ אֶפְרָתָה הִוא בֵּית לָחֶם:

20 וַיַּצֵּב יַעֲקֹב מַצֵּבָה עַל־קְבֻרָתָהּ הִוא מַצֶּבֶת קְבֻרַת־רָחֵל עַד־הַיּוֹם:

15 כֹּה אָמַר יְהוָה קוֹל בְּרָמָה נִשְׁמָע נְהִי בְּכִי תַמְרוּרִים רָחֵל מְבַכָּה עַל־בָּנֶיהָ מֵאֲנָה לְהִנָּחֵם עַל־בָּנֶיהָ כִּי אֵינֶנּוּ:

16 כֹּה אָמַר יְהוָה מִנְעִי קוֹלֵךְ מִבֶּכִי וְעֵינַיִךְ מִדִּמְעָה כִּי יֵשׁ שָׂכָר לִפְעֻלָּתֵךְ נְאֻם־יְהוָה וְשָׁבוּ מֵאֶרֶץ אוֹיֵב:

17 וְיֵשׁ־תִּקְוָה לְאַחֲרִיתֵךְ נְאֻם־יְהוָה וְשָׁבוּ בָנִים לִגְבוּלָם: ס

QUESTIONS ABOUT THE BIBLICAL TEXT

Why was Bet-Lehem the right place to bury Rahel? (Why not bring her to the Cave of the Makhpela which was less than two days' journey away?)

_____

_____

_____

_____

_____

_____

THE MIDRASH ANSWERS THESE SAME QUESTIONS

A MIDRASH [Bereshit Rabbah 84.2]

When Yosef was being carried into slavery, the caravan passed Ra<u>h</u>el's tomb. Yosef threw himself on the ground and cried: "Mother, Mother—your son has been taken from his father and sold into slavery." He hugged the stones and cried. A voice came up from inside the tomb: "I know of your suffering my son, but do not be afraid to go to Egypt. God is with you and will protect you."

In 586 BCE, the Babylonian empire captured and destroyed Jerusalem. They carried away much of the Jewish community. They took them to Babylonia as slaves. Jews spent about 70 years there. Then Persia conquered Babylon and those Jews who wished to return were allowed to do so. Many Jews, however, remained in Babylonia. The Babylonian exile ended around 430 B.C.E. when Ezra returned to Yisrael and began to organize things.

A MIDRASH [Pesikta Rabbati 3:69]

Before he died, Yaakov explained to Yosef: "I really wanted to bury your mother in the cave of the Makhpela, but God ordered her buried at the crossroads of Bet-Lehem. She was placed there to give comfort to B'nai Yisrael when they are carried away into the Babylonian exile. She will plead to God, God will listen to her prayers and B'nai Yisrael will indeed return from that exile." This indeed came to pass.

Separating the P'shat from the Drash

1. Overline/Underline the parts of these midrashim which can be found in the Bible. (Hint: look at Genesis 46.3-4.)

2. What information do the rabbis "lift" from other places in the Bible?

3. What story does this midrash add to the Torah?

Separating the Answers from the Messages

4. According to these midrashim, why was Rahel buried outside of Bet-Lehem?

5. What do these midrashim teach about Jewish history? Can you learn a lesson from the parallel stories of Rahel and Josef and Rahel and the Babylonian Exile?

6. What message about God can you draw from this midrash?

_____

_____

_____

_____

_____

_____

_____

BEYOND THIS LESSON:

[1] Think about writing your own midrashim about Rahel's death: (a) What did Yaakov tell Binyamin about his mother? (b) Why did Rahel give her son a sad name? (c) What did it mean to her? (d) What did Yosef say at his mother's funeral?

[2] Some other VAYISHLAH midrashim which need writing are: (a) What did the messengers say to each other before and after meeting with Esav? (b) Where did Yaakov's wrestling partner learn to fight? (c) What was Yitzhak's funeral like? What did Esav do? What did Yaakov do? (d) Did Yaakov inherit anything physical from Yitzhak?

[3] What other questions about parashaht VAYISHLAH would be good triggers for midrashim? Which one would you like to write?

9. Va-Yeshev

Genesis 37:1-40:23

Yaakov settled in the land of his father's sojournings, in the land of Canaan (Genesis 37:1).

[1] VAYESHEV is the *sidrah* which begins the Yosef story. It starts when Yosef is 17 years old. *(Remember that number, see if you can find where it pops up again.)* Yosef has a poor relationship with his brothers (except for Binyamin) because he is his father's favorite. Yisrael has had a special coat made for him. **Yosef has two dreams**, one about sheaves of grain and the other about the heavens. Both of these dreams show the whole family bowing down to Yosef. This makes his brothers hate him more.

[2] Now the plot thickens. Yisrael sends Yosef out to join his brothers in the field. **The brothers rip off his special coat and throw him in a pit.** They sell him to traders who eventually sell him to Potifar in Egypt.

Before the Yosef story continues, we have a short story about Yehuda, his son Onan, and a side adventure between Yehuda and Tamar.

[3]. Then, the *parashah* returns to Egypt where Yosef makes good in the house of Potifar, but is then thrown in prison when **Potifar's wife invents a story about Yosef seducing her**.

[4] In prison, he meets two of Pharaoh's servants, a cupbearer and a baker, both of whom Pharaoh had thrown in prison. Both of these men have dreams and Yosef interprets them. He tells the cupbearer that he will be returned to Pharaoh's service. He tells the baker that he will be executed. His interpretations come true.

The cliffhanger on this *sidrah* leaves Yosef in the dungeon. What will happen?

CJ'S COMMENTS

Once again I notice that the character whom we all see as the hero, is really contributing to the crime. You say that *"Yosef has a poor relationship with his brothers (except for Binyamin) because he was his father's favorite."* I'm not saying that Yisrael didn't contribute to the problem, he put in his share (as usual). No father should favor one child, even if they do they shouldn't show it. It will make Yosef's brothers mad enough that their father favors one over all. Now the younger brother must be rubbing it in. It's characteristic of the younger child (I would know, I am one) to annoy their older siblings before they mature. What does Yisrael care? He probably just likes the kid because he's Rahel's (and the youngest, like daddy dearest) even if he's annoying. Now maybe they were able to tolerate Yosef. But he just keeps getting himself into trouble. He would've been fine if he could have kept his dreams to himself! **[C.J.]**

I think it is really hard to keep dreams to one-self—especially when they feel like they come from God. But the idea that biblical characters are 3-D, that they have deep flaws along with virtues is an important idea. I think that is what you are getting at here. The problem feels like Yosef making too big a deal out of his dreams—and not noticing his brother's reactions.**[GRIS]**

Yosef	= Joseph
Potifar	= Potiphar
Cupbearer	= Butler
Yehudah	= Judah

THE BIBLICAL TEXT

This is the Torah's story of the cupbearer and the baker whom Yosef meets in prison. As you read the story, see if you can figure out why the cupbearer is saved and the baker is executed.

Genesis 40: 6-19

6. When Yosef came to them in the morning and saw them, here, they were dejected!

7. So he asked Pharaoh's officials who were with him in custody in the house of his lord, saying:
   Why are your faces in such ill-humor today?

8. They said to him:
   We have dreamt a dream, and there is no interpreter for it!
   Yosef said to them:
   Are not interpretations from God?
   Pray recount them to me!

9. The chief cupbearer recounted his dream to Yosef, he said to him:
   In my dream—
   here, a vine was in front of me,

10. and on the vine, three winding-tendrils,
    and just as it was budding, the blossom came up,
    (and) its clusters ripened into grapes.

11. Now Pharaoh's cup was in my hand—
    I picked the grapes
    and squeezed them into Pharaoh's cup
    and put the cup in Pharaoh's palm.

12. Yosef said to him:
    This is its interpretation:
    The three windings are three days—

13. in another three days
    Pharaoh will lift up your head,
    he will restore you to your position
    so that you will put Pharaoh's cup in his hand (once more),
    according to the former practice, when you were his cupbearer.

14. But keep me in mind with you, when it goes well for you,
    pray deal kindly with me and call me to mind to Pharaoh,
    so that you have me brought out of this house.

15. For I was stolen, yes, stolen from the land of the Hebrews,
    and here too I have done nothing
    that they should have put me in the pit.

16. Now when the chief baker saw that he had interpreted for good,
    he said to Yosef:
    I, too, in my dream—
    here, three baskets of white-bread were on my head,

17. and in the uppermost basket, all sorts of edibles for Pharaoh, baker's work,
    and birds were eating them from the basket, from off my head.

18. Yosef gave answer, he said:
    This is its intepretation:

The three baskets are three days—
19. in another three days
Pharaoh will lift up your head
from off you,
he will hang you on a tree,
and the birds will eat your flesh from off you...

6 וַיָּבֹא אֲלֵיהֶם יוֹסֵף בַּבֹּקֶר וַיַּרְא אֹתָם וְהִנָּם זֹעֲפִים:

7 וַיִּשְׁאַל אֶת־סְרִיסֵי פַרְעֹה אֲשֶׁר אִתּוֹ בְמִשְׁמַר בֵּית אֲדֹנָיו לֵאמֹר מַדּוּעַ פְּנֵיכֶם רָעִים הַיּוֹם:

8 וַיֹּאמְרוּ אֵלָיו חֲלוֹם חָלַמְנוּ וּפֹתֵר אֵין אֹתוֹ וַיֹּאמֶר אֲלֵהֶם יוֹסֵף הֲלוֹא לֵאלֹהִים פִּתְרֹנִים סַפְּרוּ־נָא לִי:

9 וַיְסַפֵּר שַׂר־הַמַּשְׁקִים אֶת־חֲלֹמוֹ לְיוֹסֵף וַיֹּאמֶר לוֹ בַּחֲלוֹמִי וְהִנֵּה־גֶפֶן לְפָנָי:

10 וּבַגֶּפֶן שְׁלֹשָׁה שָׂרִיגִם וְהִיא כְפֹרַחַת עָלְתָה נִצָּהּ הִבְשִׁילוּ אַשְׁכְּלֹתֶיהָ עֲנָבִים:

11 וְכוֹס פַּרְעֹה בְּיָדִי וָאֶקַּח אֶת־הָעֲנָבִים וָאֶשְׂחַט אֹתָם אֶל־כּוֹס פַּרְעֹה וָאֶתֵּן אֶת־הַכּוֹס עַל־כַּף פַּרְעֹה:

12 וַיֹּאמֶר לוֹ יוֹסֵף זֶה פִּתְרֹנוֹ שְׁלֹשֶׁת הַשָּׂרִגִים שְׁלֹשֶׁת יָמִים הֵם:

13 בְּעוֹד שְׁלֹשֶׁת יָמִים יִשָּׂא פַרְעֹה אֶת־רֹאשֶׁךָ וַהֲשִׁיבְךָ עַל־כַּנֶּךָ וְנָתַתָּ כוֹס־פַּרְעֹה בְּיָדוֹ כַּמִּשְׁפָּט הָרִאשׁוֹן אֲשֶׁר הָיִיתָ מַשְׁקֵהוּ:

14 כִּי אִם־זְכַרְתַּנִי אִתְּךָ כַּאֲשֶׁר יִיטַב לָךְ וְעָשִׂיתָ־נָּא עִמָּדִי חָסֶד וְהִזְכַּרְתַּנִי אֶל־פַּרְעֹה וְהוֹצֵאתַנִי מִן־הַבַּיִת הַזֶּה:

15 כִּי־גֻנֹּב גֻּנַּבְתִּי מֵאֶרֶץ הָעִבְרִים וְגַם־פֹּה לֹא־עָשִׂיתִי מְאוּמָה כִּי־שָׂמוּ אֹתִי בַּבּוֹר:

16 וַיַּרְא שַׂר־הָאֹפִים כִּי טוֹב פָּתָר וַיֹּאמֶר אֶל־יוֹסֵף אַף־אֲנִי בַּחֲלוֹמִי וְהִנֵּה שְׁלֹשָׁה סַלֵּי חֹרִי עַל־רֹאשִׁי:

17 וּבַסַּל הָעֶלְיוֹן מִכֹּל מַאֲכַל פַּרְעֹה מַעֲשֵׂה אֹפֶה וְהָעוֹף אֹכֵל אֹתָם מִן־הַסַּל מֵעַל רֹאשִׁי:

18 וַיַּעַן יוֹסֵף וַיֹּאמֶר זֶה פִּתְרֹנוֹ שְׁלֹשֶׁת הַסַּלִּים שְׁלֹשֶׁת יָמִים הֵם:

QUESTIONS ABOUT THE BIBLICAL TEXT

a. In your opinion, why was the cupbearer returned to power and the baker put to death?

b. Was this a fair verdict?

_____

_____

_____

_____

57

A MIDRASH [Midrash Lekakh Tov]

Both the cupbearer and the baker had seemed to do their jobs poorly. The cupbearer handed Pharaoh a goblet of wine with a fly in it. The baker had delivered bread with splinters of wood in it. Eventually Pharaoh's counselors figured out the difference. The cupbearer's error could have been an honest mistake—he could have poured the cup carefully, but a fly could have landed in it at the last moment. The baker's mistake was clearly a careless one. If he had sifted the flour carefully, there was no way for splinters to get in the bread. The baker was responsible for his negligence. Therefore, the baker was hanged while the cupbearer was returned to his duties.

Separating the P'shat from the Drash

1. Overline/Underline the parts of this midrash which are based on facts found in the biblical text.

2. How much of this story is added by the midrash?

Separating the Answers from the Messages

3. How does this midrash explain why the cupbearer was saved and the baker was killed?

4. What does this midrash teach us about Pharaoh's sense of justice?

5. What is the message being taught by this midrash? What sermon could you base on it?

_____
_____
_____
_____
_____
_____
_____
_____
_____
_____
_____
_____
_____
_____
_____

BEYOND THIS LESSON:

[1] Think about writing your own cupbearer and baker midrashim: a) What was the cupbearer's story—how did he get the job? (b) What was the baker's story—how did he get the job? (c) Why did Pharaoh put the cupbearer in jail? (d) Why did Pharaoh put the baker in jail? (d) What did the baker do with his last three days? (e) What did the cupbearer do during those same three days? (f) What did Yosef do during those same three days?

[2] Some other VA-YESHEV midrashim which need writing include: (a) Why did Yosef dream about grain—what did the grain mean? (b) Why did Yosef dream about stars—what did the stars mean? (c) Where did Yaakov get the coat he gave to Yosef? What is the coat's story? (d) Why did Potifar buy Yosef? (e) What did Potifar's wife see in him? (f) What happened to Potifar's marriage and house once Yosef was in jail?

[3] What other questions about parashat VA-YESHEV would be good triggers for midrash? Which one are you going to think about? Are you going to write it?

10. Miketz

Genesis 41:1-44:17

Now at the end of two years' time it was that Pharaoh dreamt: here, he was standing by the Nile-Stream (Genesis 41:1).

[1] MIKETZ continues the story of Yosef. (*When we left Yosef last sidrah, he was still in the dungeon.*) Meanwhile, Pharaoh has two dreams which no one can interpret. The cupbearer finally remembers Yosef, tells Pharoah about his ability to interpret dreams, and Yosef is taken from prison. He successfully explains that Pharaoh's two dreams warn that there will be seven years of plenty followed by seven years of famine.

[2] **Pharaoh puts Yosef in charge of preparing Egypt for the famine.** Yosef takes an Egyptian wife, Osnat, and she gives him two sons: Efraim and Manashe.

[3] Seven years of plenty come to pass, and now there is famine. Back in Canaan, **Yaakov sends ten of his sons** (but not Binyamin) **down to Egypt to buy food.** When they get to Egypt, they are forced to buy food from Yosef, a man whom they don't recognize. He gives them a hard time and even accuses them of being spies. In the end, he gives them sacks of grain, hides their money in the sacks, and warns them that if they return for more food, they must bring Binyamin with them.

CJ'S COMMENTS

[1]: In the first paragraph of the summary we see that Yosef marries an Egyptian, Osnat. This brings up a few questions: (1) Is intermarriage right? (2) Does this "bond" to Osnat symbolize a later "bondAGE" to the Egyptians? (3) Would Yaakov have approved of the intermarriage? **[C.J.]**

How do you know that she is a non-Jew? In the midrash, the rabbis (who are bothered by the same questions) weave a path which makes her the daughter of Dinah (who was seduced by Shekhem). This way she has a Jewish mother! This daughter, too, makes her way to Egypt as a slave. Joseph discovers her at just the right moment. It is very romantic—and not an intermarriage, either. **[GRIS]**

[2]: We have to wonder: Was Yosef only trying to lead his brothers along, to play a game with them? Or was he trying to get revenge on them for the wrongs they had done? **[C.J.]**

I don't see a difference between "playing a game" and "taking revenge." They both are pretty negative views of Yosef. When the rabbis want to picture him in a better light, they suggest that this was a "growth opportunity." The definition of *t'shuvah* (repentance) is "changing so much that when you have the chance to repeat the sin/crime and get away with it—you still don't do it." Yosef is testing his brothers. They have the chance to abandon another one of Ra<u>h</u>el's kids and profit in the end (more inheritance). That may be why he returned silver the first time in their bags, before he set up Binyamin with the cup. "Here is that crazy Egyptian who framed us— we couldn't help it Dad!" They pass the test with flying colors. I think the big question was: Was the test for Yosef to know that his brothers had changed—or for them to realize that they had become different people? **[GRIS]**

CONTINUED ON PAGE **185**

Efraim	= Ephraim
Manashe	= Manasseh

[4] The famine, of course, continues, and the brothers are forced to return to Egypt. After a long bargaining session, Yisrael agrees to let Binyamin go. When they arrive in Egypt, Yosef invites them to a banquet. (At one point he starts to cry, but hides his tears from the brothers.) This time, **he hides a goblet in Binyamin's pack.**

The *sidrah* ends with a new cliffhanger. Binyamin is caught, and with his fate still unknown. As Yosef did, he sits in the dungeon.

THE BIBLICAL TEXT

This is the Torah's explanation of how Yosef distributed grain during the famine. As you read it, see if you can figure out what principles he was using to distribute the grain.

Genesis 41:47-57

47. In the seven years of abundance the land produced in handfuls.
48. And he collected all kinds of provisions from those seven years that occurred in the land of Egypt, and placed provisions in the towns.
    The provisions from the fields of a town, surrounding it, he placed in it (as well).
49. So Yosef piled up grain like the sand of the sea, exceedingly much, until they had to stop counting, for it was uncountable.
53. There came to an end the seven years of abundance that had occurred in the land of Egypt,
54. and there started to come the seven years of famine, as Yosef had said.
    Famine occurred in all lands, but in all the land of Egypt there was bread.
55. But when all the land of Egypt felt the famine, and the people cried out to Pharaoh for bread, Pharaoh said to all the Egyptians:
    Go to Yosef, whatever he says to you, do!
56. Now the famine was over all the surface of the earth.
    Yosef opened up all (storehouses) in which there was (grain), and gave out rations to the Egyptians, since the famine was becoming stronger in the land of Egypt.
57. And all lands came to Egypt to buy rations, to Yosef,
    for the famine was strong in all lands.

47 וַתַּעַשׂ הָאָרֶץ בְּשֶׁבַע שְׁנֵי הַשָּׂבָע לִקְמָצִים:

48 וַיִּקְבֹּץ אֶת־כָּל־אֹכֶל שֶׁבַע שָׁנִים אֲשֶׁר הָיוּ בְּאֶרֶץ מִצְרַיִם וַיִּתֶּן־אֹכֶל בֶּעָרִים אֹכֶל שְׂדֵה־הָעִיר

אֲשֶׁר סְבִיבֹתֶיהָ נָתַן בְּתוֹכָהּ:

49 וַיִּצְבֹּר יוֹסֵף בָּר כְּחוֹל הַיָּם הַרְבֵּה מְאֹד עַד כִּי־חָדַל לִסְפֹּר כִּי־אֵין מִסְפָּר:

50 וּלְיוֹסֵף יֻלַּד שְׁנֵי בָנִים בְּטֶרֶם תָּבוֹא שְׁנַת הָרָעָב אֲשֶׁר יָלְדָה־לּוֹ אָסְנַת בַּת־פּוֹטִי פֶרַע כֹּהֵן אוֹן:

51 וַיִּקְרָא יוֹסֵף אֶת־שֵׁם הַבְּכוֹר מְנַשֶּׁה כִּי־נַשַּׁנִי אֱלֹהִים אֶת־כָּל־עֲמָלִי וְאֵת כָּל־בֵּית אָבִי:

52 וְאֵת שֵׁם הַשֵּׁנִי קָרָא אֶפְרָיִם כִּי־הִפְרַנִי אֱלֹהִים בְּאֶרֶץ עָנְיִי:

53 וַתִּכְלֶינָה שֶׁבַע שְׁנֵי הַשָּׂבָע אֲשֶׁר הָיָה בְּאֶרֶץ מִצְרָיִם:

QUESTIONS ABOUT THE BIBLICAL TEXT

a. How did Yosef distribute grain?

b. What was behind Yosef's plan for distributing grain?

_____

_____

_____

_____

_____

THE MIDRASH ANSWERS THESE SAME QUESTIONS

A MIDRASH [Bereshit Rabbah 91.4]

Yosef introduced these laws for the distribution of food:

*   Not only Egyptians but any hungry people can buy grain.

*   A master must come and buy the food for his household—
    a slave cannot be sent.

*   No one will be sold more grain than can be carried on one
    donkey.

*   Food may only be bought for personal use, anyone trying to
    make a profit will be put to death.

*   The names of anyone buying grain from outside of Egypt
    will be recorded.

The Egyptians thought that Yosef did all of this to be fair and just. Little did they know that he had other reasons. Yosef was sure that his brothers would need to come to Egypt to buy food and this would let him locate his father. Since slaves could not be sent, and since no one could carry more than one donkey's worth of grain, Yisrael had to send the whole family. In addition, the recording of names made sure that Yosef could locate them.

In the past, food was only distributed to Egyptians, Yosef saw to it that all who were hungry could buy food. This was an intentional act of ḥesed by Yosef.

Separating the P'shat from the Drash

1. What facts from the Torah does this midrash use? Underline/overline the parts which have biblical roots.

2. What elements does this midrash add to the story?

Separating the Answers from the Messages

3. In this midrash there are two different explanations of the rules which Yosef establishes. What are the two different explanations?

4. Each explanation gives Yosef a different motive. What are his two motivations?

5. What values can be learned from this midrash? In what ways do we want to imitate Yosef?

_____

_____

_____

_____

BEYOND THIS LESSON:

[1] Think about writing your own midrash on the famine: (a) What did Pharaoh eat every day during the famine? (b) How did other Egyptians treat Yosef during the seven years of plenty? Did this change during the seven years of famine? (c) What did Yosef tell his wife and children about his brothers and the rest of his family?

[2] Some other MIKETZ midrashim which need writing are: (a) What were some of the wrong interpretations of Pharaoh's dream that his wizards, fortune tellers, and advisors came up with? (b) Whatever happened to the nice jailer? (c) Did Yosef ever see Potifar or his wife again, now that he was an Egyptian big shot? (d) Why did Yosef choose a "cup" as the thing to put in Binyamin's sack?

[3] What other questions about parashat MIKETZ would be good triggers for midrash? What are you going to do about it?

11. Va-Yigash

Genesis 44:18-47:27

Now Yehuda came closer to him and said: Please, my lord, pray let your servant speak a word in the ears of my lord, and do not let your anger flare up against your servant, for you are like Pharaoh! (Genesis 44:18)

[1] VA-YIGASH brings us to the conclusion of the Yosef story. When last we left the brothers, Yosef was going to keep Binyamin for a slave (after framing him with a goblet). This *sidrah* opens as Yehuda pleads for Binyamin and even offers to remain in his place. **At this point Yosef begins to cry, and reveals himself to his brothers.**

[2] Pharaoh is informed that Yosef's brothers have come to Egypt and he welcomes them and the rest of the family in Egypt. The brothers return, **inform Yaakov that his son Yosef is still alive,** and Yaakov decides to go to Egypt.

DRAW YOUR OWN PICTURE

[3] **Yisrael offers sacrifices in Be'er-Sheva**, sees God in a vision, and then goes down to Egypt. They settle in the land of Goshen.

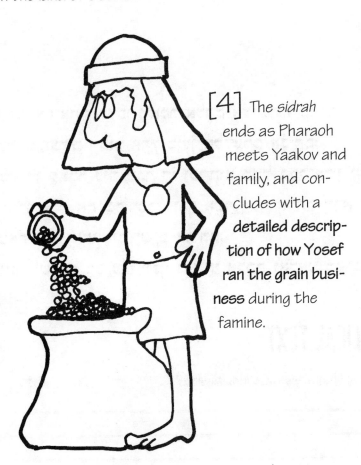

[4] The *sidrah* ends as Pharaoh meets Yaakov and family, and concludes with a **detailed description of how Yosef ran the grain business** during the famine.

CJ'S COMMENTS

[1]: Yosef might have sent his brothers away with no food had he really wanted to. They had been cruel to him, selling him off to a caravan. There were three things which made him decide to reveal himself. [1] Yosef hadn't seen his brothers in years, and although they had been cruel, he had missed them. [2] Yosef loved his father Yisrael very much, so he did not want his father to starve. [3] This was the immediate cause: Yehudah was once a mean person. He headed the idea of getting rid of Yosef. The Torah explains that Yehudah changed for the better. Yosef sees this when Yehudah offers to take Binyamin's place as prisoner. This makes Yosef happy enough to reveal himself. Do you realize now why we are called the Yehudim? **[C.J.]**

You got three choices here: [1] Get Even-Yosef, [2] Better-Safe-Than-Sorry-Yosef or [3] Sensitive-Yosef. [1] It is a *midah k'neged midah*—a measure for measure getting even. He was in jail—they have to think that one of them is in jail. etc. They made him suffer—he will make then suffer. [2] Yosef is checking his brothers out, making sure that it is safe to deal with them. If they take the bait and sacrifice Binyamin, they still don't have any sense of family with Raḥel's kids. [3] Yosef is giving them a chance to do *t'shuvah*. Remember, one of the indicators is when you have the chance to repeat a sin—and then don't. He gives them the chance to abandon another one of Raḥel's sons to prison in Egypt—and this time they don't do it. Any-which-way his dreams of the family bowing down to him come true. **[GRIS]**

[2]: Yisrael finally realized that Yosef was alive when he saw his wagons. He knew that since Yosef was a righteous man, being alive meant that he had to do good things, too. Sending the wagons for his father was something that Yosef would do out of kindness, so his father realized the truth. **[C.J.]**

Nice! **[GRIS]**

See you next *parashah*. **[C.J.]**

THE BIBLICAL TEXT

This passage tells how the brothers told their father Yisrael that Yosef was still alive. Read the text and see if you can figure out why he finally believes them.

Genesis 45:24-28

24. Then he (Yosef) sent his brothers off, and they went;
    he said to them:
    Do not be agitated on the journey!

25. They went up from Egypt and came to the land of Canaan, to
    Yaakov their father,

26. and they told him, saying:
    Yosef is still alive!
    Indeed, he is ruler of all the land of Egypt!
    His heart failed,
    for he did not believe them.

27. But when they spoke to him of Yosef's words which he had spoken to them,
    and when he saw the wagons that Yosef had sent to carry them down,
    their father Yaakov's spirit came to life.

28. Yisrael said:
    Enough!
    Yosef my son is still alive;
    I must go and see him before I die!

24 וַיְשַׁלַּח אֶת־אֶחָיו וַיֵּלֵכוּ וַיֹּאמֶר אֲלֵהֶם אַל־תִּרְגְּזוּ בַּדָּרֶךְ:

25 וַיַּעֲלוּ מִמִּצְרָיִם וַיָּבֹאוּ אֶרֶץ כְּנַעַן אֶל־יַעֲקֹב אֲבִיהֶם:

26 וַיַּגִּדוּ לוֹ לֵאמֹר עוֹד יוֹסֵף חַי וְכִי־הוּא מֹשֵׁל בְּכָל־אֶרֶץ מִצְרָיִם וַיָּפָג לִבּוֹ כִּי לֹא־הֶאֱמִין לָהֶם:

27 וַיְדַבְּרוּ אֵלָיו אֵת כָּל־דִּבְרֵי יוֹסֵף אֲשֶׁר דִּבֶּר אֲלֵהֶם וַיַּרְא אֶת־הָעֲגָלוֹת אֲשֶׁר־שָׁלַח יוֹסֵף
לָשֵׂאת אֹתוֹ וַתְּחִי רוּחַ יַעֲקֹב אֲבִיהֶם:

28 וַיֹּאמֶר יִשְׂרָאֵל רַב עוֹד־יוֹסֵף בְּנִי חָי אֵלְכָה וְאֶרְאֶנּוּ בְּטֶרֶם אָמוּת:

QUESTIONS ABOUT THE BIBLICAL TEXT

What do you think finally convinced Yisrael that Yosef was indeed alive?

_____

_____

_____

_____

THE MIDRASH ANSWERS THESE SAME QUESTIONS

A MIDRASH [Yalkut: Aleph 152, Gen R. 94.5, and other sources]

Yosef told his brothers to tell Yaakov the following: "When we left Egypt, Yosef insisted on escorting us, because the last halakhah you taught him was the law of escorting a guest." At first Yaakov did not believe the brothers, but when they told him all that Yosef had done, including his message about the halakhah—Yaakov finally believed them. He said: "YOSEF IS STILL ALIVE," but he also meant "YOSEF IS STILL A TZADIK,"

Yaakov was happier to find that his son was still a *tzadik* than he was to discover that he was like a king.

Separating the P'shat from the Drash

1. Underline/Overline the parts of this story which are also found in the Torah text.

Separating the Answers from the Messages

2. According to this midrash, what caused Yaakov to believe that Yosef was still alive?

3. What is the "sermon" found in this midrash?

_____

_____

_____

_____

_____

_____

_____

BEYOND THIS LESSON:

[1] **Think about writing your own "telling Yisrael" midrashim.** (a) Why didn't Yosef actually go to his father? (b) Why did his brothers not fight this time on the trail? Would they have fought on earlier journeys together? (c) What did Yaakov do at the moment he actually stepped or rode out of Canaan?

[2] **Some other VA-YIGASH midrashim which the text invites are:** (a) Why was Yehuda the one brother who spoke up? (b) When did Yosef tell Binyamin who he was? Did he make him sit in jail? (c) Why did Yisrael need to see God before he went to Egypt?

[3] **What other questions about parashat VA-YIGASH would be good triggers for midrash?**

12. Va-Ye<u>h</u>i

Genesis 47:28-50:26

And Yaakov lived in the land of Egypt for seventeen years. And the days of Yaakov, the years of his life, were seven years and a hundred and forty years (Genesis 47:28).

[1] VA-YE<u>H</u>I brings to an end the stories of Yosef and Yaakov. At the beginning of the *parashah*, Yaakov sends for Yosef and makes him swear that **Yosef will not bury him in Egypt**, but rather will have his body returned to the cave of the Makhpela in Canaan.

[2] Yaakov blesses Yosef's two **sons**: Ephraim and Manashe—blessing the younger in the place of the older. Then **Yaakov blesses each of the 12 sons**. These are now the 12 tribes of Yisrael.

CJ'S COMMENTS

[1]: I like the use of the number 17; more specifically that we were told to look where it would reappear when you summarized VA-YESHEV. It is interesting that Yosef was sent to Egypt at the age of 17 and Yaakov lived in Egypt for 17 years. **[C.J.]**

Sure, it is interesting. But what does it mean? Here is a very deep clue. Rashi looks at Genesis 37.2 (VA-YESHEV). Here it says: "THESE ARE THE BEGETTINGS OF YAAKOV. YOSEF, SEVENTEEN, USED TO TEND SHEEP." He notices that this is a change in pattern. Compare it with "AND THESE ARE THE BEGETTINGS OF ESAV—THAT IS EDOM. ESAV TOOK HIS WIVES FROM THE WOMEN OF CANAAN, ADA, DAUGHER OF ELON THE HITTITE, AND OHOLIVAMA DAUGHTER OF ANA...ADA BORE ELIFAZ TO ESAV..." (Gen 36.1-4). The normal pattern in a genealogy is to list the person's wives and then their children in birth order. But in this genealogy of Yaakov we skip straight to Yosef. Rashi says: Everything which happened to Yaakov happened to Yosef. Both were hated by brothers. Both had brothers who wanted to kill them, etc. (Look it up in Bereshit Rabbah.) The parallel seventeens is one of Rashi's clues. But for the deep secret, look at Genesis 41.31. After interpreting Pharaoh's dreams. Yosef says: "NOW AS FOR THE TWOFOLD REPETITION OF THE DREAM TO PHARAOH; IT MEANS THAT THE MATTER IS DETERMINED BY GOD." In other words, why do many things happen twice in the Torah? They do it to serve as a pair of kosher witnesses ('cause Jewish courts always need two witnesses) that God is really acting here. How many "two times" can you find in Genesis? What "thing" from God do they point to? **[GRIS]**

[2]: There is something I've been wondering about. Whenever you write the cave of the Makhpela I say to myself "I thought it was the cave of Makhpela, not the cave of THE Makhpela." Which one is correct? **[C.J.]**

The JPS translation that we used when I originally wrote *Torah Toons* calls it, "THE CAVE OF THE FIELD OF MACHPELAH." Everett Fox does the same thing (except he spells it Makhpela).

CONTINUED ON PAGE 185

[3] Yaakov dies after living 17 years in Egypt (*Remember the number 17?*) and Yosef fulfills his wishes, burying him in Canaan. After Yaakov's death, the brothers are fearful that Yosef will now take revenge—but he reassures them that all is forgiven.

[4] The *sidrah* ends (ending the book of BERESHIT) with Yosef's death. He is embalmed and buried in Egypt. Before his death, he makes **the Families-of-Yisrael swear to bring his bones up to Canaan from Egypt.**

Our cliffhanger for the next book—will the Jewish people survive the pressures of Egypt?

HAZAK HAZAK V'NITHAZEK

THE BIBLICAL TEXT

Just before Yaakov dies, he brings his sons together for a blessing. There seems to be something different about this blessing—different from other blessings we have seen. As you read this Torah text, see if you can figure out:

a. What is different about these blessings?

b. What is Yaakov trying to communicate?

Genesis 49: 1-12 and 27-28

1. Now Yaakov called his sons and said:
   Gather round, that I may tell you
   what will befall you in the aftertime of days.

2. Come together and hearken, sons of Yaakov,
   hearken to Yisrael your father.

3. Reuven,
   my firstborn, you,
   my might, first-fruit of my vigor!
   Surpassing in loftiness, surpassing in force!

4. Headlong like water—surpass no more!
   For when you mounted your father's bed,
   then you defiled it—he mounted the couch!

5. Shim'on and Levi,
   such brothers,
   wronging weapons are their ties-of-kinship!

6. To their council may my being never come,
   in their assembly may my person never unite!
   For in their anger they kill men,
   in their self-will they maim bulls.

7. Damned be their anger, that is so fierce!
   Their fury, that it is so harsh!
   I will split them up in Yaakov,
   I will scatter them in Yisrael.

8. Yehuda,
   you—your brothers will praise you,
   your hand on the neck of your enemies!
   Your father's sons will bow down to you.

9. A lion's whelp, Yehuda—
   from torn-prey, my son, you have gone up!
   He squats, he crouches,
   like the lion, like the king-of-beasts,
   who dares rouse him up?

10. The scepter shall not depart from Yehuda,
    nor the staff-of-command from between his legs,
    until they bring him tribute,

—the obedience of peoples is his.

11. He ties up his foal to a vine,
    his young colt to a crimson tendril;
    he washes his raiment in wine,
    his mantle in the blood of grapes;

12. his eyes, darker than wine,
    his teeth, whiter than milk....

27. Binyamin,
    a wolf that tears-to-pieces.
    In the morning he devours prey,
    and then, in the evening, divides up the spoils.

28. All these are the tribes of Yisrael, twelve,
    and this is what their father spoke to them;
    he blessed them,
    according to what belonged to each as blessing, he blessed them.

1 וַיִּקְרָא יַעֲקֹב אֶל־בָּנָיו וַיֹּאמֶר הֵאָסְפוּ וְאַגִּידָה לָכֶם אֵת אֲשֶׁר־יִקְרָא אֶתְכֶם בְּאַחֲרִית הַיָּמִים:

2 הִקָּבְצוּ וְשִׁמְעוּ בְּנֵי יַעֲקֹב וְשִׁמְעוּ אֶל־יִשְׂרָאֵל אֲבִיכֶם:

3 רְאוּבֵן בְּכֹרִי אַתָּה כֹּחִי וְרֵאשִׁית אוֹנִי יֶתֶר שְׂאֵת וְיֶתֶר עָז:

4 פַּחַז כַּמַּיִם אַל־תּוֹתַר כִּי עָלִיתָ מִשְׁכְּבֵי אָבִיךָ אָז חִלַּלְתָּ יְצוּעִי עָלָה:

5 שִׁמְעוֹן וְלֵוִי אַחִים כְּלֵי חָמָס מְכֵרֹתֵיהֶם:

6 בְּסֹדָם אַל־תָּבֹא נַפְשִׁי בִּקְהָלָם אַל־תֵּחַד כְּבֹדִי כִּי בְאַפָּם הָרְגוּ אִישׁ וּבִרְצֹנָם עִקְּרוּ־שׁוֹר:

7 אָרוּר אַפָּם כִּי עָז וְעֶבְרָתָם כִּי קָשָׁתָה אֲחַלְּקֵם בְּיַעֲקֹב וַאֲפִיצֵם בְּיִשְׂרָאֵל:

8 יְהוּדָה אַתָּה יוֹדוּךָ אַחֶיךָ יָדְךָ בְּעֹרֶף אֹיְבֶיךָ יִשְׁתַּחֲווּ לְךָ בְּנֵי אָבִיךָ:

9 גּוּר אַרְיֵה יְהוּדָה מִטֶּרֶף בְּנִי עָלִיתָ כָּרַע רָבַץ כְּאַרְיֵה וּכְלָבִיא מִי יְקִימֶנּוּ:

10 לֹא־יָסוּר שֵׁבֶט מִיהוּדָה וּמְחֹקֵק מִבֵּין רַגְלָיו עַד כִּי־יָבֹא שִׁילֹה שִׁילֹה וְלוֹ יִקְּהַת עַמִּים:

11 אֹסְרִי לַגֶּפֶן עִירֹה וְלַשֹּׂרֵקָה בְּנִי אֲתֹנוֹ כִּבֵּס בַּיַּיִן לְבֻשׁוֹ וּבְדַם־עֲנָבִים סוּתֹה סוּתוֹ:

12 חַכְלִילִי עֵינַיִם מִיָּיִן וּלְבֶן־שִׁנַּיִם מֵחָלָב:

27 בִּנְיָמִין זְאֵב יִטְרָף בַּבֹּקֶר יֹאכַל עַד וְלָעֶרֶב יְחַלֵּק שָׁלָל:

28 כָּל־אֵלֶּה שִׁבְטֵי יִשְׂרָאֵל שְׁנֵים עָשָׂר וְזֹאת אֲשֶׁר־דִּבֶּר לָהֶם אֲבִיהֶם וַיְבָרֶךְ אוֹתָם אִישׁ אֲשֶׁר כְּבִרְכָתוֹ בֵּרַךְ אֹתָם:

QUESTIONS ABOUT THE BIBLICAL TEXT

a. What makes these blessings different from other biblical blessings?

b. What is Yaakov trying to tell his sons?

_____

_____

_____

_____

_____

THE MIDRASH ANSWERS THESE SAME QUESTIONS

A MIDRASH [Tanhuma, Vayehi 11]

Yaakov was afraid that God's presence had left him because his sons were unworthy of a Divine blessing. He therefore asked his sons: "How do I know if your hearts are full with God's will?"

All of Yisrael's children said, "*Shema Yisrael YHWH Eloheynu YHWH Ehad*—HEARKEN O YISRAEL (DAD), YHWH IS OUR GOD, YHWH ALONE." (Deuteronomy 6.4)

Yaakov bowed in thanks to God and quietly answered, "*Baruch Shem K'vod Malkhuto l'Olam va'Ed*—PRAISED BE "THE NAME"—WHOSE HONORED EMPIRE WILL LAST FOREVER." Then he blessed his 12 sons.

Separating the P'shat from the Drash

1. What facts from the Torah does this midrash use?

2. What words in the Torah hint that the Shema might first have been said at this moment in history?

Separating the Answers from the Messages

3. According to the midrash, what fear was behind these blessings?

4. What does this midrash teach us about the Shema?

5. How would you spin this midrash into a sermon? What lesson would it teach?

_____

_____

_____

_____

BEYOND THIS LESSON:

[1] Think about writing your own "Yaakov's Blessing" midrashim: (1) Did Yaakov's blessings come true? Were they supposed to? (b) Which brother got the best blessing and why? Which one got the worst blessing and why?

[2] Some other VA-YEHI midrashim which need writing are: (a) What did Yaakov do every day for 17 years? (b) Why did the Sons of Yisrael stay in Egypt after the seven years of famine were over? (c) C.J.'s question: "Why didn't they bury Yosef in Egypt when he died? (d) What makes the Yosef story the right thing to study during the shortest and darkest days of the year (it always falls out around the end of December)?

[3] What other questions about parashat VA-YEHI would be good triggers for midrashim?

13. Shemot

Exodus 1.1-6.1

Now these are the names of the Children of Yisrael coming to Egypt, with Yaakov, each-man and his household they came (Exodus 1:1).

[1] SHEMOT begins the story of the Exodus from Egypt. At the end of the book of Genesis, we left the Families-of-Yisrael, all 70 of their clan, in Egypt. As the book of Exodus begins, a whole number of changes have taken place. Yosef and all his generation have died, and the **Families-of-Yisrael have multiplied from a family to a nation.** A new king has arisen over Egypt who doesn't know about Yosef and his special relationship with the old Pharaoh.

[2] **The new Pharaoh begins a 5-point process of persecution which includes:** (a) taskmasters, (b) enslavement, (c) bitter oppression, (d) having the midwives kill male children, and then (e) ordering all the people to do the same.

[3] Next, Moshe is born, set afloat on the Nile, and then adopted by Pharaoh's daughter. When he is grown, he kills a taskmaster who was beating a Hebrew slave and then flees from Egypt.

[4] Moshe flees to Midian, saves the daughters of the local priest Yitro, and marries one of them—Tzipora. They have a son named Gershom. Moshe becomes a shepherd, and one day while tending the flocks by Mt. Sinai, he sees a burning bush and talks with God. After a long dialogue, he is given orders to return to Egypt and release the Jewish people from slavery.

[5] Moshe begins his mission. He bids Yitro farewell and has an encounter with God over the fact that Gershom was not circumcised. **He joins with his brother Aharon and they present their demands to Pharaoh to 'Let the people go.'** Pharaoh reacts by making the Hebrews now bake their bricks without straw. The Families-of-Yisrael blame Moshe and Aharon for the harder work.

CJ'S COMMENTS

[1]: We can tell that Pharaoh is obviously afraid of Yisrael. He would only set up these laws if he were afraid of them. When there was slavery in America, those in control had to punish bad behavior and would sometimes punish ordinary behavior, just to keep control of all those slaves—because they were fewer in number. Pharaoh was afraid of war with these "strangers in the land." **[C.J.]**

[2]: It is strange how relations with other religions have changed over the generations. Yitro and Moshe seemed to have a pretty good relationship with each other (I mean, Moshe married his daughter). How upsetting that all encounters with other religions could not be this peaceful. I am not encouraging intermarriage—this is intermarriage in a sense—but I'm just saying that we don't really need a war of the religions. **[C.J.]**

The midrash plays an important game with Yitro. The gematria for Yitro is 606. (That is when you turn letters into numbers and add them up). If you add the 7 mitzvot given to Noah, Yitro comes out as 613, the total number of mitzvot. The idea being that (a) Yitro was a virtual Jew, and (b) he was a righteous gentile—and righteous gentiles (who get a place along side us in the world to come) are our allies. Midrash Halakhah solves the problem in another way. The other solution is that laws about intermarriage begin at Mount Sinai. Everyone pre-Sinai was "grandpawed" or "grandmawed" into the Jewish people. **[GRIS]**

[3]: Does Moshe ever do anything about the fact that Gershom was not circumcised? **[C.J.]**

No, Tzipora did it! That is an explanation of the "bridgegroom of blood" story. (See Ex. 4.24). **[GRIS]**

CONTINUED ON PAGE 187

Moshe	=	Moses
Aharon	=	Aaron
Tzipora	=	Zipporah
Yitro	=	Jethro
Midyan	=	Midian

THE BIBLICAL TEXT

After Moshe fled from Egypt, he came to Midian and became a shepherd. The Torah tells this short story about his experience as a shepherd. As you read, see if you can decide:

a. Why was it important training for Moshe to be a shepherd?

b. Why did he lead his flock all the way from Midian to Mount Horev (a.k.a. Mount Sinai)?

Exodus 3: 1-8

1. Now Moshe was shepherding the flock of Yitro his father-in-law, priest of Midian. He led the flock behind the wilderness—
   and he came to the mountain of God, to Horev.

2. And YHWH's messenger was seen by him
   in the flame of a fire out of the midst of a bush.
   He saw:
   here, the bush is burning with fire,
   and the bush is not consumed!

3. Moshe said:
   Now let me turn aside
   that I may see this great sight—
   why the bush does not burn up!

4. When YHWH saw that he had turned aside to see,
   God called him out of the midst of the bush,
   He said:
   Moshe! Moshe!
   He said:
   Here I am.

5. He said:
   Do not come near to here,
   put off your sandal from your foot,
   for the place on which you stand—it is holy ground!

6. And he said:
   I am the God of your father,
   the God of Avraham,
   the God of Yitzhak,
   and the God of Yaakov.
   Moshe concealed his face,
   for he was afraid to gaze upon God.

7. Now YHWH said:
   I have seen, yes, seen the affliction of my people that is in Egypt,
   their cry have I heard in the face of their slave-drivers;
   indeed, I have known their sufferings!

8. So I have come down
   to rescue it from the land of Egypt,
   to bring it up from that land
   to a land, goodly and spacious, to a land flowing with milk and honey,

to the place of the Canaanite and the Hittite,
of the Amorite and the Perizzite,
of the Hivvite and the Yevusite.

1 וּמֹשֶׁה הָיָה רֹעֶה אֶת־צֹאן יִתְרוֹ חֹתְנוֹ כֹּהֵן מִדְיָן וַיִּנְהַג אֶת־הַצֹּאן אַחַר הַמִּדְבָּר וַיָּבֹא אֶל־הַר הָאֱלֹהִים חֹרֵבָה:

2 וַיֵּרָא מַלְאַךְ יְהוָה אֵלָיו בְּלַבַּת־אֵשׁ מִתּוֹךְ הַסְּנֶה וַיַּרְא וְהִנֵּה הַסְּנֶה בֹּעֵר בָּאֵשׁ וְהַסְּנֶה אֵינֶנּוּ אֻכָּל:

3 וַיֹּאמֶר מֹשֶׁה אָסֻרָה־נָּא וְאֶרְאֶה אֶת־הַמַּרְאֶה הַגָּדֹל הַזֶּה מַדּוּעַ לֹא־יִבְעַר הַסְּנֶה:

4 וַיַּרְא יְהוָה כִּי סָר לִרְאוֹת וַיִּקְרָא אֵלָיו אֱלֹהִים מִתּוֹךְ הַסְּנֶה וַיֹּאמֶר מֹשֶׁה מֹשֶׁה וַיֹּאמֶר הִנֵּנִי:

5 וַיֹּאמֶר אַל־תִּקְרַב הֲלֹם שַׁל־נְעָלֶיךָ מֵעַל רַגְלֶיךָ כִּי הַמָּקוֹם אֲשֶׁר אַתָּה עוֹמֵד עָלָיו אַדְמַת־קֹדֶשׁ הוּא:

6 וַיֹּאמֶר אָנֹכִי אֱלֹהֵי אָבִיךָ אֱלֹהֵי אַבְרָהָם אֱלֹהֵי יִצְחָק וֵאלֹהֵי יַעֲקֹב וַיַּסְתֵּר מֹשֶׁה פָּנָיו כִּי יָרֵא מֵהַבִּיט אֶל־הָאֱלֹהִים:

7 וַיֹּאמֶר יְהוָה רָאֹה רָאִיתִי אֶת־עֳנִי עַמִּי אֲשֶׁר בְּמִצְרָיִם וְאֶת־צַעֲקָתָם שָׁמַעְתִּי מִפְּנֵי נֹגְשָׂיו כִּי יָדַעְתִּי אֶת־מַכְאֹבָיו:

8 וָאֵרֵד לְהַצִּילוֹ מִיַּד מִצְרַיִם וּלְהַעֲלֹתוֹ מִן־הָאָרֶץ הַהִוא אֶל־אֶרֶץ טוֹבָה וּרְחָבָה אֶל־אֶרֶץ זָבַת חָלָב וּדְבָשׁ אֶל־מְקוֹם הַכְּנַעֲנִי וְהַחִתִּי וְהָאֱמֹרִי וְהַפְּרִזִּי וְהַחִוִּי וְהַיְבוּסִי:

QUESTIONS ABOUT THE BIBLICAL TEXT

a. Why do you think it was "good for Moshe" to spend time as a shepherd?

b. Why would Moshe take his flock as far as Sinai? (A HINT: Think about what Avraham did with his sheep.)

_____

_____

_____

_____

THE MIDRASH ANSWERS THESE SAME QUESTIONS

A MIDRASH [Shemot Rabbah 1.40,2.2-3]

As soon as Moshe took over Yitro's flocks they were blessed. Not a single animal was ever injured by a wild beast. Moshe used to graze his flocks in ownerless land to insure that they would not steal by grazing on lands which were not Yitro's.

Once a lamb ran away from the flock. Moshe followed it until it reached some bushes near a pond. It stopped to drink. Moshe said: "I didn't know you ran all this way because you were thirsty. You must be tired too." He lifted the lamb on his shoulder and carried it back to the flock.

A MIDRASH [Ibid 2.2]

God trained two people to be great leaders by making them shepherds. One of them was King David, who used to protect the smaller sheep from the attacks of the larger ones, and who would make sure that each animal got the food which was best for it. God said: "A man who cares for the needs of each individual sheep will do the same for My people the Families-of-Yisrael."

Moshe was also tested. God said: "A man who tends sheep with such mercy will be a compassionate leader for My sheep, Yisrael."

Separating the P'shat from the Drash

1. Underline/overline the parts of these midrashim which are based on facts in the Bible.

2. What parts of this story do we learn only in the midrash?

Separating the Answers from the Messages

3. How do these midrashim explain why it was good for Moshe to be a shepherd?

4. How do these midrashim explain why Moshe led his herd as far as Mt. Sinai?

5. What "sermon" could you write using each midrash? What would be your message?

_____

_____

_____

_____

_____

BEYOND THIS LESSON:

[1] Be creative—use the idea of being a shepherd as good training to write your own midrash on why Moshe went to Mt. Sinai. What is the moral of your midrash?

[2] Some other midrashim that this sidrah invites are: (a) What happened to the "new Pharaoh" that he started to fear the Families-of-Yisrael? (b) What made Pharaoh's daughter willing to accept a Jewish child into her house? (And the answer to that other question is that she knew because he was circumcised. While most Jews in Egypt abandoned circumcision, the tribe of Levi, Moshe's tribe, didn't). (c) Why didn't the Jews rebel earlier against the moves which made them slaves? (d) Why did God pick a bush as a way to meet Moshe? (e) Why were these events staged at Mt. Sinai?

[3] What other questions about SHEMOT would be good triggers for midrashim?

14. Va-Era

Exodus 6:2-9:35

God spoke to Moshe, He said to him: I am YHWH (Exodus 6:2).

[1] In this *sidrah*, Moshe and Aharon go into action and begin to organize the slave revolt. Va-Era begins with God giving Moshe, and then Moshe and Aharon, a pep talk. Then the Torah lists the major leaders of the Families-of-Yisrael. It is here that Moshe complains about not being able to speak properly. **Moshe and Aharon** then **go to Pharaoh and do the old staff-into-snake trick.** They ask Pharaoh to allow their people to go into the wilderness to sacrifice to their God. He says no, so they introduce the first plague. **Aharon holds his staff over the Nile river and all the water in Egypt is turned into blood.** Pharaoh's heart is hard and he doesn't respond.

[2] Next, **Aharon holds out his staff over the canals and frogs fill the land.** This is the second plague. This time Pharaoh gives in and the frogs are removed. Then, Pharaoh changes his mind and Aharon brings the third plague. **He strikes the ground with his staff and lice filled the land.** Pharaoh's heart remains hardened.

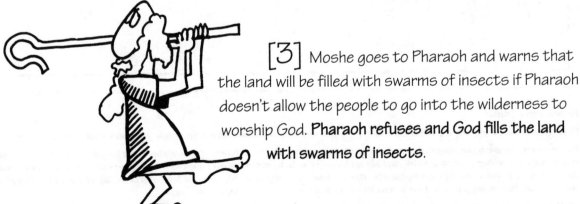

[3] Moshe goes to Pharaoh and warns that the land will be filled with swarms of insects if Pharaoh doesn't allow the people to go into the wilderness to worship God. **Pharaoh refuses and God fills the land with swarms of insects.**

[4] Pharaoh sends for Moshe and Aharon and agrees to let the Families-of-Yisrael go 3 days into the wilderness to worship. The swarms of insects vanish. Afterwards, Pharaoh changes his mind and won't let them go. Next God has **all of the sheep and cattle in Egypt die of the pestilence**. Still Pharaoh won't let them go. Next **Moshe and Aharon take handfuls of soot, throw it in the air**, and **boils began to break out on every Egyptian**. But Pharaoh's heart remained hardened and he would not let them go. Then Moshe warns Pharaoh that the seventh plague will be hail. **He holds out the staff to the sky** and **hail strikes down people and animals who are outside, and destroys all the crops.** This parashah ends with Pharaoh's heart still hardened and with him refusing to let the Jewish people go.

C.J.'S COMMENTS

[1]: Was Moshe's speech problem that he couldn't really speak well, or that he couldn't speak properly? I wonder whether the reason for that midrash wherein Moshe burns his tongue is based on a misinterpretation of the text. You ask: Why do you think that Aharon was the one to bring the plagues to Egypt while Moshe gave the warnings? (Remember, Aharon was suposed to do the talking and Moshe the leading.) The following midrash is my answer to that question:

Moshe: (*standing before the Pharaoh of Egypt and next to his brother Aharon*): Watch Pharaoh, as I turn my s-s-s-staff into a s-s-s-snake!

Pharaoh: So, it turns out this supposed liberator also does animal sounds! (With this, Pharaoh and his men laugh.)

Moshe: Sheket!

(*Pharaoh eyes his wizards, they throw their staffs on the ground, making snakes.*)

Pharaoh: Oh my!

Moshe: And now Mr. Pharaoh sir, I'd like to introduce you to a friend of mine…Blood!

Pharaoh: Hello there, Mr. Blood, nice to meet you.

Blood: Why thank you, Pharaoh. Now, if you don't mind, I think I'll go for a dip.

Pharaoh: Okay…Hey! Wait a sec! (Pharaoh becomes red in the face and doesn't answer.)

Aharon: I guess this is our cue, let's leave. (Moshe and Aharon walk out to the canals.)

Aharon: Gee, arguing with Pharaoh sure does make me sleepy! Yawn! (*Aharon stretches his hand out over the canals.*)

Frog: Hey, guys! Riiiiibit!

Moshe: Cool! Can we keep it?

Aharon: No, it's the next plague. Hey you there! (calling Pharaoh's servant). Fetch us the Pharaoh!

Servant: Yes sir!

Pharaoh: Oh, not you two!

CONTINUED ON PAGE **187**

THE BIBLICAL TEXT

This text is the Torah's version of how the first plague happened. As you read it, see if you can figure out why Aharon starts this plague rather than Moshe.

Edited Exodus 7:17-19

17. Thus says YHWH:

    By this shall you know that I am YHWH:

    here, I will strike—with the staff that is in my hand—upon the water that is in the Nile,

    and it will change to blood.

18. The fish that are in the Nile will die, and the Nile will reek,

    and the Egyptians will be unable to drink water from the Nile.

19. YHWH said to Moshe:

    Say to Aharon:

    Take your staff

    and stretch out your hand over the waters of Egypt, over their tributaries, over their Nile-canals,

    over their ponds and over all their bodies of water,

    and let them become blood!

    There will be blood through out all the land of Egypt—in the wooden-containers, in the stoneware.

17 כֹּה אָמַר יְהוָה בְּזֹאת תֵּדַע כִּי אֲנִי יְהוָה הִנֵּה אָנֹכִי מַכֶּה בַּמַּטֶּה אֲשֶׁר־בְּיָדִי עַל־הַמַּיִם
אֲשֶׁר בַּיְאֹר וְנֶהֶפְכוּ לְדָם:

18 וְהַדָּגָה אֲשֶׁר־בַּיְאֹר תָּמוּת וּבָאַשׁ הַיְאֹר וְנִלְאוּ מִצְרַיִם לִשְׁתּוֹת מַיִם מִן־הַיְאֹר:

19 וַיֹּאמֶר יְהוָה אֶל־מֹשֶׁה אֱמֹר אֶל־אַהֲרֹן קַח מַטְּךָ וּנְטֵה־יָדְךָ עַל־מֵימֵי מִצְרַיִם
עַל־נַהֲרֹתָם עַל־יְאֹרֵיהֶם וְעַל־אַגְמֵיהֶם וְעַל כָּל־מִקְוֵה מֵימֵיהֶם וְיִהְיוּ־דָם וְהָיָה
דָם בְּכָל־אֶרֶץ מִצְרַיִם וּבָעֵצִים וּבָאֲבָנִים:

QUESTIONS ABOUT THE BIBLICAL TEXT

a. Why do you think that Aharon was the one to bring the plague to Egypt while Moshe gave the warning? (Remember, Aharon was supposed to do the talking and Moshe the leading).

_____

_____

_____

THE MIDRASH ANSWERS THESE SAME QUESTIONS
A MIDRASH (SHEMOT RABBAH 20.1)

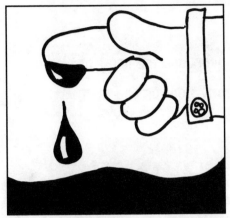

Moshe repeated God's words to Pharaoh and warned him that the Nile would turn to blood. When Pharaoh ignored the warning, God ordered Moshe to strike the river and bring the plague. Moshe objected: "How can I strike the Nile? Can someone who drank from a well throw stones into it? As a baby I was saved by the waters of the Nile—how can I strike these same waters?"

Separating the P'shat from the Drash

1. Underline/overline the parts of this midrash which can also be found in the Torah.

2. What other Torah facts does it use?

Separating the Answers from the Messages

3. How does this midrash explain why Aharon brought this plague?

4. How does it connect two different Biblical stories (using something found elsewhere to solve a problem here)?

5. What value does this midrash teach?

_____

_____

_____

_____

_____

_____

_____

_____

_____

_____

BEYOND THIS LESSON:

[1] Think about writing your own "first plague" midrash? (a) Why did the plagues start in the Nile? (b) Why did the plagues start with blood? (c) Why did God decide on ten plagues? Why not 5, 7, 12, or 40, etc.?

[2] Some other midrashim that this *sidrah* invites are: (a) Why did God pick "death of the firstborn" as the severest plague? (Why not death of everyone who killed an Israelite, etc?) (b) Why did God harden Pharaoh's heart? (c) Why the order of the plagues? (d) Which plagues didn't God choose?

[3] What other questions about the plagues would be good triggers for midrash? Pick your favorite plague and explain it. Why did God pick this plague? What lesson does it teach?

15. Bo

Exodus 10:1-13:16

YHWH said to Moshe: Come to Pharaoh! For I have made his heart and the heart of his servants heavy-with-stubbornness, in order that I may put these my signs among them...(Exodus 10:1).

[1] Continuing with the adventures of the Exodus, we come to *parashat* BO. So far, 7 of the 10 plagues have hit Egypt. We start with the eighth plague. Again Moshe warns Pharaoh, the warning is ignored, and **Moshe holds up the staff** and **brings the locust swarms.**

[2] Pharaoh sends for Moshe and Aharon, agrees to let the Families-of-Yisrael go, then changes his mind once the plague is over. God has **Moshe hold out his staff,** which **brings** the ninth plague—**darkness.** Pharaoh sends for Moshe, they fail to work out a deal, and Moshe then follows God's order to warn them of the 10th plague—the death of the firstborn.

[3] God then teaches Moshe the first mitzvah given to all of Yisrael, the marking of the new month. This is then followed by rules for **the observance of the first Passover.** While these Seders are going on in **homes marked with blood of lambs on the mezuzot,** the 10th plague, **the death of the firstborn,** hits Egypt. At this point Pharaoh tries to rush the Families-of-Yisrael out of Egypt.

[4] At last the Exodus has begun. Before we finish the *sidrah* however, the Torah teaches rules about **who can celebrate Passover** and rules about the mitzvah to sanctify the firstborn male of both people and animals.

CONTINUED ON PAGE **188**

85

CJ'S COMMENTS

[1]: And here we meet Pharaoh: a child trapped in a king's body. Here sits the little child (Pharaoh) playing with his toys (the Yisraelites). But the little boy never puts his toys away (lets the Yisraelites leave). The boy's Parent (God) gets mad, and uses a puppet (Moshe) to warn him that there will be punishments if the he keeps leaving his toys out (keeps the Yisraelites in bondage). The boy believes that he is only talking with a puppet, and he knows the puppet can't hurt him. So the boy goes about his business and leaves the toys on the floor. Enraged, the Parent picks up His son and gives him a good whack. The boy cries that he will pick up his toys, and so his Parent lets him go. But as soon as he is free he leaves his toys on the floor. This repeats itself over and over again. The boy does not at all believe that anything really bad can or will happen, so he never obeys the Parent. Finally, the parent destroys the boy's favorite belonging (firstborn son) as a punishment. The boy quickly picks up all of his toys. I think you get the picture. **[C.J.]**

[2]: A confusing part of parashat Bo is that Nisan is considered the first month because of Pesah, while Tishre would seem to be the first month because it has Rosh ha-Shanah (the New Year) in it. The answer will make sense if you view what is said in terms of many years instead of one. Nisan will be the first month. Not necessarily the first month in the year, but the first month in history. Tishre will be the first month of the year. But Nisan will be celebrated as a new month as well, because it was the first month for the Yisraelites. It marks the beginning of their freedom. **[C.J.]**

A great interpretation of a wrong understanding. Tishre is the seventh month. The truth is, if you look at the Mishnah on Rosh ha-Shanah (1.1), it says that there are four new years every year: one for kings and festivals (Nisan), one for animal tithes (Elul), one for Sabbatical years (Tishre), and one for trees/planting (Shevat). Each new year does start a different aspect of the year. **[GRIS]**

THE BIBLICAL TEXT

In the middle of the ten plagues, God introduces the first mitzvot which are directly taught to Yisrael. Here is the way the Torah presents these mitzvot. See if you can figure out:

[a] Why fixing the calendar is an important first mitzvah.

[b] Why the month which contains Passover should be the first month—rather than the month of Tishre—which has Rosh ha-Shanah. Read on.

Exodus 12.1-3

1. Yhwh said to Moshe and to Aharon in the land of Egypt, saying:
2. Let this New-Moon be for you the beginning of New-Moons,
   the beginning-one let it be for you of the New-Moons of the year.
3. Speak to the entire community of Yisrael, saying:
   On the tenth day after this New-Moon
   they are to take them, each-man, a lamb, according to their father's house, a lamb per household.

וַיֹּאמֶר יְהוָה אֶל־מֹשֶׁה וְאֶל־אַהֲרֹן בְּאֶרֶץ מִצְרַיִם לֵאמֹר: 1

הַחֹדֶשׁ הַזֶּה לָכֶם רֹאשׁ חֳדָשִׁים רִאשׁוֹן 2

הוּא לָכֶם לְחָדְשֵׁי הַשָּׁנָה:

דַּבְּרוּ אֶל־כָּל־עֲדַת יִשְׂרָאֵל לֵאמֹר בֶּעָשֹׂר לַחֹדֶשׁ הַזֶּה 3

וְיִקְחוּ לָהֶם אִישׁ שֶׂה לְבֵית־אָבֹת שֶׂה לַבָּיִת:

QUESTIONS ABOUT THE BIBLICAL TEXT

1. Why would a mitzvah about a new month be the first commandment taught to all of Yisrael?
2. How can *Nisan* be the first month, when the month of *Tishre* has Rosh ha-Shanah (the New Year)?

_____

_____

_____

_____

_____

_____

THE MIDRASH ANSWERS THESE SAME QUESTIONS

A MIDRASH [Shemot Rabbah 15:30]

God informed Moshe: "For 2,448 years I have proclaimed every new month in heaven, but now that you have become a nation—I give you the responsibility."

To what can this be compared? This can be compared to a King who carefully guarded the keys to his treasury and would allow no one to touch them. However, as soon as the King's son came of age, the King gave him the keys and said: "In the future you will be responsible for them."

Separating the P'shat from the Drash

1. None of this midrash is directly based on facts from the Torah. What question about the text is this midrash trying to answer?

Separating the Answers from the Messages

2. This midrash is a parable. Figure out what each of the following represent:

   The King_____

   The Prince_____

   The Key_____

3. What is the message of this midrash? What does it teach us about the Jewish vision of time?

   _____

   _____

   _____

   _____

A MIDRASH [Shemot Rabbah 15.10]

On the first of Nisan (the month of *Pesah*), God told Moshe that this will be the first of all months in the Jewish calendar.

To what can this be compared? This can be compared to a country where the birthday of the King's son was a national holiday every year. One day, when the prince was grown up, he visited a foreign country and was taken prisoner for many years. Finally he was released. The whole country celebrated his return. The king ordered that from now on, the day the prince was set free would be a national holiday rather than his birthday.

Separating the P'shat from the Drash

4. What facts from the Torah does this midrash use?

Separating the Answers from the Messages

5. This midrash too is a parable. It too, is not directly based on any specific Torah text. What do each of these represent?

   The King_____

   The Prince_____

   The birthday_____

   The liberation day_____

6. What is the message of this midrash? What does it teach us about Passover?

   _____

   _____

   _____

BEYOND THIS LESSON:

[1] Think about writing your own calendar midrash. (a) Write a midrash about the fight between the months, each of whom wanted to be first. (b) Invent your own king/prince midrash about how Passover got its date. (c) Write the story of the first Passover in Egypt.

[2] Some other midrashim that BO invites are: (a) Why did Moshe use his staff to make the plagues? (b) Why did the Yisraelites need blood on the doorposts in order to protect their homes? Why were seven plagues put in one *sidrah* and three put in another?

[3] What other questions about BO would be good triggers for midrash?

16. Beshalla<u>h</u>

Exodus 13:17-17:16

Now it was, when Pharaoh had sent the people free, that God did not lead them by way of the land of the Philistines, which indeed is nearer, for God said to himself: Lest the people regret it, when they see war, and return to Egypt! (Exodus 13:17).

[1] With *parashat* BESHALLA<u>H</u>, **the Families-of-Yisrael are off and running** from Egypt. God leads them the long way, avoiding the land of the Philistines. Meanwhile back in Egypt, **Pharaoh has a change of heart and gives chase.**

[2] It is at the Reed Sea that Pharaoh catches the Families-of-Yisrael. God tells Moshe to stop praying and lift his staff. **The sea divides and the Families-of-Yisrael cross,** but Pharaoh and his army are drowned when the sea closes.

[3] On the other side of the sea, Moshe and the Families-of-Yisrael sing a song of praise—The Song of the Sea—to God. Miriam, Moshe and Aharon's sister, simulta-neously leads the women in song and dance. As soon as they move into the wilderness, **the people begin to complain**, so Moshe makes bitter water sweet to ease their complaints. **God also introduces manna—**the special food which falls from the sky daily (except Shabbat). To complete the menu, God also sees to it that quail can be easily caught.

[4] Before the Families-of-Yisrael can move even another chapter into the *sidrah*, they again complain about the lack of water. **Moshe** follows God's instructions and **hits a rock—bringing forth water.**

To end this parashah, **Yehoshua** fights a battle with Amalek. Moshe, Aharon and Hur go up on a hill. **As long as Moshe can keep his arms in the air—the Families-of-Yisrael win the battle...**

CJ'S COMMENTS

[1]: I have often wondered why it was that God chose to send B'nai Yisrael the long way to Canaan. Here it is: they avoided the Philistines. I always thought that it was unfair that the Yisraelites should have to go the long way. I admit though, I would rather go the long way than put up with war in the midst of all the troubles of such a long, hard journey. **[C.J.]**

Your question triggers one of my favorite midrashim of all times. It says, "If God had led them directly to Mt. Sinai and then directly to Yisrael, they would have forgotten the Torah. Everyone would have shouted "Me" and "Mine." Instead, they had to strug-gle in the desert together, drink measured water and eat rationed manna. In the process they developed a sense of discipline and a sense of community, the things they needed to hold onto and live by Torah. Otherwise, these former slaves would have been lost in saying "My field. My vineyard. My needs come first." The Sinai wilderness experience was a spiritual "Outward Bound" vision quest to develop the tools to live cor-rectly by Torah in the land of Yisrael. Without the wilderness of Sinai, Torah can't come true. **[GRIS]**

I heard what C.J. said and I heard what GRIS said, and it made me think of a difficult question. Perhaps if the Israelites were busy fighting the Philistines—that could make them forget Torah. A nation at war has a hard time thinking about Torah. That may have a lot to do with what is going on in Israel today. There may be no more important question than this: Can Israel continue to maintain its security without sacrificing its devotion to Torah? **[Rabbi Yosi Gordon]**

[2]: We now see that Pharaoh has changed his mind. Who does he think he is, the ancient, evil version of Bill Clinton? The one thing I don't understand is why Pharaoh decided to chase B'nai Yisrael into the Red

CONTINUED ON PAGE 189

Yehoshua = Joshua

THE BIBLICAL TEXT

At the edge of the Reed Sea, the Families-of-Yisrael sang a song of praise to God. Read the text of part of this song. See if you can find anything wrong with it. See if you can explain why it was the right song for the Families-of-Yisrael to sing.

Exodus 15: 1-6

1. Then sang Moshe and the Children of Yisrael
   this song to YHWH,
   they uttered (this) utterance:
   I will sing to YHWH,
   for he has triumphed, yes, triumphed,
   the horse and its charioteer he flung into the sea!

2. My fierce-might and strength is YAH,
   he has become deliverance for me.
   This is my God—I honor Him,
   the God of my father—I exalt Him.

3. YHWH is a man of war ,
   YHWH is His name!

4. Pharaoh's chariots and his army
   He hurled into the sea,
   his choicest teams-of-three
   sank in the Sea of Reeds.

5. Oceans covered them,
   they went down in the depths
   like a stone.

6. Your right-hand, O YHWH,
   majestic in power,
   Your right-hand, O YHWH,
   shattered the enemy.

7. In Your great triumph
   You smashed Your foes,
   You sent forth Your fury,
   consumed them like chaff.

8. By the breath of Your nostrils
   the waters piled up,
   the gushing-streams stood up like a dam,
   the oceans congealed in the heart of the sea.

9. Uttered the enemy:
   I will pursue,
   overtake,
   and apportion the plunder,
   my greed will be filled on them,
   my sword I will draw,
   my hand—dispossess them!

10. You blew with Your breath,

the sea covered them,
they plunged down like lead
in majestic waters.

11. Who is like You among the gods, O Yʜᴡʜ!
Who is like You, majestic among the holy-ones,
Feared-One of praises, Doer of Wonders!

12. You stretched out your right-hand,
the Underworld swallowed them.

1 אָז יָשִׁיר־מֹשֶׁה וּבְנֵי יִשְׂרָאֵל אֶת־הַשִּׁירָה הַזֹּאת לַיהוָה וַיֹּאמְרוּ לֵאמֹר אָשִׁירָה לַיהוָה כִּי־גָאֹה
גָּאָה סוּס וְרֹכְבוֹ רָמָה בַיָּם:

2 עָזִּי וְזִמְרָת יָהּ וַיְהִי־לִי לִישׁוּעָה זֶה אֵלִי וְאַנְוֵהוּ אֱלֹהֵי אָבִי וַאֲרֹמְמֶנְהוּ:

3 יְהוָה אִישׁ מִלְחָמָה יְהוָה שְׁמוֹ:

4 מַרְכְּבֹת פַּרְעֹה וְחֵילוֹ יָרָה בַיָּם וּמִבְחַר שָׁלִשָׁיו טֻבְּעוּ בְיַם־סוּף:

5 תְּהֹמֹת יְכַסְיֻמוּ יָרְדוּ בִמְצוֹלֹת כְּמוֹ־אָבֶן:

6 יְמִינְךָ יְהוָה נֶאְדָּרִי בַּכֹּחַ יְמִינְךָ יְהוָה תִּרְעַץ אוֹיֵב:

7 וּבְרֹב גְּאוֹנְךָ תַּהֲרֹס קָמֶיךָ תְּשַׁלַּח חֲרֹנְךָ יֹאכְלֵמוֹ כַּקַּשׁ:

8 וּבְרוּחַ אַפֶּיךָ נֶעֶרְמוּ מַיִם נִצְּבוּ כְמוֹ־נֵד נֹזְלִים קָפְאוּ תְהֹמֹת בְּלֶב־יָם:

9 אָמַר אוֹיֵב אֶרְדֹּף אַשִּׂיג אֲחַלֵּק שָׁלָל תִּמְלָאֵמוֹ נַפְשִׁי אָרִיק חַרְבִּי תּוֹרִישֵׁמוֹ יָדִי:

10 נָשַׁפְתָּ בְרוּחֲךָ כִּסָּמוֹ יָם צָלְלוּ כַּעוֹפֶרֶת בְּמַיִם אַדִּירִים:

11 מִי־כָמֹכָה בָּאֵלִם יְהוָה מִי כָּמֹכָה נֶאְדָּר בַּקֹּדֶשׁ נוֹרָא תְהִלֹּת עֹשֵׂה פֶלֶא:

12 נָטִיתָ יְמִינְךָ תִּבְלָעֵמוֹ אָרֶץ:

QUESTIONS ABOUT THE BIBLICAL TEXT

1. What might make this song a poor thing for Moshe and the Families-of-Yisrael to sing?

2. What makes it the right thing to sing?

_____

_____

_____

_____

_____

_____

THE MIDRASH ANSWERS THESE SAME QUESTIONS

A MIDRASH [Shemot Rabbah 23.8]

When the Egyptian army was chasing the Families-of-Yisrael, the angels in heaven wanted to sing the Song of the Sea to God. God would not let them. God said: "How can you sing My praises when the Families-of-Yisrael are scared to death while crossing the Reed Sea?"

After the Families-of-Yisrael had safely crossed the sea, the angels once again wanted to sing the Song of the Sea. God still said no. God told them: "How can you sing when My creatures are drowning? My mercy goes out to all people."

A MIDRASH [Shemot Rabbah 23.8]

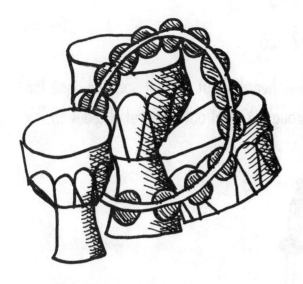

Even though God prevented the angels from singing the Song of the Sea, the Families-of-Yisrael were given permission to sing it. God did this because the Families-of-Yisrael had actually experienced the miracles and had the obligation to thank and praise God for saving them.

Separating the P'shat from the Drash

1   What facts from the Torah do these midrashim use?

Separating the Answers from the Messages

2.   Here we have two midrashim which are based on a question about the Torah. What is that question?

3.   According to the first midrash, what seems wrong with the Song of the Sea?

4.   According to the second midrash, why was it right for the Families-of-Yisrael to sing the Song of the Sea?

5.   These midrashim express two conflicting values—what are they?

6.   What lessons can you draw from these midrashim?

_____

_____

_____

_____

_____

_____

_____

BEYOND THIS LESSON:

[1] Think about writing your own Reed Sea midrash: (a) There is a very famous midrash about Na<u>h</u>shon being the first Jew into the sea—now write one about who was the last Jew into the sea. (b) A student at Adat Ari El Day School (whose name has been lost over five or so years) once asked: "I understand why the Egyptians deserved to die for what they did to the Jewish babies—but what did the horses do wrong that they deserved to drown, too? (c) And now, my favorite question— where did the women get the drums and timbrels they played at the edge of the sea?

[2] Some other midrashim that parashat BESHALLA<u>H</u> invites are: (a) What makes Pharaoh change his mind? (b) How did God invent manna? Test manna? What is the secret formula or ingredient of manna? (c) Why manna and not other foods? (d) Why does God want Moshe to hit the rock this time—and tell him to talk to it later? (e) Why did Moshe have to hold up his hands for Yehoshua to win the battle—what did the hands do?

[3] What other questions about BESHALLA<u>H</u> would be good triggers for midrashim?

17. Yitro

Exodus 18:1-20:26

Now Yitro, the priest of Midian, Moshe's father-in-law, heard about all that God had done for Moshe and for Yisrael his people, that YHWH had brought Yisrael out of Egypt (Exodus 18:1).

[1] In *sidrah* YITRO, **Yitro makes a return entrance.** Moshe and the Families-of-Yisrael are camped at Mount Sinai. Yitro, having heard of all the wonders which have taken place in Egypt, takes Tzipora, Gershom and Eliezer, and brings them to Moshe. Yitro offers sacrifices to God.

[2] While he is around camp, Yitro sees how busy Moshe is—serving as a judge for all the people. He suggests that **Moshe set up a system of judges.** Moshe follows his suggestion.

CJ'S COMMENTS

[1]: Yitro: Yitro definitely is a righteous gentile (good non-Jew who has helped Jews and mythologically has a spot in the world to come: the Mashia_h_'s world). It was nice of him to bring Tzipora and Gershom to Moshe. It was also nice that he made sacrifices. It also was smart of him to advise for a team of judges. **[C.J.]**

In the midrash—Yitro is sort of confusing. They are not quite sure what to do with him. They don't know if he is a good guy or a bad guy pretending to be good. The problem starts later in the Torah with Bil'am and then works backwards. Bil'am is the wizard who tries to curse Yisrael and then God zaps the curse into the *Mah Tovu*. (See Balak, Numbers 22). Bil'am is a Midianite, so is Yitro. The Midianites, just a few chapters later, mess with the Families-of-Yisrael again at Baal Pe'or. They almost destroy Israel. So the question is "How could the Big Kahuna (The High Priest) of the Midianites have different values than the rest of the nation?" So, either (1) Yitro is the one good Midianite, or (2) He is fooling and really is trying to get something from Moshe. Here is the way the stories are told.

Yitro was one of Pharaoh's advisors who told him to throw the Jewish baby boys into the Reed Sea. Later he repented (*Shemot Rabbah* 27.6) Another version of the the same story says that Pharaoh had three advisors: Job, Bil'am, and Yitro. Bil'am said, "Throw them in the river." Job remained silent (and took the fifth). And, Yitro fled town and went to Midian. (*Sanhedrin* 106a) Generally it is assumed that to be a Midianite Priest you have to believe in pagan gods and do idols, but—just like Bil'am—they also assumed that he had some kind of knowledge about or connection with Y_HWH_.

My favorite story about Yitro has to do with Moshe's staff. One version said it got passed down from Adam all the way to Yosef and was then taken by Pharaoh as part of his treasures. On it was the secret full name of God (which gave it its power). Yitro recognized it, and took it with him when he fled.

CONTINUED ON PAGE **190**

[3] God then presents the Families-of-Yisrael with a set of conditions for a special event which is to take place. **The Ten Commandments are then given from Mount Sinai.** All the people witness the thunder and lightning, the smoking mountain and the other effects and they are afraid. They ask Moshe to serve as a go-between with God.

At the end of the *sidrah* are two short laws: (1) Make no idols, and (2) Use no stones in an altar which have been shaped by metal tools.

THE BIBLICAL TEXT

This *sidrah* has the Ten Commandments given to the Families-of-Yisrael. Before the laws are given, there is a description of how God had selected the Families-of-Yisrael to be a chosen people. As you read this text, see if you can figure out why Mount Sinai was the chosen mountain.

Exodus 19:1-6

1. On the third New-Moon after the going-out of the Children of Yisrael from the land of Egypt,
   on that (very) day
   they came to the Wilderness of Sinai.

2. They moved on from Refidim and came to the Wilderness of Sinai,
   and encamped in the wilderness.
   There Yisrael encamped, opposite the mountain.

3. Now Moshe went up to God,
   and YHWH called out to him from the mountain,
   saying:
   Say thus to the House of Yaakov,
   (yes,) tell the Children of Yisrael:

4. You yourselves have seen
   what I did to Egypt,
   how I bore you on eagles' wings and brought you to me.

5. So now,
   if you will hearken, yes, hearken to my voice
   and keep my covenant,
   you shall be to me a special-treasure from among all peoples.
   Indeed, all the earth is mine,

6. but you, you shall be to me
   a kingdom of priests,
   a holy nation.
   These are the words
   that you are to
   speak to the
   Children of Yisrael.

1 בַּחֹדֶשׁ הַשְּׁלִישִׁי לְצֵאת בְּנֵי־יִשְׂרָאֵל מֵאֶרֶץ מִצְרָיִם בַּיּוֹם הַזֶּה בָּאוּ מִדְבַּר סִינָי:

2 וַיִּסְעוּ מֵרְפִידִים וַיָּבֹאוּ מִדְבַּר סִינַי וַיַּחֲנוּ בַּמִּדְבָּר וַיִּחַן־שָׁם יִשְׂרָאֵל נֶגֶד הָהָר:

3 וּמֹשֶׁה עָלָה אֶל־הָאֱלֹהִים וַיִּקְרָא אֵלָיו יְהוָה מִן־הָהָר לֵאמֹר כֹּה תֹאמַר לְבֵית יַעֲקֹב
וְתַגֵּיד לִבְנֵי יִשְׂרָאֵל:

4 אַתֶּם רְאִיתֶם אֲשֶׁר עָשִׂיתִי לְמִצְרָיִם וָאֶשָּׂא אֶתְכֶם עַל־כַּנְפֵי נְשָׁרִים וָאָבִא אֶתְכֶם אֵלָי:

5 וְעַתָּה אִם־שָׁמוֹעַ תִּשְׁמְעוּ בְּקֹלִי וּשְׁמַרְתֶּם אֶת־בְּרִיתִי וִהְיִיתֶם לִי סְגֻלָּה מִכָּל־הָעַמִּים כִּי־לִי
כָּל־הָאָרֶץ:

6 וְאַתֶּם תִּהְיוּ־לִי מַמְלֶכֶת כֹּהֲנִים וְגוֹי קָדוֹשׁ אֵלֶּה הַדְּבָרִים אֲשֶׁר תְּדַבֵּר אֶל־בְּנֵי יִשְׂרָאֵל:

QUESTIONS ABOUT THE BIBLICAL TEXT

Why was Mount Sinai the right place for God to give the Ten Commandments to the Families-of-Yisrael?

_____

_____

_____

_____

_____

_____

_____

THE MIDRASH ANSWERS THIS SAME QUESTION

A MIDRASH [Bereshit Rabbah 79.1]

When God was picking the place to be the place where the Torah was given, a quarrel broke out among the mountains. Each one insisted that "The Torah should have been given on me." Mount Tavor and Mount Carmel both claimed to be the right mountain. God, however, told the mountains—none of you is right, because each of you served as a place where idols were worshiped. Mount Sinai is a low mountain, it never served as a place of idol worship, therefore it is the chosen place.

A MIDRASH
[Targum/Tosefta]

All of the mountains expected to be chosen to be the place where the Torah was given. Mount Tavor said: "I am so tall that the flood didn't even cover half of me. I am the right place. Mount Hermon said: "I am the right choice, God used me to divide the Reed Sea. Mount Carmel said: "My location is perfect, right for either land or sea." Mount Sinai didn't say anything. God chose Mount Sinai because of its humility. This made it the right place.

Separating the P'shat from the Drash

1. What facts from the Torah do these midrashim use?

Separating the Answers from the Messages

2. These midrashim add to the Torah without being based on specific verses. What question are they trying to answer?

3. The rabbis wrote two different midrashim for the same question. How could they believe that both were true?

4. What value does each of these midrashim teach?

_____

_____

_____

_____

_____

_____

BEYOND THIS LESSON:

[1] Think about writing your own Mount Sinai midrash: (1) What did they put at the exact spot of the burning bush? (b) Why did God decide to have 10 commandments? (c) What commandments didn't make the top ten (but came close)? (d) Why did God pick a mountain as a place to give Torah?

[2] Some other midrashim that YITRO invites are: (a) How does Yitro know that Moshe & Co. are at Mount Sinai? (b) What is Moshe's reunion with his family like? (c) How does Yitro figure out that appointing judges is a good idea? (d) Two Torah portions are named after non-Jews YITRO and BALAK (a bad guy)? Why do non-Jews get Torah portions?

[3] What other questions about YITRO would be good triggers for midrash?

18. Mishpatim

Exodus 21:1-24:18

Now these are the regulations that you are to set before them...(Exodus 21:1)

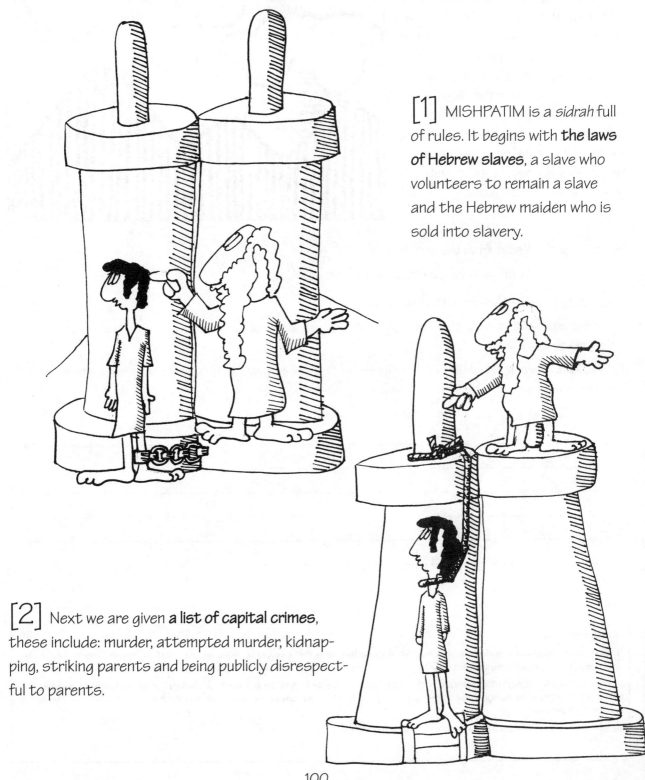

[1] MISHPATIM is a *sidrah* full of rules. It begins with **the laws of Hebrew slaves**, a slave who volunteers to remain a slave and the Hebrew maiden who is sold into slavery.

[2] Next we are given **a list of capital crimes**, these include: murder, attempted murder, kidnapping, striking parents and being publicly disrespectful to parents.

Ox

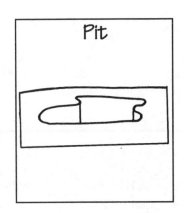

Pit

Tooth

Fire

[3] Following that we are given **a set of rules of damages**. Here we meet four famous Jewish characters: **the goring ox**, **the pit**, **the tooth** and **the fire**.

[4] Moving along, we have rules of theft and fraud. Also included are rules about witchcraft, treatment of animals, oppressing the stranger, lending money, first-born, carrying false rumors, fair courts, the sabbatical year and even the 3 pilgrimage festivals.

[5] Together these rules form the foundation for a basic Jewish society. At the end the *sidrah*, God warns the people about following the pagan customs of the nations around them, and promises to send an angel ahead of them to protect them. Finally, the Families-of-Yisrael accept the law and Moshe goes up Mount Sinai to receive the Tablets of the Law.

CJ'S COMMENTS

[1]: MISHPATIM: From the name, I would think that Mishpatim would have to do more with families than with rules. But seeing as the names of these parashot come from the beginning words, we can't judge a parashah by its title. **[C.J.]**

The word for family מִשְׁפָּחָה *Mishpahah* comes from the root: [שפח] which means spill. In a certain sense, a family is a "blood spill." The word for judgement/laws is מִשְׁפָּטִים from the root [שפט]—close but no cigar. They are homonyms but nothing else. **[GRIS]**

[2]: I have taken a look at the capital crimes and I realize that many of these rules are still considered to be crimes in today's (non-Jewish) society. The only one that isn't considered a crime is publicly disrespecting parents. I have mixed feelings about this. Many kids disrespect their parents unjustly. Their parents give them everything. Other times, though, kids' lives are ruined by their parents. I think that in most cases, kids should be respectful of their parents; but that won't keep any kids, me included, from having private opinions of what their parents do sometimes. **[C.J.]**

The Talmud makes a very big deal out of this law. In the Mishnah they say that a son can only be considered rebellious from the time he can grow two pubic hairs until the time he can grow a beard (while he is a teenager). (Girls are let off the hook this time.) In the Gemara, they tighten it and say that a child can only be liable for punishment for crimes committed on his 13th birthday (I won't go into the legal details here). But the bottom line is that the Talmud says, "There never was and there never will be a son rebellious enough to merit stoning." And I add, but the law is there to teach us that a lot of sons come close at least once or twice in their lives. **[GRIS]**

[3]: Most of the punishments for these crimes are death. The only times the punishment does not include death is under accidental circumstances, or when damage is not at a certain level. Eye for eye, tooth for tooth. **[C.J.]** CONTINUED ON PAGE 191

THE BIBLICAL TEXT

This *sidrah* describes the Families-of-Yisrael becoming the choosing people—the people who chose to accept the Torah. As you read the description of their acceptance, see if you can figure out what made them worthy.

Exodus 24: 3-4

3. So Moshe came
   and recounted to the people all the words of YHWH and all the regulations.
   And all the people answered in one voice, and said:
   All the words that YHWH has spoken, we will do.
4. Now Moshe wrote down all the words of YHWH…

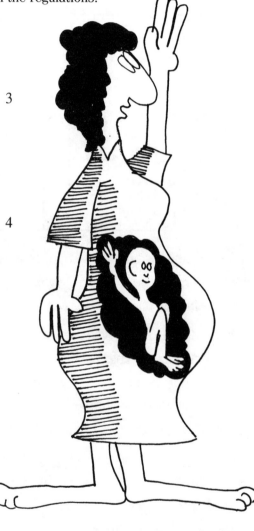

3 וַיָּבֹא מֹשֶׁה

וַיְסַפֵּר לָעָם אֵת כָּל־דִּבְרֵי יהוה וְאֵת כָּל־הַמִּשְׁפָּטִים

וַיַּעַן כָּל־הָעָם קוֹל אֶחָד

וַיֹּאמְרוּ כָּל־הַדְּבָרִים אֲשֶׁר־דִּבֶּר יהוה נַעֲשֶׂה:

4 וַיִּכְתֹּב מֹשֶׁה אֵת כָּל־דִּבְרֵי יהוה

QUESTIONS ABOUT THE BIBLICAL TEXT

What made the Families-of-Yisrael the right people to receive God's law?

_____

_____

_____

_____

_____

_____

THE MIDRASH ANSWERS THIS SAME QUESTION

A MIDRASH [Pirke d' Rabbi Eliezer 41]

The people listened and unanimously answered: "*Na'aseh v'Nishma*—we will do and we will hearken." They said, we will observe and fulfill all the mitzvot in the Torah, even though we have not yet heard them.

(CLUE: Notice that it says We will DO before it says we will LISTEN. An act of blind faith.)

A MIDRASH [Song of Songs R. 1:24]

God asked the Families-of-Yisrael: "Even though you want to accept the Torah, who will guarantee that you will keep your commitment?"

The Families-of-Yisrael answered: "Our ancestors will be our guarantors."

God answered: "Your forefathers need their own guarantors. Each of them doubted me. AVRAHAM doubted that he would have a son, YITZHAK favored Esav over Yaakov, and YAAKOV doubted when Yosef disappeared."

The Families-of-Yisrael then said: "How about the prophets?"

God answered: "Your prophets often spoke for me but sometimes they fled like Jonah."

At this point, the children still in the wombs of their mothers spoke to God. "We will be the guarantors that the Torah will be studied and observed."

God answered: "This I will accept."

Separating the P'shat from the Drash

1. What single fact from the Torah does this midrash use?

Separating the Answers from the Messages

2. What is the literal question these two midrashim are answering? (It is a question of language!)

3. How does the midrash answer this question?

4. The deeper question is why were the Families-of-Yisrael trusted with the Torah? What two answers are given to this question?

_____

_____

_____

_____

_____

BEYOND THIS LESSON:

[1] Think about writing your own "Receiving the Torah" midrash: (a) The Families-of-Israel said "We will do" before they said "We will listen." When they got around to "listening" what was the first law they studied? (b) God knew in advance that Israel would break their promise to "obey" the law—why did God still give it to them? (c) Look at the order of the laws taught in this *sidrah*—explain why God chose that order.

[2] Some other midrashim that this sidrah invites are: (a) In this *sidrah* God gives rules for slavery—explain why God let the Families-of-Israel have slavery. (b) In this law, God starts with slavery and then moves to capital crimes—why did the death penalty come near the top of this code? (c) God puts Jewish holidays at the end of a criminal law code—explain the connection.

[3] What other questions about MISHPATIM would be good triggers for midrash?

19. Terumah
Exodus 25:1-27:19

Now YHWH spoke to Moshe, saying: Speak to the Children of Yisrael that they may take me a raised-contribution... (Exodus 25:1).

[1] TERUMAH begins the description of the *Mishkan*. The *sidrah* opens with *God* directing Moshe to tell the Families-of-Yisrael **to bring gifts for the Mishkan.** The *Mishkan* was to be a "dwelling place" for *God* within the Families-of-Yisrael's camp. It was a portable sanctuary. *God* asked for 13 different kinds of materials: (1) gold, (2) silver, (3) copper, (4) blue yarn, (5) purple yarn, (6) crimson yarn, (7) fine linen, (8) goats' hair, (9) tanned ram skins, (10) dolphin skins, (11) acacia wood, (12) oil and spices. and (13) stones for the breast plate.

[2] The Torah then describes three items which will be used in the *Mishkan*. These are the ARON—the ark which will be used to hold the Torah, the SHULHAN—the table which holds the 12 loaves of shew bread which were brought daily, and the MENORAH—the candlestick with seven branches which was lighted in the sanctuary.

CJ'S COMMENTS

[1]: At the beginning of TERUMAH we see God's instructions for Moshe to instruct B'nai Yisrael to bring gifts for the Mishkan. Listed afterward are materials that were/are valuable, and were probably hard to get for a traveling religion. Caravans, however, might have had some of these materials. God asked for freewill donations instead of fixed ones because some people might not have had the connections or the money to afford these items. God did not want to embarrass these people. So, if God knew these things would be hard to get, why didn't God provide them? It is another test. God wants the Yisraelites to get serious because now the real work will start. God needs some trust and this is how it will be tested. **[C.J.]**

[3] Next the Torah describes **the Mishkan** itself. It is a tent with 20 columns on each of the long sides, and 6 on the one closed wall. The top and the open side were covered with curtains. The *Mishkan* was divided into two rooms, the holy of holies where the ark was stored, and the holy—which was the remaining two-thirds of the tent. There was a complicated plan of connectors and fasteners which allowed it to be constructed and taken apart—just like an erector set.

The midrash has fun with these donations—because they seem so out of line for a people wandering in the desert. Where does a Bedouin get "dolphin skin?" They give a number of fun answers: (1) That much of the booty came from the Egyptians—the jewels that Israel "borrowed" as payment for 400 years of slavery, (2) That gems and other goodies were pulled out of the Red Sea when it was crossed, (3) That for the righteous, pearls rained down with the manna, etc. The idea, as stated below, is that each of the 13 items donated by Israel either cleansed a specific sin or brought a specific merit—and that for each item donated, Yisrael got a specific blessing. **[GRIS]**

[4] In addition, the *sidrah* describes **a copper altar** with horns which was used for sacrifices.

[2]: The next thing we see (at least in Joel's summary) happens to be three items: The ARON, the SHULḤAN, and the MENORAH. I'm going to concentrate on the third one. This menorah may not be one that many of you reading this book are familiar with. Maybe you know about a menorah which has nine branches and we use on Hannukah. This is the Ḥannukiyah, a more modern version of the menorah. The ancient menorah was lighted in the sanctuary. How

CONTINUED ON PAGE 191

Mishkan = Tabernacle

THE BIBLICAL TEXT

This week, the Torah describes the donations requested by God for the *Mishkan*. As you read the list, see (1) if you can believe that all of these things were findable in the wilderness, and (2) if you can figure out the reason for each item.

Exodus 25:1-9

1. Now YHWH spoke to Moshe, saying:
2. Speak to the Children of Yisrael,
   that they may take me a raised-contribution;
   from every man whose heart makes-him-willing, you are to take my contribution.
3. And this is the contribution that you are to take from them:
   gold, silver, and bronze,
4. blue-violet, purple, and worm-scarlet (yarn), byssus, and goats'-hair,
5. rams' skins dyed-red, tanned-leather skins,
   acacia wood,
6. oil for lighting,
   spices of oil of anointing and for fragrant smoking-incense,
7. onyx stones, stones for setting
   for the *efod* and for the breastpiece.
8. Let them make me a Holy-Shrine
   that I may dwell amidst them.
9. According to all that I grant you to see,
   the building-pattern of the Dwelling and the building-pattern of all its implements,
   thus are you to make it.

1 וַיְדַבֵּר יְהוָה אֶל־מֹשֶׁה לֵּאמֹר:

2 דַּבֵּר אֶל־בְּנֵי יִשְׂרָאֵל וְיִקְחוּ־לִי תְּרוּמָה מֵאֵת כָּל־אִישׁ אֲשֶׁר יִדְּבֶנּוּ לִבּוֹ תִּקְחוּ אֶת־תְּרוּמָתִי:

3 וְזֹאת הַתְּרוּמָה אֲשֶׁר תִּקְחוּ מֵאִתָּם זָהָב וָכֶסֶף וּנְחֹשֶׁת:

4 וּתְכֵלֶת וְאַרְגָּמָן וְתוֹלַעַת שָׁנִי וְשֵׁשׁ וְעִזִּים:

5 וְעֹרֹת אֵילִם מְאָדָּמִים וְעֹרֹת תְּחָשִׁים וַעֲצֵי שִׁטִּים:

6 שֶׁמֶן לַמָּאֹר בְּשָׂמִים לְשֶׁמֶן הַמִּשְׁחָה וְלִקְטֹרֶת הַסַּמִּים:

7 אַבְנֵי־שֹׁהַם וְאַבְנֵי מִלֻּאִים לָאֵפֹד וְלַחֹשֶׁן:

8 וְעָשׂוּ לִי מִקְדָּשׁ וְשָׁכַנְתִּי בְּתוֹכָם:

9 כְּכֹל אֲשֶׁר אֲנִי מַרְאֶה אוֹתְךָ אֵת תַּבְנִית הַמִּשְׁכָּן וְאֵת תַּבְנִית כָּל־כֵּלָיו וְכֵן תַּעֲשׂוּ:

QUESTIONS ABOUT THE BIBLICAL TEXT

1. Do you believe that it was really possible for the Families-of-Yisrael to donate all of these things in the wilderness? (Clue: Ex. 11.1-3).

2. What was the reason for asking for freewill donations (and not demanding a fixed donation)?

THE MIDRASH ANSWERS THESE SAME QUESTIONS

A MIDRASH [Shemot Rabbah 36.9]

When Moshe heard that a *Mishkan* was to be built in the midst of the desert, he doubted that the community had enough materials with which to build it. God told him: "Not only do the Families-of-Yisrael collectively possess all the necessary materials to build a *Mishkan,* but in fact—every single Jew is capable of providing all that is needed to build a *Mishkan.*"

A MIDRASH [Midrash Ha Gadol 25.1]

God asked for donations of 13 different kinds of materials because each type of material was selected to help Yisrael atone for a specific sin. This makes sense, because among other things, the *Mishkan* was a place for making atonement.

Gold = the golden calf

Silver = the sale of Yosef for 22 pieces of silver

Copper = impurities in their hearts (NOTE: This midrash then goes through the remainder of the 13 items.)

Separating the P'shat from the Drash

1   What facts from the Torah does this midrash use?

Separating the Answers from the Messages

2.   According to these midrashim, how was it possible to build the *Mishkan* in the wilderness?

3.   According to these midrashim, why did God ask for freewill offerings?

4.   What values are taught by these two midrashim? What lesson could you teach about the *Mishkan* based on them?

_____

_____

_____

_____

_____

BEYOND THIS LESSON:

[1] Think about writing your own midrashim on the collecting for the *Mishkan*: God asks the people to donate 13 kinds of things. What was the lesson of donating each kind of thing? (1) gold, (2) silver, (3) copper, (4) blue yarn, (5) purple yarn, (6) crimson yarn, (7) fine linen, (8) goats' hair, (9) tanned ram skins, (10) dolphin skins, (11) acacia wood, (12) oil and spices. and (13) stones for the breast plate.

[2] Some other midrashim that this *sidrah* invites are: (a) Shaye Horowitz asked: "If God said no idols, why are there golden cherubim on the ark?" (b) What lesson is supposed to be learned from keeping a menorah with 7 lights in the *Mishkan*? (3) If the *Shulḥan* could talk, how would it explain its strange collection of trays and loaves?

[3] What other questions about TERUMAH would be good triggers for midrash?

20. Tetzaveh

Exodus 27:20-30:10

Now you, command the Children of Yisrael, that they may fetch you oil of olives, clear, beaten, for the light, to draw up a lampwick, regularly (Exodus 27:20).

[1] TETZAVEH is the second *parashah* which involves preparing the *Mishkan*. This time most of our focus is on the *Kohanim*. First we have a special responsibility for **the Families-of-Yisrael to bring olive oil for the** Menorah.

[2] Then **Aharon, and his sons Nadav, Avihu, Elazer and Itamar are chosen to serve as priests—Kohanim.** Next we begin a long description of the special clothing a *kohain* was to wear. It included: the tunic, the breeches (the world's earliest description of underwear), the belt, the hat, the mantle (the overgarment), the apron, the breast plate, and the head plate.

[1]: My biggest summary question is: Why was an altar built to burn incense? Incense smells nice and all, but is there any particular reason? **[C.J.]**

Let's look at four clues: Clue One: Think of the spicebox used at havdalah. The spicebox replaces the "hallah" used in the welcoming of Shabbat triptych (along with candles and wine). It is the spiritual component, soul food rather than stomach food. Likewise, the incense (smoke and smell) represents the soul sacrifice rather than the food sacrifice on the big altar. On Yom Kippur when the *Kohein ha-Gadol* went into the Holy-of-Holies to ask God's forgiveness face to not-face, the incense smoke was used to mask God's presence. Clue Two: The altar is also called (a) the Golden Altar and (b) the Interior Altar. The Golden Altar name comes from the fact that it was covered in gold. The Interior Altar name comes from the fact that it was placed in the interior of the *Mishkan*. But, both names may also be symbolic—incense representing our inner-gold. Clue Three: Midrash *Tanhuma* teaches that the other sacrifices on the other altar atone for various kinds of sin, but the incense sacrifice is a symbol of pure joy and happiness. When the *Mishkan* was first set up and the sacrifices offered, the regular sacrifices did not bring God. The *Shekhinah* (the part of God that gets close) only showed up when the incense was burned. Clue Four: The rule is that the incense smoke must rise up to heaven as a column of smoke. A direct connection between Torah and God. But here is the final secret: When Noah offers the first sacrifice ever, the Torah says, "THE ETERNAL SMELLED THE SOOTHING ODOR..." Evidently, God likes smells. They have a direct spiritual connection. **[GRIS]**

[2]: Olive oil might be used because it emphasizes cleanliness, and olive oil is generally pure. **[C.J.]**

[3]: The first midrash doesn't seem important nor does it say anything to me. I'd take it out. The second, however, is a good

CONTINUED ON PAGE 192

[3] Following this there is a long description of the sacrifices and **ceremonies which were used to ordain the Kohanim.** At the end of the *sidrah* we are introduced to the altar for burning incense.

THE BIBLICAL TEXT

In last week's *sidrah*, TERUMAH, we were introduced to the *Mishkan* and three of its major furnishings: The *Aron*, the *Shulhan* and the *Menorah*. This week's *sidrah* mainly talks about the *kohanim*. However, at the beginning of this parashah is a passage dealing with the mitzvah of bringing olive oil. As you read it, think about these two questions:

a. Why does God make a point of inserting this mitzvah here, right in the middle of the designs for the *Mishkan* and its furnishings?

b. Why is the Torah so specific about the kind of oil which is to be used?

Exodus 27.20-21

20. Now you,
    command the Children of Yisrael,
    that they may fetch you
    oil of olives, clear, beaten,
    for the light,
    to draw up a lampwick, regularly.

21. In the Tent of Appointment,
    outside the curtain that is over the Testimony,
    Aharon and his sons are to arrange it,
    from sunset until daybreak
    before the presence of Yнwн—
    a law for the ages, throughout your generations,
    on the part of the Children of Yisrael.

20 וְאַתָּה תְּצַוֶּה אֶת־בְּנֵי יִשְׂרָאֵל וְיִקְחוּ אֵלֶיךָ שֶׁמֶן זַיִת זָךְ כָּתִית לַמָּאוֹר לְהַעֲלֹת נֵר תָּמִיד:

21 בְּאֹהֶל מוֹעֵד מִחוּץ לַפָּרֹכֶת אֲשֶׁר עַל־הָעֵדֻת יַעֲרֹךְ אֹתוֹ אַהֲרֹן וּבָנָיו מֵעֶרֶב עַד־בֹּקֶר לִפְנֵי יְהוָה חֻקַּת עוֹלָם לְדֹרֹתָם מֵאֵת בְּנֵי יִשְׂרָאֵל:

QUESTIONS ABOUT THE BIBLICAL TEXT

a. Why do you think the Torah adds this mitzvah about olive oil after the plans for the *Mishkan* and before the designs for the *kohanim*?

b. What is so special about 'pure/clear beaten olive oil'? Why do you think the Torah is so specific about this kind of oil?

_____

_____

_____

_____

_____

_____

THE MIDRASH ANSWERS THESE SAME QUESTIONS

A MIDRASH
[Midrash Hagadol 27.2]

God said to Moshe: "Let the Families-of-Yisrael eternally occupy themselves with the mitzvah of bringing the olive oil. Through it they will gain merit, and remember that the *Mishkan* is for them and not just for the *kohanim*."

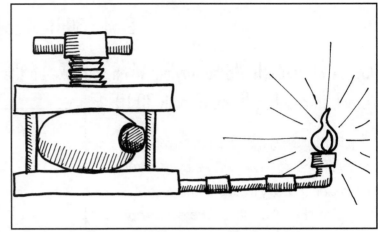

A MIDRASH
[Shemot Rabbah 36.1]

What kind of olive oil was usable in the *Mishkan*? Only the oil which came from the first pressing of an olive could be used. These first few drops were clear and had no sediment. So, when you beat the olives, you got the clear oil. After this, the olives needed to be ground and then filtered.

Why did God choose this oil for lighting? The prophet Jeremiah taught (11.15) that Yisrael is like an olive. He said: "A fresh olive, a fruit of beautiful shape, did God call your name."

How is Yisrael like olive oil? Just as olive oil is the finest of all oils, so Yisrael is the holiest of all nations. Most liquids when you mix them, mix together, but like oil Yisrael will never be absorbed into the other nations. When you put liquids together, oil rises to the top, so too, Yisrael rises when they follow the Torah. Just as oil serves to give light, Yisrael is a light to the nations.

Separating the P'shat from the Drash

1. Overline/highlight the stuff from the Bible used in this midrash.

Separating the Answers from the Messages

2. How *do* these midrashim explain why this mitzvah is taught here?

3. The second midrash uses a number of comparisons to show that olive oil is used because it is like Yisrael. What *do* these comparisons teach about Yisrael?

4. What *Divrei Torah* could you write based on these midrashim?

_____

_____

_____

BEYOND THIS LESSON:

[1] Think about writing your own "olive oil" midrash: (a) Tell the story of the first olive oil that Adam and Eve made (or whoever made the first source of light by fire). (b) Tell the story of the olive tree from which Noah's dove plucked its post-flood olive branch. (c) Explain where the Families-of-Israel found olive oil in the wilderness. (d) Write the story of the competition between olives, corn, animal fat, and other kinds of oil to be the source of the eternal light. Why did God pick the olive?

[2] Some other Midrashim that this sidrah invites are: (a) The lesson to be learned from each of the garments that the *kohanim* wore: The shirt, the underwear, the belt, the turban, the mantle, the apron, the breastplate, and the headplate. (b) Look at the order of the twelve stones on the breastplate (Exodus 28:17-21) and see if you can explain the meaning of the pattern and the colors. (c) Look up—then explain—the secret of the *Urim* and *Tumim*. (Exodus 28:30)

[3] What other questions about TETZAVEH would be good triggers for midrash?

21. Ki Tissa

Exodus 30:11-34:35

Now YHWH spoke to Moshe, saying: When you take up the head-count of the Children of Yisrael, in counting them. (Exodus 30:11)

[1] In KI TISSA we have new rules, more parts of the *Mishkan* and we even return to the ongoing story of the Families-of-Yisrael in the wilderness. The *sidrah* opens with rules for taking census. Moshe is told to **collect a coin for each person rather than count the numbers directly.**

[2] Then we are introduced to a new *Mishkan* part—the KIYOR, a laver for washing—and we are given the formula for making incense and the formula for making anointing oil.

DRAW YOUR OWN IMAGE HERE

[3] Next **we meet Betzalel**, the skilled craftsman who headed the actual construction of the *Mishkan*. Next the focus changes and **God restates the rules for observing Shabbat.**

[4] Now, the scene changes. We find Moshe still up on Mount Sinai (the end of the 40 days and 40 nights). **God gives him the two tablets of the Law.** He takes them, heads down the mountain **and finds the golden calf**. Aharon had made the calf because the people were restless while Moshe was away. Moshe dropped the tablets. Then he had the calf destroyed. Both were destroyed.

[5] **Moshe then grinds up the calf, mixes it with water and makes the people drink.** He then criticizes Aharon and all the people. God then complains about the people. Moshe takes his tent and moves it away from everyone else. Moshe and God talk about the Families-of-Yisrael and what to do with them and then **Moshe is sent back up the mountain to get a second set of commandments.** At the end of the portion, we get **a restatement of the covenant**, a restatement of some key rules and a look at Moshe working on the new commandments on Mount Sinai.

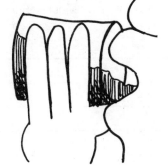

CJ'S COMMENTS

[1]: Maybe we should explain what anointing oil is. We covered incense before. Anointing oil was poured over people's heads to make them pure. They used this when new kings were introduced. It was also used on the *kohanim*. **[C.J.]**

Are you ready for a treasure hunt? There is a midrash which teaches that Moshe made two gallons of anointing oil—which is all that has ever been used. It miraculously was enough to serve the needs of every anointment. When the Temple was destroyed, the remaining oil was hidden away to wait for the *Mashiah* (the anointed one) who will be anointed with this very Mosaic oil. Rashi also reports that the anointing oil included a blend of 12 spices—11 sweet smelling, and 1 bitter—explaining that even difficult Jews have an important role within the Families-of-Israel. **[GRIS]**

[2]: Now we meet the real Ben Hur: Betzalel. Funny how grandfather and grandson are here in the same *parashah* (at least midrashically). It's also funny that right after we get focused on building and working, we become occupied with rest. **[C.J.]**

Good insight. The rabbis learn the connection between the two parts of this portion— rules for building the *Mishkan* and the "Keep Shabbat" restatement to develop the 39 categories of labor which cannot be done on Shabbat. Basically, this *sidrah* teaches the lesson that, if it was done to build the *Mishkan*, it is forbidden on Shabbat. If God wouldn't let the most holy work in the world be done on Shabbat, no work can be done. Or as Abraham Joshua Heschel put it, "Six days a week we build a *Mishkan* in space, on the Seventh Day we build a *Mishkan* in time, in eternity." All that we learn from the juxtaposition you noticed. **[GRIS]**

[3]: My favorite quote from the Ten Commandments: "Those who do not live by the law...shall die by the law! Kaboom!" Here we see Moshe coming down from the mountain, only to be infuriated and then throw the tablets at the calf, destroying both.

CONTINUED ON PAGE 192

THE BIBLICAL TEXT

NOW A TRUTH CAN BE TOLD. When you read the Torah, it seems that God gave Moshe the Ten Commandments on Mount Sinai. When you hear people talk (and that talking is usually based on midrashim) you hear them speak about God giving the Torah to Moshe on Mount Sinai. Did God give just the Ten Commandments or the whole Torah on Mount Sinai? When you read the midrashim (and the Torah text) closely, you can figure out that during the 40 days and 40 nights God taught the Torah to Moshe on Mount Sinai and gave him the Ten Commandments to take back to the Families-of-Yisrael. As you read this text, here is the question for you to think about:

Why did God only give 10 of the mitzvot in written form (at this point in time)?

Exodus 31:18

18. Now he gave to Moshe
    when he had finished speaking with him on Mount Sinai
    the two tablets of Testimony,
    tablets of stone,
    written by the finger of God.

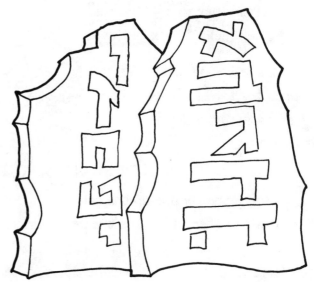

18 וַיִּתֵּן אֶל־מֹשֶׁה
כְּכַלֹּתוֹ לְדַבֵּר אִתּוֹ בְּהַר סִינַי
שְׁנֵי לֻחֹת הָעֵדֻת לֻחֹת אֶבֶן כְּתֻבִים
בְּאֶצְבַּע אֱלֹהִים:

QUESTIONS ABOUT THE BIBLICAL TEXT

If God spent 40 days and 40 nights teaching Moshe on Mount Sinai, why was Moshe only given 10 commandments to bring back to the Families-of-Yisrael?

_____

_____

_____

_____

_____

_____

THE MIDRASH ANSWERS THIS SAME QUESTION

A MIDRASH [Midrash HaGadol 41.8]

Why did God only give the Families-of-Yisrael the Ten Commandments at Mount Sinai and not the whole Torah?

To what can this be compared? This can be compared to a child who just begins to go to school. At first, the teacher only shows him the letters of the alphabet on the blackboard. Later, when he has mastered these, the teacher gives him books. God gave the Families-of-Yisrael the Ten Commandments first, to teach them the basic Torah concepts; later God gave them the entire five books of the Torah.

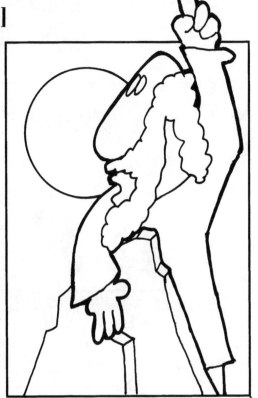

Separating the P'shat from the Drash

1. What facts from the Torah does this midrash use?

Separating the Answers from the Messages

2. This midrash works by comparison. Write down what is being compared to what.

3. Here are two questions to use to figure out what this midrash teaches about the Ten Commandments:

   How important are the Ten Commandments?

   Is it enough just to know the Ten Commandments?

---

22. Va-Yakhel

Exodus 35:1-38:20

Now Moshe assembled the entire community of the Children of Yisrael and said to them: These are the words that YHWH has commanded, to do them:...(Exodus 35:1).

[1] In VAYAKHEL Moshe gathers the Families-of-Yisrael in order to teach two things. First he teaches **the rules for Shabbat** (again), then he teaches **the rules for donating to the** *Mishkan* (again).

[2] Then comes a description of the actual work done by Betzalel and Company. At one point, Moshe has to tell the Families-of-Yisrael to **stop the donations, there are too many**.

[3] Among the interesting details, the *kiyor*—the laver—was made out of the copper taken from mirrors donated by the women.

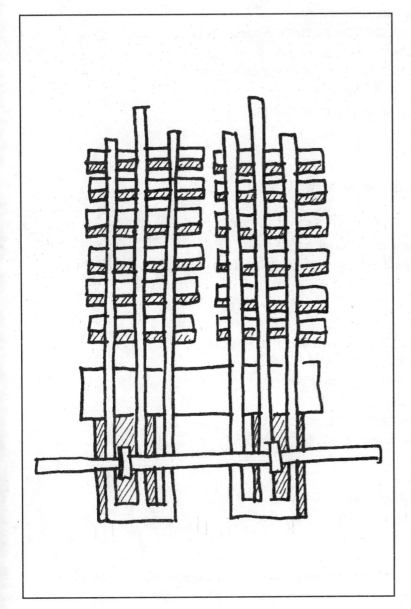

CJ'S COMMENTS

[1]: Why did Moshe reteach the rules concerning Shabbat and the *Mishkan* twice? Were the people not understanding the instructions, disobeying them, or did they need the review? **[C.J.]**

This answer is going to be confusing. But so is the passage. The Torah tells this story out of order. The picking of Betzalel and the building of the Tabernacle comes after the Golden Calf story in history—but part of the story is told before that happens. Think of it like being the "clips" shown at the beginning of a TV show, which show action from the middle and the end of the episode—before you ever begin watching this week's adventure. The preview gets you ready to anticipate the rest of the story. Rashi teaches that some "clips" which showed God's forgiveness following the sin of the Golden Calf were shown before the terror of the punishment which followed the sin. The explanations of Shabbat and the Building were "previewed" there as a way of letting us know that this passage would follow, that even the worst sins are followed by new starts, if you are willing to do *t'shuvah*. **[GRIS]**

[2]: I could undertand some people taking mirrors along with them, but enough to make a laver (basically the equivalent of a washbasin)? It seems that the Israelites were being a little arrogant to take such needless things as mirrors. With the need to bring all their flocks and such, wouldn't they have realized that the little things didn't matter? It is nice to know, though, that people brought too much. It shows the willingness to contribute to Judaism. **[C.J.]**

Your asking this question shows that you know little about women—and even less about men. Most people care about their looks. For them, a mirror was an essential. Their willingness to give up their outward

CONTINUED ON PAGE 193

Mishkan = Dwelling = The Tabernacle

THE BIBLICAL TEXT

What follows is the description of the actual work done on the *Mishkan*. As you read it, see if you can figure out:

1. What it actually looked like.

2. Why the Torah teaches us all this detail about a place of worship which was used only in ancient times.

Exodus 38:1-23

1. Then he made the slaughter-site of offering-up, of acacia wood,
   five cubits its length, five cubits its width, square,
   and three cubits its height.

2. He made its horns on its four points,
   from it were its horns.
   He overlaid it with bronze.

3. He made all the implements for the slaughter-site,
   the pails, the scrapers, the bowls, the flesh-hooks, and the pans;
   all its implements, he made of bronze.

4. He made for the slaughter-site a lattice, as a netting of bronze is made,
   beneath its ledge, below, (reaching) to its halfway-point.

5. He cast four rings on the four edges of the netting of bronze,
   as holders for the poles.

6. He made the poles of acacia wood
   and overlaid them with bronze.

7. He brought the poles through the rings on the flanks of the altar,
   to carry it by (means of) them;
   hollow, of planks, did he make it.

8. He made the basin of bronze, its pedestal of bronze,
   with the mirrors of the women's working-force that was doing-the-work at the entrance of the Tent of Appointment.

9. And he made the courtyard:
   on the Negev border, southward,
   the hangings of the courtyard, of twisted byssus, a hundred by the cubit,

10. with their columns, twenty, their sockets, twenty, of bronze,
    the hooks of the column and their binders, of silver.

11. And on the northern border, a hundred by the cubit,
    their columns, twenty, their sockets, twenty, of bronze,
    the hooks of the columns and their binders, of silver.

12. And on the sea border, hangings, fifty by the cubit,
    their columns, ten, their sockets, ten,
    and the hooks of the columns and their binders, of silver.

13. And on the eastern border, toward sunrise, fifty by the cubit,

14. (namely:) hangings of fifteen to the shoulder-piece,
    their columns, three, their sockets, three,

15. and for the second shoulder-piece—(over) here and (over) there for the gate of the courtyard—

hangings of fifteen cubits,

their columns, three, their sockets, three.

16. All the hangings of the courtyard all around, of twisted byssus,

17. and the sockets for the columns, of bronze,

the hooks of the columns and their binders, of silver,

and the overlay for their tops, of silver, they themselves bound with silver,

all the columns of the courtyard.

18. The screen of the courtyard gate, of embroiderer's making,

of blue-violet, purple, worm-scarlet, and twisted byssus,

twenty cubits in length,

their height along the width, five cubits,

corresponding to the hangings of the courtyard,

19. their columns, four, their sockets, four, of bronze,

their hooks, of silver,

and the overlay for their tops and their binders, of silver,

20. and all the pins for the Dwelling and for the courtyard all around, of bronze.

21. These are the accountings of the Dwelling,

the Dwelling of Testimony,

that were accounted by Moshe

for the service of the Levites,

under Itamar, son of Aharon the priest:

22. So Betzalel son of Uri, son of Ḥur, of the tribe of Yehuda

had made

all that Yhwh had commanded Moshe,

23. and with him, Oholiav son of Ahisamakh, of the tribe of Dan,

carver, designer, embroiderer in the blue-violet, purple and work, scarlet and byssus.

QUESTIONS ABOUT THE BIBLICAL TEXT

BASED ON THIS TEXT, DRAW BLUEPRINTS FOR THE *MISHKAN* ON THE NEXT PAGE.

Why do you think the Torah goes into this much detail about the *Mishkan*?

_____

_____

_____

_____

_____

_____

_____

_____

_____

_____

Draw your Mishkan Blueprints Here!

THE MIDRASH ANSWERS THESE SAME QUESTIONS

A MIDRASH [Rav Bechi 38.9]

Although the mitzvot of the *Mishkan* are not ones that we can practice today, God gives us a reward for learning them. We are rewarded for studying the layout of the *Mishkan* and the design of furnishings and especially for studying their symbolic meaning.

The rabbis taught that someone who studies the laws of the sacrifices is considered to be equal to one who actually offered sacrifices. That means that by studying about how people thanked God and made atonement through the *Mishkan,* we learn how to thank God and make atonement.

A MIDRASH [Talmud, Brakhot 55a]:

The book of Proverbs says: "YHWH FOUNDED THE EARTH BY **WISDOM**, GOD ESTABLISHED THE HEAVENS BY **UNDER-STANDING**, BY GOD'S KNOWLEDGE THE DEPTHS BURST APART." (Proverbs 3:19-20). When Betzalel enters the text, God says: "I HAVE FILLED HIM WITH THE SPIRIT OF GOD IN PRACTICAL-**WISDOM**, DISCERNMENT AND **KNOWLEDGE**." (Ex. 31.1-2) When Betzalel created the *Mishkan*, he was just like God creating the world, using **WISDOM** and **KNOWLEDGE**. When Betzalel finished the *Mishkan*, God said: "THUS WERE FINISHED THE HEAVENS AND THE EARTH, WITH ALL THEIR ARRAY." (Gen 2.1) The creation of the *Mishkan* was just like the creation of the world. In a spiritual sense, the *Mishkan* was a model for the universe.

A HASIDIC TEACHING [Menahem Mendel of Kotzk]: When God tells Israel: "LET THEM MAKE ME A HOLY-SHRINE/*MISHKAN* THAT I MAY DWELL AMIDST THEM," (Ex. 25.8) the Torah is teaching that by building the physical *Mishkan*, we are turning our hearts into a *Mishkan*, a place where God can dwell and be our neighbor.

Separating the P'shat from the Drash

1. What facts from the Torah does this midrash use?

2. How do these link different parts of the Torah to find an answer?

Separating the Answers from the Messages

3. These midrashim are really comments on a problem. They try to answer a question. Restate "the big question."

4. According to these midrashim, why are the plans for the *Mishkan* so important? Each midrash suggests something different we can learn from the specifics and the details.

5. What *Davar Torah* would you give based on this problem and these answers?

_____

_____

BEYOND THIS LESSON:

[1] Think about writing your own *Mishkan* midrash: (a) Where is the human holy of holies? (b) What kind of sacrifices do we offer in our lives? (c) What is our burning incense? (d) With what do we light the menorah of our soul? (e) What is written on the tablets in your heart?

[2] Some other midrashim that this *sidrah* invites are: (a) What was the first gathering to start the *Mishkan* like—given all that had gone on before? (b) What was it like to be building the *Mishkan*—was there singing or silence, cooperation or bickering? (c) What happened to the extra donations that weren't used in building the *Mishkan* or the holy garments?

[3] What other questions about Va-Yak-hel would be good triggers for midrash?

23. Pekudei

Exodus 38:21-40:38

These are the accountings of the Dwelling, the Dwelling of Testimony, that were accounted by Moshe for the service of the Levites, under Itamar, son of Aharon the priest (Exodus 38:21).

[1] PEKUDEI brings us to **the end of the construction of the Mishkan**, and the end of the book of Exodus. It begins with Moshe reporting to the Families-of-Yisrael how all the donations which were given were actually utilized in the *Mishkan*.

[2] Then **Moshe sets up the Mishkan** and Aharon and his sons are established as the *kohanim*.

CJ'S COMMENTS

[1]: It is the end of the construction of the *Mishkan*, it is also the end of Exodus. This, however, is the beginning of God's presence among the people. It sends us a nice message to feel that the people were safe with God's presence among them. Then the *sidrah* ends. That's it: *Hazak Hazak V'Nithazek*. Aren't there a few unanswered questions? Why did Moshe inform the people of how their donations were used? Did he think they'd get mad if they had to give up something without knowing why? Besides, this would be a long and boring task. This is a lot like modern day Bar Mitzvah thank-you notes, yet those have purpose. **[C.J.]**

Listen to this quote from *Midrash Tanhuma*; see if it answers your question. The person who collected money for the Holy Temple did not wear a double-hemmed garment, a hollow belt, or even pants. Because, that way, if he later became rich, no one could say he became rich by stealing from the Temple. Just as such a person must be flawless before God, so too he must be flawless in the sight of the entire people. It was to model honesty. But I like the thank-you note metaphor. Where did you come up with that idea—so original for a thirteen-year-old?**[GRIS]**

[2]: Another question is why cloud and fire? Aside from the easy answer: "Why not?" can you think of any other reasons? **[C.J.]**

This one is easy. The fire and the cloud were like "on the air" signs on the *Mishkan*. It was an indication to the Families-of-Yisrael that "God is in the House." But let's work backwards. We have seen the fire and the cloud twice before. Second, they led Israel when they walked through the wilderness. The cloud led them by day, the fire led them by night. First, when God gave the Torah on Mt. Sinai, the mountain was covered by a cloud and by fire. The fire, of course, goes back even earlier, to the burning bush. There are two ideas here. One, that the fire and the cloud keep people from seeing God's face. Remember, you can't see God's face and

[3] At the end of the work, **a cloud covers the Mishkan.** The *sidrah* ends with a report that a cloud always covered the *Mishkan* by day and a fire would appear in it at night. This symbolizes God's presence. "*Mishkan*" means dwelling place, and this shows that **God dwelled within the camp of the Families-of-Yisrael.**

HAZAK HAZAK V'NITHAZEK

CONTINUED ON PAGE **193**

THE BIBLICAL TEXT

At the end of the *sidrah*, the *Mishkan* is erected and God's presence comes to rest on it. As you read the Torah's description of this moment, see if you can figure out what makes this moment so special.

Exodus 40:33-38

33. He erected the courtyard all around the Dwelling and the slaughter-site,
    and put up the screen for the courtyard gate.
    So Moshe finished the work.
34. Now the cloud covered the Tent of Appointment,
    and the Glory of YHWH filled the Dwelling.
35. Moshe was not able to come into the Tent of Appointment,
    for the cloud took-up-dwelling on it, and the Glory of YHWH filled the Dwelling.
36. Whenever the cloud goes up from the Dwelling,
    the Children of Yisrael march on, upon all their marches;
37. if the cloud does not go up,
    they do not march on, until such time as it does go up.
38. For the cloud of YHWH (is) over the Dwelling by day,
    and fire is by night in it,
    before the eyes of all the House of Yisrael
    upon all their marches.

33 וַיָּקֶם אֶת־הֶחָצֵר סָבִיב לַמִּשְׁכָּן וְלַמִּזְבֵּחַ וַיִּתֵּן אֶת־מָסַךְ שַׁעַר הֶחָצֵר
וַיְכַל מֹשֶׁה אֶת־הַמְּלָאכָה:

34 וַיְכַס הֶעָנָן אֶת־אֹהֶל מוֹעֵד וּכְבוֹד יְהוָה מָלֵא אֶת־הַמִּשְׁכָּן:

35 וְלֹא־יָכֹל מֹשֶׁה לָבוֹא אֶל־אֹהֶל מוֹעֵד כִּי־שָׁכַן עָלָיו הֶעָנָן וּכְבוֹד יְהוָה מָלֵא אֶת־הַמִּשְׁכָּן:

36 וּבְהֵעָלוֹת הֶעָנָן מֵעַל הַמִּשְׁכָּן יִסְעוּ בְּנֵי יִשְׂרָאֵל בְּכֹל מַסְעֵיהֶם:

37 וְאִם־לֹא יֵעָלֶה הֶעָנָן וְלֹא יִסְעוּ עַד־יוֹם הֵעָלֹתוֹ:

38 כִּי עֲנַן יְהוָה עַל־הַמִּשְׁכָּן יוֹמָם וְאֵשׁ תִּהְיֶה לַיְלָה בּוֹ לְעֵינֵי כָל־בֵּית־יִשְׂרָאֵל בְּכָל־מַסְעֵיהֶם:

QUESTIONS ABOUT THE BIBLICAL TEXT

Why do you think this is the first time that God's presence is in the midst of the Families-of-Yisrael?

_____

_____

_____

_____

_____

THE MIDRASH ANSWERS THESE SAME QUESTIONS

A MIDRASH
[Pesikta d'Rav Kahana 1.2]:

(CLUE: SHEKHINAH=the presence of God which dwells among people)

God created the world so that the *Shekhinah* could dwell there. However, when Adam sinned, the *Shekhinah* moved to the first heaven. When the generation of Enosh sinned, the *Shekhinah* moved to the second heaven. When the generation of the flood was wicked, the *Shekhinah* moved to the third heaven. The evil of the tower of Bavel moved the *Shekhinah* to the fourth heaven. When Egypt was corrupt in Avraham's time, the *Shekhinah* moved to the fifth heaven. The sins of Sedom moved the *Shekhinah* to the sixth heaven. And the wickedness of the Egyptians in the generation of Moshe moved the *Shekhinah* to the seventh heaven.

Avraham's goodness brought the *Shekhinah* back to the sixth heaven. Yitzhak's faithfulness brought the *Shekhinah* back to the fifth heaven. Yaakov's returned the *Shekhinah* to the fourth heaven. Levi, who was founder of Moshe's tribe, brought the *Shekhinah* back to the third heaven. Kahat, Moshe's grandfather, brought the *Shekhinah* back to the second heaven. Amram, Moshe's father, brought the *Shekhinah* back to the first heaven. When Moshe set up the *Mishkan*, the *Shekhinah* again returned to dwell on earth.

Separating the P'shat from the Drash

1. List the Torah facts this midrash uses.

2. The ideas of the *Shekhinah* and the layers of heaven are not in the Torah. Underline/Overline the other non-Torah ideas this midrash uses.

Separating the Answers from the Messages

3. According to this midrash, what makes God further away from people? According to this midrash, what makes God closer to people?

4. How does this midrash explain why God waited to appear till the *Mishkan* was finished?

5. What does this midrash teach about the importance of family tradition?

_____

_____

_____

ON ANOTHER PAGE, DESIGN A VIDEO GAME CALLED SEVEN HEAVENS

BEYOND THIS LESSON:

[1] Think about writing your own "*Shekhinah* over the *Mishkan*" midrash: (a) Make your own list of things in history which brought the *Shekhinah* near, or moved it further from us. (b) C.J.'s question: Why did God choose to have a cloud and a fire appear over the *Mishkan*? (c) How is God's presence like a cloud? How is God's presence like a fire?

[2] Some other midrashim that this *sidrah* invites are: (a) Why did God pick Aharon and his family to be the *kohanim*? (b) Tell the story of the spot on which the *Mishkan* was first erected and the cloud first came down. (c) Tell the story of what happened to that spot after the *Mishkan* was moved.

[3] What other questions about PEKUDEI would be good triggers for midrash?

24. Va-Yikra

Leviticus 1:1-5:26

Now he called to Moshe—YHWH spoke to him from the Tent of Appointment,
saying:...(Leviticus 1:1).

VA-YIKRA starts the third book of the Torah. The book of VA-YIKRA is also called **TORAT HA-KOHANIM**, the Torah of the *Kohanim*. VA-YIKRA is also a Torah portion which talks about sacrifices. Now that the *Mishkan* is completed, and now that the *kohanim* are in service—we are ready for a description of their tasks. In VA-YIKRA we are introduced to 5 kinds of sacrifices:

[1] **THE OLAH**—The burnt offering. This is the regular daily offering which is given as a freewill offering. This can be an ox, a lamb, a goat, a turtledove, or a pigeon.

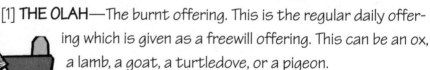

[2] **THE MINHAH**—The meal offering. This is an offering of flour and oil which is given by someone who cannot afford to give an animal.

DRAW YOUR OWN IMAGE HERE.

[3] THE SHLAMIM—The peace offering. This is an offering which is given like the Olah except that it is devoted to peace. In *Midrash Tanhuma* it says: "It is used by two friends who want to share a meal."

[4] THE HATAT—The sin offering. This is the offering of a person who broke a commandment—by doing something that was forbidden—and wants to atone.

[5] THE ASHAM—The guilt offering. This is an offering of forgiveness for someone who stole, lied, oppressed his neighbors or otherwise dealt falsely.

CJ'S COMMENTS

[1]: If you thought the chapters before were exciting, then here is the "climax". Actually not much takes place in VA-YIKRA except for the description of five kinds of sacrifices (one of my *favorite* subjects). If some of my assumptions are correct on the meanings of the names of the sacrifices, you can figure out why some of these names were chosen. You also get a little linguistics lesson (a linguist is someone who studies languages and their roots). **[C.J.]**

Personally I think that we modern folk can never really explain the sacrifices well enough that we will feel good about them—and actually imagine wanting to do them. (Though there are Jews who can't wait to start broasting *korbanot* in the third Temple—the one they want to burn down the Mosque of Omar to build.) Not even Maimonides felt that good about the sacrifices.

The Talmud points out that little kids should start studying Torah with Va-Yikra and the sacrifices rather than with Bereshit and the creation. Rabbi Assi explains this by saying "Children are pure and the sacrifices are pure. Let the pure come and occupy themselves with the pure." Somehow, for the Rabbis, the process of sacrifice, which is dirty and bloody (think about cleaning the barbecue at the end of the summer), brings a kind of cleanliness. I know about it, but I don't quite get it.

Rambam, however, seems to be on my side. He says in the *Guide to the Perplexed* "It is impossible to go suddenly from one extreme to the other. Human nature doesn't work in such a way that people can immediately reject everything which has been common. So when God sent Moshe to make the Israelites into a "Kingdom of Priests and a holy nation" it was to be a religion based on the knowledge of God...But the pattern of worship in those days was animal sacrifices. It was in God's plan to discontinue this practice...but to do so slowly... The sacrificial portions of the Torah were designed to get

CONTINUED ON PAGE 194

127

THE BIBLICAL TEXT

Here is the beginning of the Torah's description of the laws of sacrifice. As you read it, see if you can figure out which animals were chosen for sacrificing and why?

Leviticus 1:1-3 & 10

וַיִּקְרָא אֶל־מֹשֶׁה 1
מֵאֹהֶל וַיְדַבֵּר יְהוָה אֵלָיו מוֹעֵד לֵאמֹר:

דַּבֵּר אֶל־בְּנֵי יִשְׂרָאֵל וְאָמַרְתָּ אֲלֵהֶם 2
אָדָם כִּי־יַקְרִיב מִכֶּם קָרְבָּן לַיהוָה
מִן־הַבְּהֵמָה מִן־הַבָּקָר וּמִן־הַצֹּאן
תַּקְרִיבוּ אֶת־קָרְבַּנְכֶם:

אִם־עֹלָה קָרְבָּנוֹ מִן־הַבָּקָר 3
זָכָר תָּמִים יַקְרִיבֶנּוּ
אֶל־פֶּתַח אֹהֶל מוֹעֵד יַקְרִיב אֹתוֹ
לִרְצֹנוֹ לִפְנֵי יְהוָה:

וְאִם־מִן־הַצֹּאן קָרְבָּנוֹ 10
מִן־הַכְּשָׂבִים אוֹ מִן־הָעִזִּים לְעֹלָה
זָכָר תָּמִים יַקְרִיבֶנּוּ:

1. Now he called to Moshe—
   YHWH spoke to him from the Tent of Appointment,
   saying:
2. Speak to the Children of Yisrael and say to them:
   Anyone—when (one) among you brings-near a near-offering for YHWH
   from domestic-animals: from the herd or from the flock you may
   bring-near your near-offering.
3. If an offering-up is his near-offering, from the herd,
   (then) male, wholly-sound, let him bring-it-near,
   to the entrance of the Tent of Appointment let him bring-it-near,
   as acceptance for him, before the presence of YHWH.
10. Now if from the flock of his near-offering,
    from the sheep or from the goats, for an offering-up,
    (then) male, wholly-sound, let him bring-it-near.

QUESTIONS ABOUT THE BIBLICAL TEXT

1. List the three kinds of animals which were used for sacrifice (in biblical terms birds are not animals—
   they are birds).

2. Why do you think these three animals were chosen?

_____

_____

_____

THE MIDRASH ANSWERS THESE SAME QUESTIONS

A MIDRASH [Pesikta d'Rav Kahana]

God said: "There are 10 kinds of kosher animals, but only three of them are domesticated. Because I don't want you hunting the wild beasts of the hills and fields, I will take only the three domesticated animals: the ox, the sheep, and the goat as my sacrifices."

A MIDRASH [Sifre 54]

Each of these three animals teaches us something about our forefathers. The ox reminds us of AVRAHAM's welcoming guests, because he ran and got an ox to serve his three guests. The lamb reminds us of YITZHAK who had a ram sacrificed instead of him. And the goat reminds us of YAAKOV who served his father two kid goats when he received the blessing.

ABRAHAM

ISAAC

JACOB

Separating the P'shat from the Drash

1. Underline the parts of these midrashim which are taken directly from the Torah.

Separating the P'shat from the Drash

2. According to these midrashim, why were these three animals chosen? CLUE: The first midrash teaches why only some animals were chosen (and not all animals could be used). The second midrash explains why these specific animals could be used.

3. What is the message of only using three animals for sacrifices?

4. What is the message of sacrificing the ox, the lamb, and the goat?

_____

_____

_____

_____

BEYOND THIS LESSON:

[1] Think about writing your own Sacrifice midrash: (a) Why does the altar have horns? (b) What happens when God smells a sacrifice? (c) What is it like in the *kohanim's* locker room after a hard day of offerings?

[2] Some other midrashim that this *sidrah* invites are: The midrash is big on telling the story of the first time everything happened. Connect the story of the five sacrifices to the book of Genesis. What Genesis character offered the first of each of the five kinds of sacrifices? Why did they decide to offer it?

[3] What other questions about parashat VA-YIKRA would be good triggers for midrash?

25. Tzav

Leviticus 6:1-8:36

YHWH spoke to Moshe, saying: Command Aharon and his sons, saying: "This is the Instruction for the offering-up... (Leviticus 6:1).

[1] In TZAV we are introduced to what the *kohanim* have to do in the *Mishkan*. We are introduced to the ritual of the **OLAH sacrifice**. Here, the offering is left burning all through the night, and in the morning the *kohein* must remove the ashes. The *kohein* must keep the fire burning constantly, and the fat parts of the *Olah* are turned into the smoke of the **SHLAMIM**.

[2] Then the rules for the **MINHAH offering** are given. The *kohanim* make cakes out of flour and oil and put them on the altar with frankincense. That which is left over they may eat. As part of the rules of the *Minhah* offering we learn about the special offering which is made when a *kohein* is anointed.

[3] Next come the rules of the <u>HATAT</u> **offering.** This offering is slaughtered, sacrificed and eaten by the *kohanim*. The rules for the *Asham* offering are similar except that key parts of the animal are burnt totally into smoke.

[4] Finally we get the rules for the **SHLAMIM sacrifice.** This includes the commandment to eat that which is sacrificed on the day it was offered (or in the case of a freewill offering within two days).

[5] As long as we have been talking about sacrificing animals, the Torah introduces some **rules of how to eat meat**. No meat may be eaten from an animal which died naturally or which was torn by wild animals. Also, no blood may ever be consumed. TZAV ends with the inauguration of Aharon, the *kohanim*, and the *Mishkan*.

CJ'S COMMENTS

[1]: Tzav is the next chapter. Is it possible that you could use excerpts from my Bar Mitzvah speech? [C.J.]

Sure. **[GRIS]**

[2]: My Torah portion, Tzav, and the Haftarah portion for this Sabbath, *Shabbat Ha-Gadol*, concentrate on two very different topics; but I find that coincidentally they have a lot in common.

Tzav tells us about the different offerings brought into the Sanctuary daily. Meanwhile, the Haftarah informs us of the wrongs we have done and how we should improve. It says that our fate will not be a good one on the "GREAT AND AWESOME DAY OF THE L-RD" (hence the name *Shabbat Ha-Gadol* "the great Sabbath") if we do not. The general summaries don't really show any connection. Maybe by taking a look at more specific details you will understand the connection….

First, let's take a look at the sacrifices that Tzav focuses on…These sacrifices united the Jews and G-d. But when the Temple was destroyed, Jews could no longer make sacrifices. G-d said that when the Jews could no longer make sacrifices they could recite the order of the sacrifices and it would be as if the offerings had actually been made. But it seems that in Malachi, the last of the prophets writes that these prayers are not working.

The portion starts with the mention of an offering, but then goes on to talk about judgment against those who do wrong; those who oppress. It continues saying that we have been betraying G-d right from the start. But, if we return to G-d, G-d will return to us. However, it continues to list how we have done wrong by robbing G-d in offerings; how we're so bad that even if G-d slipped a miracle under our noses we wouldn't notice it. It looks pretty bad for us as a group. As we go further, though, we see that those who pray and do good things, in the "GREAT AND AWESOME DAY OF THE L-RD," will live to triumph over those who do evil. And we see that when we all become good we will have earned the right of a blessed nation.

CONTINUED ON PAGE **195**

THE BIBLICAL TEXT

To understand something about this text, you will have to go back and look at *parashat* VAYIKRA. Notice to whom all the commands are directed. Who is left out? As you read this text, see if you can find a new emphasis.

Leviticus 6:1-6

1. Yнwн spoke to Moshe, saying:
2. Command Aharon and his sons, saying:
   This is the Instruction for the offering-up—
   that is what goes-up on the blazing-hearth on the slaughter-site all night, until daybreak,
   while the fire of the slaughter-site is kept-blazing on it:…

5. Now the fire on the slaughter-site is to be kept-blazing upon it—it must not go out!—
   and the priest is to stoke on it (pieces-of-)wood, in the morning, (every) morning, and he is to arrange on it the offering-up,
   and is to turn into smoke on it the fat-parts of the *shalom*-offering.
6. A regular fire is to be kept-blazing upon the slaughter-site—it is not to go out!

1 וַיְדַבֵּ֥ר יְהוָ֖ה אֶל־מֹשֶׁ֥ה לֵּאמֹֽר׃

2 צַ֤ו אֶֽת־אַהֲרֹן֙ וְאֶת־בָּנָ֣יו לֵאמֹ֔ר זֹ֥את תּוֹרַ֖ת הָעֹלָ֑ה הִ֣וא הָעֹלָ֡ה עַל֩ מוֹקְדָ֨ה עַל־הַמִּזְבֵּ֤חַ
   כָּל־הַלַּ֙יְלָה֙ עַד־הַבֹּ֔קֶר וְאֵ֥שׁ הַמִּזְבֵּ֖חַ תּ֥וּקַד בּֽוֹ׃

5 וְהָאֵ֨שׁ עַל־הַמִּזְבֵּ֤חַ תּֽוּקַד־בּוֹ֙ לֹ֣א תִכְבֶּ֔ה וּבִעֵ֨ר עָלֶ֧יהָ הַכֹּהֵ֛ן עֵצִ֖ים בַּבֹּ֣קֶר בַּבֹּ֑קֶר
   וְעָרַ֤ךְ עָלֶ֙יהָ֙ הָֽעֹלָ֔ה וְהִקְטִ֥יר עָלֶ֖יהָ חֶלְבֵ֥י הַשְּׁלָמִֽים׃

6 אֵ֗שׁ תָּמִ֛יד תּוּקַ֥ד עַל־הַמִּזְבֵּ֖חַ לֹ֥א תִכְבֶּֽה׃

QUESTIONS ABOUT THE BIBLICAL TEXT

1. Who was left out of *sidrah* Vayikra and added here?
2. Why *do* you think that "he" was left out and then added?

_____

_____

_____

_____

THE MIDRASH ANSWERS THESE SAME QUESTIONS

A MIDRASH [Tosafot HaRosh]

When God was teaching Moshe the laws which were taught in VAYIKRA, Moshe asked: "What type of wood is suitable for a sacrifice?" God informed him: "All kinds except for the wood of grapevines and olive branches. Those two may not be burned on the altar. They are special because of the fruits which they produce. Branches of the grapevine may not be used since they supply wine for the *nesaḥim* (libations); neither may olive wood, for the olive yields oil for the menorah and the *Minḥah* offerings."

Moshe immediately argued, "Master of the Universe, it seems that your words should apply to people as well. You honored the grapevine and olive tree because of their produce. Should You then not treat Aharon in an honorable way (and address him directly) in spite of Your anger at him if only for the sake of his worthy sons?"

God accepted this argument and addressed Aharon in TZAV.

Separating the P'shat from the Drash

3. What Torah facts are used by this midrash?

Separating the Answers from the Messages

4. What question is this midrash trying to answer?

5. What answer does it give?

6. What does this midrash teach about Moshe?

7. What does this midrash teach about God's relationship with Moshe? (Does it remind you of AVRAHAM?)

8. What is the "moral" of this midrash? (How should we be like Moshe?)

_____

_____

_____

_____

_____

BEYOND THIS LESSON:

[1] Think about writing your own "Aharon and God make up" midrash: (a) God was already angry at Aharon when he and his family were appointed to be *kohanim*. Why then did God choose him to be the one human who gets closest to God? (b) Tell the story of what God saw Aharon do which showed that Aharon was the right choice?

[2] Some other midrashim that this *sidrah* invites are: (a) Why does God connect sacrifices and kashrut? (b) Explain why the Torah forbids any consumption of blood.

[3] What other questions about parashat TZAV would be good triggers for midrash?

26. Shmini

Leviticus 9:1-11:47

Now it was on the eighth day, (that) Moshe called Aharon and his sons and the elders of Yisrael...(Leviticus 9:1).

[1] In SHMINI we see the final day of dedication of the *Mishkan*. There are all kinds of sacrifices and ceremonies. Following these festivities, two of Aharon's sons, **Nadav and Avihu,** enter the *Mishkan* on their own, and offer a "strange fire" before God. They **are burnt to death**. God then warns Aharon that no *kohein* should drink before doing priestly service. Then Moshe orders the *kohanim* back to work.

[2] Then God teaches Aharon and Moshe a long list of rules about what animals can be eaten. First we are given the list of permitted animals—the basic rule being that the animal must chew its cud and have a cleft hoof. Then we are told about fish. To be eaten, a fish must have both fins and scales. Next we are given rules about birds—we are given a list of birds which cannot be eaten. All of the forbidden birds are hunters. Continuing its enumeration of permissible animals, the Torah lists the kinds of insects which can be eaten. It also forbids all reptiles and a bunch of animals which are in the rat and mole category.

[3] Finally the Torah talks about things which become unclean through contact with the carcass of an unclean animal.

CJ'S COMMENTS

I'm writing to you from camp. I'm going to try to review SHMINI. I will be reviewing with two bunkmates of mine named Noah Cohen and Gabi Mitchell. I finally have the time to write because it's *Tisha B'Av*. I'm fasting till dinner when the fast ends anyway. I've been having fun here. I've led services and bensching. I've done too much to write down. Now for SHMINI:

[1]: What is the "strange fire" which Nadav and Avihu offer before God? If they "offered" the fire were they sacrificing? If God warned Aharon that no *kohanim* should drink (alcohol) before doing priestly service, were Nadav and Avihu drunk? Was the fire "strange" because they sacrificed a deformed animal? **[C.J.]**

Aharon is the boys' mentor/father so he is responsible for all of their actions before them. **[Noah Cohen]**

When God gives Aharon the command he means spiritual drunkenness, not physical. Aharon's sons were not pure enough to sacrifice an offering. The fire was "strange" because God was giving the sign of rejection to their offering. **[Gabi Mitchell]**

Noah Cohen said that because Aharon is the boys' father and mentor he is ultimately responsible for their actions. I somewhat agree. However, at what point do we take responsibility for our own actions? Yes, perhaps if Aharon had trained them at a young age to respect holy places maybe they wouldn't have played with matches in the temple and none of this would've happened. However, I think the blame lies on both Aharon and his sons. **[Dina Ackermann]**

When I was 17 or so, I obsessed on this question—what did N&A do wrong that got them fried? I thought it was a personal attack on me. I was a Reform Jew studying on an Orthodox kibbutz. I thought the commentators were telling me that if I used a guitar in a service—(especially my electric) God would have me shocked by a poorly grounded amp—a "strange fire." The passage seemed to be totally against creative

CONTINUED ON PAGE 195

THE BIBLICAL TEXT

In this *sidrah*, two of Aharon's sons are killed in an accident in the *Mishkan*. Immediately after this, God gives a set of rules to Aharon. Then Moshe gives him a set of orders. As you read the text, see if you can figure out why Moshe gave these orders rather than words of comfort.

Leviticus 10:12-14

12. Now Moshe spoke to Aharon and to Elazar and to Itamar, his sons that were left:
Take the grain-gift that is left of the fire-offerings of YHWH

    and eat it unleavened next to the slaughter-site,

    for it is a holiest holy-portion.

13. You are to eat it in a holy place,

    for it is for your allotment and your sons' allotment, from the fire-offerings of YHWH,

    for thus have I been commanded.

14. But the breast of the elevation-offering and the thigh of the contribution, you may eat in (any) pure place, you and your sons and your daughters with you,

    for as your allotment and your children's allotment they have been given (you),

    from the slaughter-offerings of *shalom* of the Children of Yisrael.

12 וַיְדַבֵּר מֹשֶׁה אֶל־אַהֲרֹן וְאֶל אֶלְעָזָר וְאֶל־אִיתָמָר בָּנָיו הַנּוֹתָרִים קְחוּ

אֶת־הַמִּנְחָה הַנּוֹתֶרֶת מֵאִשֵּׁי יְהֹוָה וְאִכְלוּהָ מַצּוֹת אֵצֶל הַמִּזְבֵּחַ כִּי קֹדֶשׁ קָדָשִׁים הוּא:

13 וַאֲכַלְתֶּם אֹתָהּ בְּמָקוֹם קָדֹשׁ כִּי חָקְךָ וְחָק־בָּנֶיךָ הוּא מֵאִשֵּׁי יְהֹוָה כִּי־כֵן צֻוֵּיתִי:

14 וְאֵת חֲזֵה הַתְּנוּפָה וְאֵת שׁוֹק הַתְּרוּמָה תֹּאכְלוּ בְּמָקוֹם טָהוֹר אַתָּה וּבָנֶיךָ וּבְנֹתֶיךָ אִתָּךְ

כִּי־חָקְךָ וְחָק־בָּנֶיךָ נִתְּנוּ מִזִּבְחֵי שַׁלְמֵי בְּנֵי יִשְׂרָאֵל:

QUESTIONS ABOUT THE BIBLICAL TEXT

Why do you think Moshe chose this moment to give these orders to Aharon and his remaining sons?

_____

_____

_____

_____

_____

_____

THE MIDRASH ANSWERS THESE SAME QUESTIONS

A MIDRASH:

Why did Moshe give orders to Aharon and his sons, that they should again perform the sacrifices?

To what can this be compared? This can be compared to a husband and wife who had a fight. The husband told the wife: "Leave the house at once." After some time, the husband's anger abated and she returned to the house. When she returned, she again did the cooking and cleaning and was happy. When Aharon and his sons could return to their Divine Service, they were again happy.

Separating the Answers from the Messages

1. This midrash is another comparison. Explain who or what each of the following represents:

    Husband = _____

    Wife = _____

    House = _____

2. How does this story relate to the death of Nadav and Avihu?

3. What is the message of this midrash? (How should we be like God in this case?)

    _____

    _____

    _____

    _____

    _____

    _____

BEYOND THIS LESSON:

[1] Think about writing your own "Nadav and Avihu" midrash: (a) What kind of "strange" fire did Nadav and Avihu light? (b) What were Nadav and Avihu like as kids?(c) What happened on the day that Aharon and his family first sacrificed again?

[2] Some other SHMINI midrashim which need writing: (a) Why does the death of an animal make someone *tamei* when the blood from a dead animal makes them pure again? (b) How did God decide what should be kosher and what shouldn't? (c) Why do the laws of kashrut immediately follow the death of Nadav and Avihu in the parashah?

[3] What other questions about parashat SHMINI would be good triggers for midrash?

27. Tazria

Leviticus 12:1-13:59

YHWH spoke to Moshe, saying (any) human being—when there is on the skin of his body a swelling or a scab or a shiny-spot and it becomes on the skin of his body an affliction of *tzara'at*, he is to be brought to Aharon the priest or to one of his sons the priests....(Leviticus 12:1-2).

[1] Welcome to TAZRIA, the first of two *sidrot* on leprosy and related topics. In this *sidrah* we have a lot of laws regarding purity. They include: A woman is impure for seven days following the birth of a son, who is then circumcised on the eighth day. She is impure for 14 days following the birth of a daughter. To become pure, she has the *kohein* offer proper sacrifices.

[2] Then the Torah introduces **rules of skin disease**. We get a list of various kinds of conditions which can be considered leprosy. This is the procedure. The person with the problem comes to the *kohein* who decides if the problem is indeed leprosy. If the *kohein* has concerns, the person is isolated and re-examined in seven days. If the condition has ended, the *kohein* calls him clean, but if the rash has spread, the *kohein* labels him a leper.

LEPER

[3] The person who has leprosy tears his clothes, shaves his head, covers his lip and must call out "Unclean, Unclean" wherever he goes. **He has to dwell outside the camp.** The *kohein* is responsible to see to it that the leper and all that comes in contact with him is separated from the rest of the community.

CJ'S COMMENTS

[1]: Why is a woman impure after the birth of a child? She didn't do anything wrong. She wasn't dealing with impure things. Is she impure so as to give her a time out? If you're impure people would stay away from you. The mother would have a nice amount of time to relax before returning to the "real world." Why is she impure seven days for a son and 14days for a daughter? **[C.J.]**

[GRIS]: Here is a question I don't want to answer. I am not afraid of the answer, I am just not sure I really understand it. Here are the things I do know. *Tumah* is a tough concept. We translate it as "impure" but it is a spiritual category—not a question of dirt. It needs a spiritual change—not soap and water. Basically, two things make you impure—contact with death-fluids and contact with sex-fluids. You can get death-slimed and sex-slimed. Both things can wipe out your spiritual state. Here is the idea. If you come in contact with death—you are slimed. Your spiritual state collapses. A depression sets in and you need to do some work in order to get your life back in balance. You are not bad. You are not dirty—rather your spirit is not *tahor* (shining/pure) at that moment. Sex can do the same thing. It is not bad or dirty—it just draws your mind/soul to a different place. Birth is a combination of both—death-blood and sex-aftermath. And, more than anything, birth wonderfully distracts a mother from her normal spiritual state. In her book, *The Voice of Sarah*, Tamar Frankiel reaches the same conclusion you do—that the days of *tumah* following birth are a gift of spiritual isolation and bonding time between mother and child—just what a woman needs.

In *Leviticus Rabbah* 14.1 Rabbi Simlai asks the same question you did: "Why do daughters make a mother impure for twice as long as a son does (implying that there was something wrong with having girls)? He answers his question by reading in context ('cause circumcision is in the same verse—Leviticus 12:1). He says: "It should have

CONTINUED ON PAGE 196

THE BIBLICAL TEXT

In TAZRIA we talk about skin disease and label some of it leprosy. This is the way the Torah introduces the topic. Read it carefully and then compare it to the passage which follows.

Leviticus 13: 1-3

1. YHWH spoke to Moshe and to Aharon, saying:

2. (Any) human being—when there is on the skin of his body a swelling or a scab or a shiny-spot
   and it becomes on the skin of his body an affliction of *tzara'at*,
   he is to be brought to Aharon the priest or to one of his sons the priests.

3. The priest is to look at the affliction on the skin of the flesh;
   should hair in the afflicted-area have turned white, and the look of the affliction is deeper
   than the skin of his flesh,
   it is an affliction of *tzara'at*;
   when the priest looks at it, he is to declare-him-*tamei*.

1 וַיְדַבֵּר יְהֹוָה אֶל־מֹשֶׁה וְאֶל־אַהֲרֹן לֵאמֹר:

2 אָדָם כִּי־יִהְיֶה בְעוֹר־בְּשָׂרוֹ שְׂאֵת אוֹ־סַפַּחַת אוֹ בַהֶרֶת וְהָיָה בְעוֹר־בְּשָׂרוֹ לְנֶגַע צָרָעַת וְהוּבָא אֶל־אַהֲרֹן הַכֹּהֵן אוֹ אֶל־אַחַד מִבָּנָיו הַכֹּהֲנִים:

3 וְרָאָה הַכֹּהֵן אֶת־הַנֶּגַע בְּעוֹר־הַבָּשָׂר וְשֵׂעָר בַּנֶּגַע הָפַךְ לָבָן וּמַרְאֵה הַנֶּגַע עָמֹק מֵעוֹר בְּשָׂרוֹ נֶגַע צָרָעַת הוּא וְרָאָהוּ הַכֹּהֵן וְטִמֵּא אֹתוֹ:

QUESTIONS ABOUT THE BIBLICAL TEXT

Now read this text from Ecclesiastes 5.5, and see what it says about skin disease.

> It is better not to make a vow at all
>
> than to vow and not fulfill.
>
> Do not let your mouth cause your flesh to feel guilt.
>
> And don't tell the messenger that it was an error.
>
> Fear God and don't let God be angered by your talk
>
> and destroy your possessions.

In TAZRIA and in the next *sidrah*, METZORA, the Torah talks about leprosy of the skin, of houses, and of clothing. Based on this text from *Kohelet* (Ecclesiastes) can you see a connection between peoples' words and these kinds of leprosy?

_____

_____

_____

_____

_____

THE MIDRASH ANSWERS THESE SAME QUESTIONS

A MIDRASH [Leviticus Rabbah 17.3]

There are 10 sins which can cause leprosy:

Serving Idols (with words). Those who worshiped the golden calf got leprosy (from Ex. 32.25).

Lack of Modesty. The daughters of Yerushalayim got leprosy for behaving poorly (from Is. 3.17).

Bloodshed. Yoav got leprosy for murder (II Sam. 3.29).

Profaning God's name. This happened to Gehazi who was Elisha's servant (from II Kings 5.27).

Cursing God. This happened to the Philistines (from 1 Sam. 7.46).

Robbing the Public. This happened to Shevna who stole from the Mishkan (from Is. 22.17).

Stealing an honor. This happened to King Uzziah (II Chron. 26.21).

Conceit. This too we learn from King Uzziah (II Chron. 26.16).

Lashon ha-Ra. This we learn from when Miriam slandered Moshe (Num. 12.1).

Being a Miser. This we learn from the description of house leprosy (in this *sidrah*).

Separating the P'shat from the Drash

1. [A MAJOR PROJECT WHICH REQUIRES A BIBLE]: When the Rabbis wrote this midrash, they found ten places in the Bible where they believed that God used leprosy as a punishment for breaking important Torah-rules. Decide which of these are really described in the Torah, and which are based on other midrashim on the passages quoted. Circle those that are examples really found in the Bible.

Separating the Answers from the Messages

2. By bringing in these 10 examples and by comparing TAZRIA to the quotation from Ecclesiastes, what have the Rabbis done to the meaning of the passage from Leviticus?

   Clue: It is moved from being a medical text to a _____.

3. What is the message of this midrash? What are we now learning from a description of the treatment of leprosy?

4. How did the passage from Ecclesiastes help unlock the one from Leviticus?

   _____

   _____

   _____

   _____

   _____

BEYOND THIS LESSON:

[1] Think about writing your own "Leprosy" midrash: (a) How did God pick leprosy as the right punishment for speech crimes? (b) Why does bathing and a week outside of camp cure speech crimes? (c) If words about others can make you sick—what words can heal you?

[2] Some other TAZRIA midrashim which need writing: (a) Why does giving birth make you *tamei*? (b) Create a list of other sins that God punishes with body dysfunction. (c) Write the story of a house that gets leprosy.

[3] What other questions about parashat TAZRIA would be good triggers for midrash?

28. Metzora

Leviticus 14:1-15:33

YHWH spoke to Moshe, saying: This is to be the Instruction for the one-with-*tzara´at*...(Leviticus 14:1).

[1] In TAZRIA, the last *sidrah*, we learned all about leprosy, in this *parashah*—METZORA, we learn how the *kohanim* are supposed to **cure leprosy**. First the *kohein* has to go and inspect the leprosy, to see if it has indeed passed. Then he performs a cleansing ritual; he has the patient wash, shave and clean his clothes. Then the patient waits in isolation for seven days. On day eight, the *kohein* performs a whole number of rituals including *Minḥah* and *Asham* offerings.

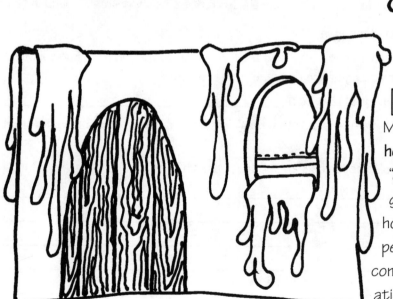

[2] Then God teaches Moshe and Aharon all about **house leprosy**. This is when "green or red stuff" starts growing on the walls of a house. Just as in the case of people leprosy, the *kohein* comes in and inspects the situation. If it is leprosy, the *kohein* has the house sealed for seven days. If it doesn't heal itself, there is a whole set of rules about isolating stones and replastering. When the matter is finished, the *kohein* has to go through other ritual actions.

[3] The *sidrah* ends with **a list of discharges from the body which require acts of purification.**

CJ'S COMMENTS

[1]: This is the second *parashah* in which we look at leprosy. Again we are told that the *kohanim* check out the situation to see if all is well. My big question is: what if a *kohein* gets leprosy? Is he treated like everyone else? Is he denied the right to work at his priestly duties? [C.J.]

A *kohein* is not allowed to work with any kind of blemish or defect, remember? If a *kohein* comes down with *metzora*, he goes outside the camp and goes into purification mode like any other Jew. That is both a medical and a spiritual understanding. If we understand *metzora* as a "medical condition," the isolation is necessary. If we understand *metzora* as spiritual impurity (loose lips cause scabs), then the *kohein* needs to do some soul searching before he can do God's work again. **[GRIS]**

[2]: House leprosy is described as "green or red stuff." Is leprosy then some sort of primitive fungus? What is the difference between skin leprosy and house leprosy? **[C.J.]**

We don't know what caused skin *metzora*—except that we know what it isn't. Milgrom, in his amazing new *Anchor Commentary on Leviticus* writes: "Biblical *tzara'at* is difficult to identify. On thing, however, is certain, it is not leprosy...." He then says, "the most recent, comprehensive medical analysis of of *tzara'at*, reaches the following conclusion: psoriasis is the disease that fulfills most (but not all) of the characteristics, except *netek* (Leviticus 13:39) resembles *favus*, a fungus infection of the skin, and the pure skin-condition called *bohak* resembles vitiligo." Then, in a personal note he adds, that in checking with a dermatologist—while the symptoms match pretty well, the Torah's description of a two-week cure is out of the context of anything we know.

Maimonides (also a doctor) writes: This affliction is a Divine sign that God is displeased with one's behavior, and that God has withdrawn God's presence from the sinner, and that there is a need to examine one's actions and to see what needs to be improved. [Laws of Cleanliness, 16.10]

House leprosy seems to be a house with fungus growing. In ancient Mesopotamia, black colored wall fungus was seen to be a sign of health and prosperity, but white, red and green (Spanish Flag) fungi are signs of trouble. Fungal houses are known as real problems in all kinds of Middle Eastern literature. In the midrash, *Pesikta Rabbati* 17, we are given the relationship of cloth, house, and skin *metzora*. All are considered to be signs from God. The classical notion is that first God attacks the house, warning a person to repent. If that does no good, then his clothes are stricken with fungus. And if that does no good, the punishment extends to his or her own skin. **[GRIS]**

Just a point of information—the Spanish flag is red and yellow. The MEXICAN flag (and Italian & Bulgarian, I think) are red, white and green. Bye, **Simon Goulden, London <aje@brijnet.org>**

[3]: If the house a family is living in has leprosy, where do they live? Are they allowed to take anything out of the house with them? **[C.J.]**

You can answer your own questions here. Just check out the Torah, Lev. 14:33-57. It gives in detail the whole treatment, but yes, stuff can be taken out. Listen to a great Rashi: House *tzara'at* came from treasures that the Canaanites hid in the walls of their houses. God would make the walls of the house break out to show the Jews where to find these treasures. Rambam, of course, connects even fungal houses to speech-crimes and similar sins. **[GRIS]**

[4]: The phrase from the text which is repeated in various spots is "THIS IS THE TORAH/ LAW OF..." What I make out of the repetition is that the phrase repeated five times represents the five books of the Torah. But this could just be a coincidence. It's like taking all the times it says "AND YHWH SPOKE UNTO MOSHE SAYING...," figuring out the numerical value and writing out a word with it. I may be wrong, but maybe we try a little too hard to find new Torah facts. **[C.J.]**

Does that mean the five times the word *light* is used in the first day of creation is just a coincidence? That it has nothing to do with the five ways that the Egyptians afflicted the Israelites and the five ways they multiplied? That it is accidental that God makes five promises about redeeming Israel from Egypt? Does it mean nothing that Moses goes up Mount Sinai five times? These fives (and a lot more) all "just happen." Right? **[GRIS]**

[5]: Looking at the Midrash I was right about one part. But that Midrash is stretching it even more than I was! My question is: how do you connect a disease to evil reports? Was the idea that leprosy was taken on by one who had said something nasty? **[C.J.]**

Here is the connection: Numbers 12:1-15: AND MIRIAM AND AARON SPOKE AGAINST MOSES ABOUT THE ETHIOPIAN WOMAN HE HAD MARRIED ...AND THEN YHWH SUDDENLY SPOKE UNTO MOSES, TO AARON, AND TO MIRIAM, YOU THREE COME OUT TO THE *MISHKAN*. AND THEY THREE CAME OUT. AND YHWH CAME DOWN IN THE PILLAR OF THE CLOUD, AND STOOD *IN* THE DOOR OF THE TABERNACLE, AND CALLED AARON AND MIRIAM: AND THEY BOTH CAME FORTH. ... AND YHWH'S ANGER WAS KINDLED AGAINST THEM...AND THE CLOUD LEFT THE

CONTINUED ON PAGE **197**

THE BIBLICAL TEXT

In this *sidrah*, you will find one phrase repeated over and over again. As you read the Torah text, (1) find the phrase, (2) see how many times it is repeated, and (3) see what conclusions you can draw.

Leviticus 13:59-14:2, 32 and 54-57

13:59. This is the Instruction for the affliction of *tzara'at* of cloth of wool or linen, or

the warp or the woof, or any vessel of skin,

for declaring-it-purified or for declaring-it-*tamei*...

14: 2. This is to be the Instruction for the one-with-*tzara'at*, on the day of his being-purified:

he is to be brought to the priest...

32. This is the Instruction for the one who has an affliction of *tzara'at*,

whose hand cannot reach (means) for his purification...

54. This is the Instruction for any affliction of *tzara'at*, for scalls,

55. for *tzara'at* of cloth or of a house,

56. for swelling, for scabs or for shiny-spots,

57. to provide-instruction, at the time of the *tamei* and at the time of the pure.

This is the Instruction for *tzara'at*.

59 זֹאת תּוֹרַת נֶגַע־צָרַעַת בֶּגֶד הַצֶּמֶר אוֹ הַפִּשְׁתִּים אוֹ הַשְּׁתִי אוֹ הָעֵרֶב אוֹ כָּל־כְּלִי־עוֹר לְטַהֲרוֹ
אוֹ לְטַמְּאוֹ:

2 זֹאת תִּהְיֶה תּוֹרַת הַמְצֹרָע בְּיוֹם טָהֳרָתוֹ וְהוּבָא אֶל־הַכֹּהֵן:

32 זֹאת תּוֹרַת אֲשֶׁר־בּוֹ נֶגַע צָרַעַת אֲשֶׁר לֹא־תַשִּׂיג יָדוֹ בְּטָהֳרָתוֹ:

54 זֹאת הַתּוֹרָה לְכָל־נֶגַע הַצָּרַעַת וְלַנָּתֶק:

55 וּלְצָרַעַת הַבֶּגֶד וְלַבָּיִת:

56 וְלַשְׂאֵת וְלַסַּפַּחַת וְלַבֶּהָרֶת:

57 לְהוֹרֹת בְּיוֹם הַטָּמֵא וּבְיוֹם הַטָּהֹר זֹאת תּוֹרַת הַצָּרָעַת:

QUESTIONS ABOUT THE BIBLICAL TEXT

1. What phrase is repeated?_____

2. How many times is it repeated?_____

3. Can you draw a conclusion from this?

_____

_____

_____

_____

_____

_____

THE MIDRASH ANSWERS THESE SAME QUESTIONS

A MIDRASH [Leviticus Rabbah 16.6]

Rabbi Yehoshua ben Levi said: "The word Torah is used five times in regard to the plague of leprosy. We know that *metzora* (leprosy) = *motze-shem-ra*—one who spreads evil reports. The repetition of Torah five times in connection to leprosy is meant to teach that one who spreads evil reports is just like someone who broke all the laws in all five books of the Torah."

Separating the P'shat from the Drash

1. Underline those parts of this midrash which are based on "Torah-facts."

2. This midrash is based on other midrashim. What midrashic pun is central to this midrash?

Separating the Answers from the Messages

3. What does this midrash notice about this *sidrah*?

4. What does Rabbi Yehoshua learn from this insight?

5. What kind of rules does this midrash use for studying Torah?

6. What would be your leprosy *Davar Torah*?

_____

_____

_____

_____

_____

BEYOND THIS LESSON:

Go back a *sidrah* and borrow any unused questions from TAZRIA.

29. Aharei Mot

Leviticus 16:1-18:30

Now YHWH spoke to Moshe after the death of the two sons of Aharon, when they came-near before the presence of YHWH and died;...(Leviticus 16:1).

[1] AHAREI MOT means after the death. After the death of Nadav and Avihu God begins this *sidrah* by giving Aharon additional rules about **the way the** *kohanim* **should perform their functions**. These include coming into the *Mishkan* only at the fixed times and wearing the proper clothing.

[2] Then we get a description of the responsibilities of the **Kohein ha-Gadol** (Big Kahuna) **on Yom Kippur**. These include his own purification, and the choosing of the two goats: the one to become the *hatat* offering, and the one to become the 'scapegoat.' Following a detailed description of all the priestly functions, we are also told how B'nai Yisrael are to fast and make atonement.

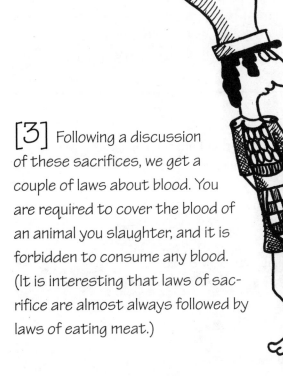

[3] Following a discussion of these sacrifices, we get a couple of laws about blood. You are required to cover the blood of an animal you slaughter, and it is forbidden to consume any blood. (It is interesting that laws of sacrifice are almost always followed by laws of eating meat.)

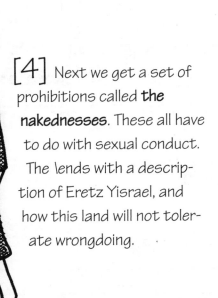

[4] Next we get a set of prohibitions called **the nakednesses**. These all have to do with sexual conduct. The \ends with a description of Eretz Yisrael, and how this land will not tolerate wrongdoing.

CJ'S COMMENTS

[1]: Most of the things in the overall *parashah* description are self-explanatory—look it up and you'll find the specifics. So far, one thing that I every so often wonder about came to mind while looking at the third paragraph. Not being allowed to consume blood is a given. Who would want to do this willingly anyway? But what if you lose a tooth or get a cut on your lip? It's your own blood, and although you try to stop the blood flow, you might swallow some along the way. **[C.J.]**

You are forgetting two or three biggies. (1) The cut finger you suck to stop the bleeding. (2) Bleeding gums. (3) The bleeding ulcer, where the stomach is serving itself blood. But none of these are a problem, because despite some fancy minor rules about spitting out rather than swallowing blood from a pulled tooth (as a fence around the basic law), the tradition concludes, "There is no prohibition about blood that is part of one's own body." **[GRIS]**

[2]: What is basically said about the land of Israel in this *parashah*: The land is good, and always will be good. If you leave, the land won't get any worse. But if you're bad, you're going to have to leave the land. The land can't be made bad, you can. This is a luxury. Show that you're worthy. The midrash explains what I say. In the land of the Jews, moral laws are the laws of the land. **[C.J.]**

You've got this only half right. For biblical thinking, rain is dependent on ethics. God says in a number of places, "If you are good, then I'll give you rain and crops." The land does get better and worse with people's actions—its just that no matter what we do, we can't wear away its basic holiness. **[GRIS]**

THE BIBLICAL TEXT

This *sidrah* includes a set of things which Jews are not supposed to do called "the nakednesses." If you want to know what they are—look them up in Leviticus 18. In that passage, God is really concerned that B'nai Yisrael not follow some of the customs of the people who lived in Canaan before they took it and made it Eretz Yisrael. Following those rules, God gives this warning about the land. As you read this text, see if you can figure out what is being said about Eretz Yisrael.

Leviticus 18: 24-29

24. You are not to make-yourselves-*tamei* through any of these,
    for through all these, they make-themselves-*tamei*, the nations that I am sending out before you.

25. Thus the land became-*tamei*, and I called it to account for its iniquity,
    so that the land vomited out its inhabitants.

26. But you are to keep, yourselves, my laws and my regulations,
    not doing any of these abominations,
    the native and the sojourner that sojourns in your midst,

27. for all these abominations did the men of the land do that were before you,
    and the land became-*tamei*—

28. that the land not vomit you out for your making it *tamei*
    as it vomited out the nation that was before you.

29. For whoever does any of these abominable-things—
    cut off shall be those persons that do (them) from amid their kinspeople!

24 אַל־תִּטַּמְּאוּ בְּכָל־אֵלֶּה כִּי בְכָל־אֵלֶּה נִטְמְאוּ הַגּוֹיִם אֲשֶׁר־אֲנִי מְשַׁלֵּחַ מִפְּנֵיכֶם:

25 וַתִּטְמָא הָאָרֶץ וָאֶפְקֹד עֲוֹנָהּ עָלֶיהָ וַתָּקִא הָאָרֶץ אֶת־יֹשְׁבֶיהָ:

26 וּשְׁמַרְתֶּם אַתֶּם אֶת־חֻקֹּתַי וְאֶת־מִשְׁפָּטַי וְלֹא תַעֲשׂוּ מִכֹּל הַתּוֹעֵבֹת הָאֵלֶּה הָאֶזְרָח
וְהַגֵּר הַגָּר בְּתוֹכְכֶם:

27 כִּי אֶת־כָּל־הַתּוֹעֵבֹת הָאֵל עָשׂוּ אַנְשֵׁי־הָאָרֶץ אֲשֶׁר לִפְנֵיכֶם וַתִּטְמָא הָאָרֶץ:

28 וְלֹא־תָקִיא הָאָרֶץ אֶתְכֶם בְּטַמַּאֲכֶם אֹתָהּ כַּאֲשֶׁר קָאָה אֶת־הַגּוֹי אֲשֶׁר לִפְנֵיכֶם:

29 כִּי כָּל־אֲשֶׁר יַעֲשֶׂה מִכֹּל הַתּוֹעֵבוֹת הָאֵלֶּה וְנִכְרְתוּ הַנְּפָשׁוֹת הָעֹשֹׂת מִקֶּרֶב עַמָּם:

QUESTIONS ABOUT THE BIBLICAL TEXT

In this passage, what is said about the land of Yisrael?

_____

_____

_____

_____

_____

THE MIDRASH ANSWERS THESE SAME QUESTIONS

A MIDRASH [Midrash Aggada 18:4/Shabbat 33b]

Of all the lands in the world, Eretz Yisrael is the most holy. She is therefore sensitive to any evil committed on her soil. If her inhabitants become evil and do wrong, she is unable to "stomach" them. She therefore inevitably "spits them up," and they are exiled. (*This happened twice to B'nai Yisrael, once in 586 BCE when the Babylonian Exile took place, and again after 210 CE when the Romans all but destroyed the Land.*).

A MIDRASH [Shabbat 36b]

Eretz Yisrael is the Palace of the King. A sin which may be tolerated elsewhere calls for immediate punishment in the Land of Holiness.

Separating the P'shat from the Drash

1. What facts from the Torah and from Jewish history do these midrashim use?

2. What rabbinic ideas do these texts use?

Separating the Answers from the Messages

3. Back in the story of Kayin and Hevel, God says: **"And now, damned be you from the soil, which opened up its mouth to receive your brother's blood from your hand. When you wish to work the soil it will not henceforth give its strength to you; wavering and wandering must you be on earth!"** How does that early biblical story connect to these midrashim?

4. One of these midrashim uses comparisons. Explain the comparisons:

5. How can this midrash truth about Eretz Yisrael become a Jewish value?

_____

_____

_____

_____

_____

_____

BEYOND THIS LESSON:

[1] Think about writing your own "Eretz Yisrael" midrash: (a) Why did God pick Eretz Yisrael to be a Holy Land? (b) Tell the story of one time that Eretz Yisrael got indigestion and spit out someone? (c) What would you find if you compared a cubic foot of Israeli soil with a cubic foot of American soil?

[2] Some other AHAREI MOT midrashim which need writing: (a) Why does the Torah fix a time for worship? (b) Does one really put sins on a scapegoat to get rid of them? Why does God want Israel to use magic? (c) Why does God set rules for who can have sex with whom?

[3] What other questions about parashat AHAREI MOT would be good triggers for midrash?

30. Kedoshim

Leviticus 19:1-20:27

YHWH spoke to Moshe, saying: Speak to the entire community of the Children of Yisrael, and say to them: Holy are you to be, for holy am I, YHWH your God!...(Leviticus 19:1-2).

[1] KEDOSHIM is the *sidrah* which is known as the Holiness Code. It begins with **Moshe gathering all of B'nai Yisrael together** and teaching them laws which will make them holy. These laws are held together by a chorus line: "I am YHWH."

[2] These laws include: **respecting parents, not worshiping idols, observing Shabbat, eating sacrifices right away, leaving the corners of your field unharvested, not stealing, not taking advantage of handicaps, judging cases fairly, not hating people,** and **loving your neighbor as yourself.**

[3] Then we move into other laws such as: mixed breeding, treatment of slaves, forbidding the fruit of new trees, not eating blood, not doing witchcraft, not shaving the corners of your head, respecting your daughter, not turning to ghosts, rising before the aged, being fair to the stranger, and using fair weights and measures.

[4] We are to follow all these laws, because (a) God took us out of Egypt, and (b) they will make us holy like God. At the end of the *sidrah* we get a few more laws. We cannot follow the cult of Molech (a cult where parents sacrificed their firstborn children), we are not to embarrass our parents, and we have a large list of unacceptable sexual relationships.

At the very end, God explains that all these laws were given to us because (1) **we are going into a land of milk and honey**, (2) **they make us different than other nations**, and (3) **they make us holy.**

[1]: I think it's cool/important that all the holiness laws are tied together by the refrain "I AM THE LORD." It shows that these are the official rules because of who's enforcing them, but it also shows that you want to be holy. "I AM THE LORD, FOLLOW MY LAWS." **[C.J.]**

I don't use the word "Lord" any more, because too many of the women in my life say that they are excluded by it. I have never found a replacement that works as easily—because when I used to say "Lord," I didn't think of a guy who was a lord over you, but of God. Now, every other "Lord" substitute (*Adonai, ha-Shem*, Eternal, YHWH) seems artificial. **[GRIS]**

[2]: I take a look at these laws and see that most of them are just normal laws of etiquette which we should be using anyway. Just as long as we're nice and proper, we're doing most of what we're supposed to anyway. Then I see the reasons why we are supposed to do these things. The second makes immediate sense: the better person you are = the holier you become = your relationship with God becomes closer. The first is a little blurry though. Maybe it shouldn't be "BECAUSE GOD TOOK US OUT OF EGYPT," but "*SINCE WE'RE OUT OF EGYPT, WE NOW RECOGNIZE THE HARDSHIPS OF SLAVERY, SO WE SHOULDN'T TREAT OTHERS THE WAY WE WERE TREATED.*" **[C.J.]**

[3]: The three reasons at the end basically sum up what I just said: going into a land of milk and honey means that the land is good, so we need to deserve it. Making us different is just another way of saying "making us special." Making us holy is obvious. **[C.J.]**

I guess I'll "C" you tomorrow, **C.J.**

THE BIBLICAL TEXT

This passage is called the Holiness Code. Most laws that were taught to B'nai Yisrael were taught to anyone who would listen to Moshe when he was teaching. As you read this text, see if you can figure out why God thought this passage was important enough for all Jews to hear, and therefore told Moshe to speak to the whole community of B'nai Yisrael.

Leviticus 19:1-18; 20:9-10

1. Yнwн spoke to Moshe, saying:
2. Speak to the entire community of the Children of Yisrael, and say to them:
   Holy are you to be,
   for holy am I, Yнwн your God!
3. **Each-man—his mother and his father you are to hold-in-awe,**
   and my Sabbaths you are to keep:
   I am Yнwн your God!
4. **Do not turn-your-faces to no-gods,**
   and molten gods you are not to make yourselves,
   I am Yнwн your God!...
9. Now when you harvest the harvest of your land,
   you are not to finish (to the) edge of your field in harvesting,
   the full-gathering of your harvest you are not to gather;
10. your vineyard you are not to glean,
    the break-off of your vineyard you are not to gather—
    rather, for the afflicted and for the sojourner you are to leave them,
    I am Yнwн your God!
11. **You are not to steal,**
    you are not to lie,
    you are not to deal-falsely, each-man with his fellow!
12. **You are not to swear by my name falsely,**
    thus profaning the name of your God—
    I am Yнwн!
13. Your are not to withhold (property from) your neighbor,
    you are not to commit-robbery.
    You are not to keep-overnight the working-wages of a hired-hand with you until morning.
14. You are not to insult the deaf,
    before the blind you are not to place a stumbling block;
    rather, you are to hold your God in awe;
    I am Yнwн!
15. You are not to commit corruption in justice;
    you are not to lift-up-in-favor the face of the poor,
    you are not to overly-honor the face of the great;
    with equity you are to judge your fellow!
16. **You are not to traffic in slander among your kinspeople.**
    You are not to stand by the blood of your neighbor,
    I am Yнwн!
17. You are not to hate your brother in your heart;

rebuke, yes, rebuke your fellow,

that you not bear sin because of him!

18. **You are not to take-vengeance, you are not to retain-anger against the sons of your kins-people—**

but be-loving to your neighbor (as one) like yourself,

I am Y<small>HWH</small>!…

20:9. Indeed, any-man, any-man that insults his father or his mother

is to be put-to-death, yes, death,

his father and his mother he has insulted, his bloodguilt is upon him!

10. **A man who adulters with the wife of (another) man, who adulters with the wife of his neigh-bor,**

is to be put-to-death, yes, death,

the adulterer and the adulteress.

1 וַיְדַבֵּר יְהֹוָה אֶל־מֹשֶׁה לֵּאמֹר׃

2 דַּבֵּר אֶל־כָּל־עֲדַת בְּנֵי־יִשְׂרָאֵל וְאָמַרְתָּ אֲלֵהֶם קְדֹשִׁים תִּהְיוּ כִּי קָדוֹשׁ אֲנִי יְהֹוָה אֱלֹהֵיכֶם׃

3 אִישׁ אִמּוֹ וְאָבִיו תִּירָאוּ וְאֶת־שַׁבְּתֹתַי תִּשְׁמֹרוּ אֲנִי יְהֹוָה אֱלֹהֵיכֶם׃

4 אַל־תִּפְנוּ אֶל־הָאֱלִילִים וֵאלֹהֵי מַסֵּכָה לֹא תַעֲשׂוּ לָכֶם אֲנִי יְהֹוָה אֱלֹהֵיכֶם׃

5 וְכִי תִזְבְּחוּ זֶבַח שְׁלָמִים לַיהֹוָה לִרְצֹנְכֶם תִּזְבָּחֻהוּ׃

6 בְּיוֹם זִבְחֲכֶם יֵאָכֵל וּמִמָּחֳרָת וְהַנּוֹתָר עַד־יוֹם הַשְּׁלִישִׁי בָּאֵשׁ יִשָּׂרֵף׃

7 וְאִם הֵאָכֹל יֵאָכֵל בַּיּוֹם הַשְּׁלִישִׁי פִּגּוּל הוּא לֹא יֵרָצֶה׃

8 וְאֹכְלָיו עֲוֺנוֹ יִשָּׂא כִּי־אֶת־קֹדֶשׁ יְהֹוָה חִלֵּל וְנִכְרְתָה הַנֶּפֶשׁ הַהִוא מֵעַמֶּיהָ׃

9 וּבְקֻצְרְכֶם אֶת־קְצִיר אַרְצְכֶם לֹא תְכַלֶּה פְּאַת שָׂדְךָ לִקְצֹר וְלֶקֶט קְצִירְךָ לֹא תְלַקֵּט׃

10 וְכַרְמְךָ לֹא תְעוֹלֵל וּפֶרֶט כַּרְמְךָ לֹא תְלַקֵּט לֶעָנִי וְלַגֵּר תַּעֲזֹב אֹתָם אֲנִי יְהֹוָה אֱלֹהֵיכֶם׃

11 לֹא תִּגְנֹבוּ וְלֹא־תְכַחֲשׁוּ וְלֹא־תְשַׁקְּרוּ אִישׁ בַּעֲמִיתוֹ׃

12 וְלֹא־תִשָּׁבְעוּ בִשְׁמִי לַשָּׁקֶר וְחִלַּלְתָּ אֶת־שֵׁם אֱלֹהֶיךָ אֲנִי יְהֹוָה׃

13 לֹא־תַעֲשֹׁק אֶת־רֵעֲךָ וְלֹא תִגְזֹל לֹא־תָלִין פְּעֻלַּת שָׂכִיר אִתְּךָ עַד־בֹּקֶר׃

14 לֹא־תְקַלֵּל חֵרֵשׁ וְלִפְנֵי עִוֵּר לֹא תִתֵּן מִכְשֹׁל וְיָרֵאתָ מֵּאֱלֹהֶיךָ אֲנִי יְהֹוָה׃

QUESTIONS ABOUT THE BIBLICAL TEXT

What about this text makes it so important that all of B'nai Yisrael had to hear it?

_____

_____

_____

_____

153

THE MIDRASH ANSWERS THESE SAME QUESTIONS

A MIDRASH: [Torah T'mima]

God told Moshe: "SPEAK TO THE ENTIRE COMMUNITY OF THE CHILDREN OF YISRAEL" in order to tell him that for this *sidrah* he should not follow his traditional teaching methods of reteaching God's lessons in the Tent of Meeting. Instead he must call an assembly of the entire people including the women and children. This *parashah* was important enough to do this for two reasons: (1) It teaches the concept: "Love your neighbor as yourself" and (2) It is a repetition of the giving of the Ten Commandments at Mt. Sinai which all Jews attended, too.

This midrash presents a puzzle. It is a challenge to see if you can find all of the Ten Commandments in this passage. Copy the passage from KEDOSHIM next to the commandment it matches. (If you need help, use the numbers to look them up.)

1. I am Yhwh (19.3) _____

2. No other Gods (19.4) _____

3. No God's name in vain (19.12) _____

4. Shabbat (19.3) _____

5. Honor Parents (19.3) _____

6. Don't Murder (19.16) _____

7. No Adultery (20.10) _____

8. Don't Steal (19.11) _____

9. No False Witness (19.16) _____

10. Don't Covet (19.18)_____

What did you learn from this *sidrah*?

_____

_____

_____

_____

_____

BEYOND THIS LESSON:

[1] Think about writing your own Holiness Code midrash: (a) How did Moshe usually teach? Describe an ordinary Moshe Torah lesson. (b) What happened in the desert that required a second, different teaching of the basic laws of the Ten Commandments? (c) How did Moshe answer the question: "What is holiness?"

[2] Some other midrashim that this *sidrah* invites are: How is Torah the recipe for Milk and Honey? (b) According to the midrash, all Jews from all time were gathered for this lesson. What was the seating plan at the Holiness Code teaching? How were all the Jewish people from all time arranged? (c) Why does God remind us over and over, "I am YHWH? What is the point of this chorus?

[3] What other questions about parashat KEDOSHIM would be good triggers for midrash?

31. Emor

Leviticus 21:1-24:23

YHWH said to Moshe: Say to the priests, the Sons of Aharon, say to them: For a dead-person among his people, one is not to make oneself *tamei*...(Leviticus 21:1).

[1] With *parashat* EMOR we are back to talking about **rules for kohanim**. God tells Aharon and sons that they may only be in the presence of a dead person if it is a close relative, because they must remain holy to offer sacrifices. A *kohein* cannot marry a harlot or a divorced woman. The ***Kohein ha-Gadol*** (The Big Kahuna) is given even stricter rules. Next, the Torah lists a long group of **physical defects which can keep a person** from the family of *kohanim* **from working as a priest**. Then it is made clear which food can only be eaten by the *kohanim* and which can be eaten by all of B'nai Yisrael.

[2] Having finished with rules of the kahuna (priesthood), the Torah moves on to **Jewish holidays**. We get the basic rules for **Shabbat**, **Pesa<u>h</u>**, **Counting the *Omer***, **Shavuot**, **Yom Kippur** and **Sukkot**. This is followed by a restatement of the commandment to leave food for those in need.

[3] Moving back to the *Mishkan*, we get another statement of the rule to **bring olive oil for light**, and the rule about the **12 loaves of the shew bread**.

[4] To end the *sidrah*, we have the story of an Israelite guy who takes God's name in vain and who is stoned by the community.

CJ'S COMMENTS

[1] Q: Why do we see a restatement of the commandment to leave food for those in need right after the rules for the holidays are listed? **A:** The holidays are a time when we should try to help those in need. One reason for this is because many of our holidays remind us of times when we were in need. Also, on some of our holidays we are supposed to repent. Doing good deeds doesn't hurt us any. **[C.J.]**

And almost every Jewish holiday has its own kind of *tzedakah*. On Purim it is *matanot la-evyonim* (gifts to the poor), on Passover it is *Me'ot H̲ittim* (the *Kosher l'Pesah̲* wheat fund.) etc. **[GRIS]**

THE BIBLICAL TEXT

In this *sidrah* we are taught the laws for many of the Jewish holidays. Read this text and see if you can figure out the rule which is being taught.

Leviticus 23:15-16

15. Now you are to number for yourselves, from the morrow of the Sabbath, from the day that you bring the elevated sheaf,

    seven Sabbaths-of-days,

    whole (weeks) are they to be;

16. until the morrow of the seventh Sabbath you are to number—fifty days,

    then you are to bring-near a grain-gift of new-crops to YHWH.

15 וּסְפַרְתֶּם לָכֶם מִמָּחֳרַת הַשַּׁבָּת מִיּוֹם הֲבִיאֲכֶם אֶת־עֹמֶר
הַתְּנוּפָה שֶׁבַע שַׁבָּתוֹת תְּמִימֹת תִּהְיֶינָה:

16 עַד מִמָּחֳרַת הַשַּׁבָּת הַשְּׁבִיעִת תִּסְפְּרוּ חֲמִשִּׁים יוֹם
וְהִקְרַבְתֶּם מִנְחָה חֲדָשָׁה לַיהוָה:

QUESTIONS ABOUT THE BIBLICAL TEXT

Write the rule here:

HERE ARE A COUPLE OF CLUES:

1. FROM THE MORROW OF THE SABBATH = the 2nd day of Pesa<u>h</u>.

2. UNTIL THE MORROW OF THE SEVENTH SABBATH = Shavuot

_____

_____

_____

_____

_____

_____

_____

_____

_____

THE MIDRASH ANSWERS THESE SAME QUESTIONS

A MIDRASH [Sefer HaḤinuch ad loc]

It is a mitzvah to count forty-nine days starting from the day of the offering of the *omer*, the sixteenth of Nisan, which is the second day of Pesaḥ. The mitzvah is to count both the number of days and the number of weeks.

What is the reason for the counting?

When B'nai Yisrael were redeemed from Egypt, Moshe told them that they were to be given the Torah after forty-nine days. They began counting on the day after the first Seder, Pesaḥ, and finished their counting on Shavuot—the day the Torah was given. In their great anticipation to receive that Divine gift, each Jew kept a daily count for himself, waiting for the great day to arrive. Thereafter, the counting was instituted by God as a permanent mitzvah.

Separating the P'shat from the Drash

1. Underline the parts of this midrash which cannot be found in the Torah or which cannot be supported directly from the Torah.

Separating the Answers from the Messages

2. What did this midrash teach you about some laws in the Torah?

3. What "message" can be learned from this law (with help from the midrash)?

_____

_____

_____

_____

_____

_____

_____

_____

BEYOND THIS LESSON:

[1] Think about writing your own *Omer* midrash: (a) Is the magic number 49? or 50? What is the lesson in this number? (b) Why was Shavuot only one day and not a week like the other pilgrimage festivals? (c) How is getting the Torah like a grain harvest?

[2] Some other midrashim that EMOR invites are: (a) Why are *Kohanim*, who kill animals for a living, made to become impure when they come in contact with dead bodies? (b) What happens to disabled *Kohanim*? What is life like in the home for wayward *Kohanim*? (c) Why do people who curse God deserve to die?

[3] What other questions about parashat EMOR would be good triggers for midrash?

32. Be-Har

Leviticus 25:1-26:2

YHWH spoke to Moshe at Mount Sinai, saying:...(Leviticus 25:1).

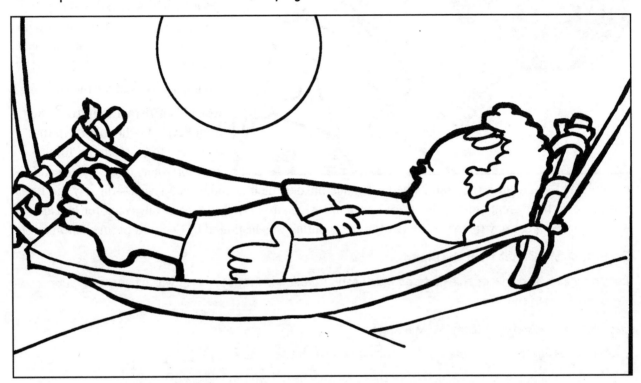

[1] BEHAR is a short *sidrah* which gives us a few new rules. We are introduced to the Sabbatical Year. Every seventh year the land is allowed to rest and no farming is done. Then we meet the Jubilee Year. The Jubilee Year is the 50th year (the year after the seventh Sabbatical Year). It is a year where not only is there no farming, but where all slaves go free and all debts are cancelled.

[2] Next we are told about the rules of owning property in Eretz Yisrael. It can never be permanently sold. It must always return to the family to whom it originally was given. This is true of houses, lands, and even people.

[3] Then, we get a strong statement about never lending money for interest. The *sidrah* ends with another warning not to worship idols.

CJ'S COMMENTS

[1] Wouldn't the Sabbatical Year be semi-destructive? When you can't harvest and get milk and do other things to get food, you'd starve. It's not always easy to keep stock of things. Also, cows can't go without milking. What happens in this situation when the Jubilee Year is the year right after the Sabbatical Year? The situation would grow worse. I must be wrong somewhere, I couldn't imagine these things being planned if people realized that they were difficult situations. [C.J.]

The Sabbatical Year was constructive to the land. It worked just like the rotation of crops did in all those Middle Ages social studies projects I used to have to do. It was not supposed to be destructive to people, either. The idea was, you had to plan and use the "layaway" plan. You're right, for the Jubilee year it took real planning. It worked in theory. Eventually, Jews had problems with making the Jubilee and Sabbatical years work. Hillel, the stand-on-one-foot rabbi, developed a legal "work-around" called the *Prozbul*. The *Prozbul* was a way that Jews could not harvest their lands during a Sabbatical Year and a Jubilee Year—and yet still eat from them. The basic deal was—you sold the land to a non-Jew, and then you rented the right to use the land which wasn't yours, and then wrote into the deal that you bought it back after the year was over. That way, the non-Jew who didn't have to follow Torah rules was doing no wrong, and you, who didn't own land, were just working in someone else's field. The *Prozbul* is (a) tricky *halakhah*, (b) difficult to understand, and (c) a good name for making a lot of sports puns. By the way, poor people could still scavenge food from land they didn't own (so they didn't starve) and milk wasn't a crop, so you could drink it. By the way, you do know that it is a mitzvah to milk a cow on Shabbat—even though it is work—because it keeps the animal from being in pain (*Tza'ar l'Ba'alei Hayyim*). The Shabbat thing is that you have to milk the cow, but you can't use the milk 'cause it was done on Shabbat. *Halakhah* can be confusing. **[GRIS]**

CONTINUED ON PAGE **197**

THE BIBLICAL TEXT

In this *parashah*, God gives a law about not lending money for interest. If you read it closely, you will notice that God connects this rule to the fact that God took B'nai Yisrael out of Egypt. As you read the text, see if you can figure out the connection.

Leviticus 25:35-38

35. Now when your brother sinks down (in poverty)
    and his hand falters beside you,
    then shall you strengthen him
    as (though) a sojourner and resident-settler,
    and he is to live beside you.
36. Do not take from him biting-interest or profit,
    but hold your God in awe,
    so that your brother may live beside you!
37. Your silver you are not to give him at interest,
    for profit you are not to give (him) your food;
38. I YHWH am your God who brought you out of the land of Egypt
    to give you the land of Canaan,
    to be for you a God!

35 וְכִי־יָמוּךְ אָחִיךָ וּמָטָה יָדוֹ עִמָּךְ וְהֶחֱזַקְתָּ בּוֹ גֵּר וְתוֹשָׁב וָחַי עִמָּךְ:

36 אַל־תִּקַּח מֵאִתּוֹ נֶשֶׁךְ וְתַרְבִּית וְיָרֵאתָ מֵאֱלֹהֶיךָ וְחֵי אָחִיךָ עִמָּךְ:

37 אֶת־כַּסְפְּךָ לֹא־תִתֵּן לוֹ בְּנֶשֶׁךְ וּבְמַרְבִּית לֹא־תִתֵּן אָכְלֶךָ:

38 אֲנִי יְהוָה אֱלֹהֵיכֶם אֲשֶׁר־הוֹצֵאתִי אֶתְכֶם מֵאֶרֶץ מִצְרָיִם לָתֵת לָכֶם אֶת־אֶרֶץ כְּנַעַן לִהְיוֹת לָכֶם לֵאלֹהִים:

QUESTIONS ABOUT THE BIBLICAL TEXT

a. What is the connection between being taken out of Egypt and not lending money at interest?

b. What do you think is so bad about collecting interest?

_____

_____

_____

_____

_____

_____

THE MIDRASH ANSWERS THESE SAME QUESTIONS

A MIDRASH [Shemot Rabbah 31.13]

The Hebrew word for interest is *neshekh*, it is very close to the word *nashakh* which means bite. God warns Yisrael, do not "bite" like the snake and offer someone a loan with interest. In the end, you will own his house, his fields, and his vineyards because he cannot make the interest payments.

A MIDRASH [Shemot Rabbah 31.15]

If a Jew takes interest on a loan, and breaks this mitzvah, that Jew denies that God took us out of Egypt. In Egypt we were forced to work and own nothing. Taking money on interest turns people back into slaves.

If a Jew breaks a mitzvah, God calls together a heavenly court to judge the actions. However, if a Jew lends money for interest, God quotes Yehezkel (18.13) and says "HE HAS GIVEN MONEY ON INTEREST...HE SHALL NOT LIVE." No court is called—the verdict was obvious.

Separating the P'shat from the Drash

A. Underline the parts of these midrashim which are based on the Torah.

B. What is the connection between "Egypt" and "interest"?

Separating the Answers from the Messages

C. Why is the Torah so concerned about "interest"?

D. How can you apply this concern today?

_____

_____

_____

_____

_____

_____

BEYOND THIS LESSON:

[1] Think about writing your own "free loan" midrash: (a) Are there times when loans (at interest) are good and not bad? (b) Was there a loan (from the snake) in the Garden of Eden? (c) Why is a loan like a slave master?

[2] Some other midrashim that BEHAR invites are: (a) What does land do when it gets some time off? (b) How do farmers survive if both year 49 and year 50 are crop-free times? (c) Why can't land be sold?

[3] What other questions about parashat BEHAR would be good triggers for midrash?

33. Be-Hukkotai

Leviticus 26:3-27:34

If by my laws you walk, and my commands you keep, and observe them...(Leviticus 26:3).

[1] BE-HUKKOTAI is the last *sidrah* in Leviticus. It comes to an end by giving **a list of blessings** which B'nai Yisrael will receive if they follow God's laws, and **a list of curses** which will happen if they don't follow the Torah.

[2] The Families-of-Yisrael are then promised **five blessings**: (1) the land giving lots of food, (2) peace in the land, (3) victory over enemies, (4) economic and population growth, and (5) God's presence among them.

[3] Then we are given a long list of more than 32 different curses. The portion ends by talking about (1) vows which a person takes, (2) vows a person makes about offering things to God, (3) dedicating things to God, and things which are to be (4) tithed or (5) redeemed. The *kohanim* were involved in all five of these functions.

HAZAK HAZAK V'NITHAZEK

[1] When this *parashah* is read the *brakhot* are read normally. But when the curses are read they are whispered. The idea is that we want to focus on doing good things and getting rewards rather than on bad things and their consequences. [C.J.]

[2] Notice that Joel lists the five blessings, then he just mentions that there is a list of over 32 curses. That way, he saves space and paper, and keeps you from dwelling on bad things. After all this, it's funny that we see vows mentioned. These can sometimes act as blessings or curses.

Busted. Last year I was doing a workshop in Orange County when a teenager said, "In my Torah portion, this Torah portion, God tells Israel that they will "eat their own children." He asked, "Why would God ever do that to anyone?" The Ramban works overtime to make the curses not so bad. He looks in the Talmud, *Gittin* 55b, and finds the story of the destruction of Jerusalem under the Romans. The Talmud says that Jerusalem was destroyed because of "groundless hate." It starts with a Jew whose servant invites his enemy Bar Kamza to a party instead of his friend Kamza. The Jew insults Bar Kamza who in turn goes to the Emperor and causes the destruction of the Temple and of Jerusalem. In the seige of Jerusalem, hunger and craziness spread. Some families do turn cannibal in order to stay alive. Ramban (not Maimonides, but the "N" guy) weaves this all together and says: "God won't make you eat your young as a punishment, but, if you forget the Torah, and forget God by not doing the mitzvot, you will begin a cycle of craziness which will end (as it did with Bar Kamza) in Jews eating their own children." The curse is not caused by God, but happens when we take God out of the equation. I hate the curses section. They make me uncomfortable too. Therefore, I go past them as quickly as possible. [GRIS]

[3] "Rains in their seasons" means that everything will happen the way it is sup-

CONTINUED ON PAGE 198

THE BIBLICAL TEXT

In this *sidrah*, God gives Yisrael a promise of blessings if they follow the laws of the Torah, and curses if they break the laws of the Torah. One of these promises is to give "rains in their season (at a set time)." As you read this text see if you can figure out what this means.

Leviticus 26:3-12

3. If by my laws you walk, and my commands you keep, and observe them,

4. then I will give-forth your rains in their set-time,

   so that the earth gives-forth its yield

   and the trees of the field give-forth their fruit.

5. Threshing will overtake vintage for you, and vintage will overtake sowing;

   you shall eat your food to being-satisfied, and be settled in security in your land.

6. I will give peace throughout the land, so that you will lie down with none to make you tremble,

   I will cause-to-cease wild beasts from the land, and a sword shall not cross through your land....

9. I will turn-my-face toward you, making-you-fruitful and making-you-many,

   and I will establish my covenant with you.

10. You will eat old-grain, the oldest-stored,

    and the old for the new you will have to clear out.

11. I will place my Dwelling in your midst,

    and I will not repel you.

12. I will walk about in your midst,

    I will be for you as a God, and you yourselves will be for me as a people.

3 אִם־בְּחֻקֹּתַי תֵּלֵכוּ וְאֶת־מִצְוֹתַי תִּשְׁמְרוּ וַעֲשִׂיתֶם אֹתָם:

4 וְנָתַתִּי גִשְׁמֵיכֶם בְּעִתָּם וְנָתְנָה הָאָרֶץ יְבוּלָהּ וְעֵץ הַשָּׂדֶה יִתֵּן פִּרְיוֹ:

5 וְהִשִּׂיג לָכֶם דַּיִשׁ אֶת־בָּצִיר וּבָצִיר יַשִּׂיג אֶת־זָרַע וַאֲכַלְתֶּם לַחְמְכֶם לָשֹׂבַע וִישַׁבְתֶּם לָבֶטַח בְּאַרְצְכֶם:

6 וְנָתַתִּי שָׁלוֹם בָּאָרֶץ וּשְׁכַבְתֶּם וְאֵין מַחֲרִיד וְהִשְׁבַּתִּי חַיָּה רָעָה מִן־הָאָרֶץ וְחֶרֶב לֹא־תַעֲבֹר בְּאַרְצְכֶם:

9 וּפָנִיתִי אֲלֵיכֶם וְהִפְרֵיתִי אֶתְכֶם וְהִרְבֵּיתִי אֶתְכֶם וַהֲקִימֹתִי אֶת־בְּרִיתִי אִתְּכֶם:

10 וַאֲכַלְתֶּם יָשָׁן נוֹשָׁן וְיָשָׁן מִפְּנֵי חָדָשׁ תּוֹצִיאוּ:

11 וְנָתַתִּי מִשְׁכָּנִי בְּתוֹכְכֶם וְלֹא־תִגְעַל נַפְשִׁי אֶתְכֶם:

12 וְהִתְהַלַּכְתִּי בְּתוֹכְכֶם וְהָיִיתִי לָכֶם לֵאלֹהִים וְאַתֶּם תִּהְיוּ־לִי לְעָם:

QUESTIONS ABOUT THE BIBLICAL TEXT

How would you explain "rains in their season?"

_____

_____

_____

_____

THE MIDRASH ANSWERS THESE SAME QUESTIONS

A MISHNAH
[Taanit 1.5]

On the third of the month of <u>H</u>eshvan they may say the prayer for rain. Rabban Gamliel taught, One can pray for rain on the seventh day of the month; this is fifteen days after the end of Sukkot and this gives enough time so that all of B'nai Yisrael who made a pilgrimage to Yerushalayim can make it back to Babylon and cross the River Euphrates. This is the right season for rain.

Separating the P'shat from the Drash

1. Where is the Torah found in this text?

Separating the Answers from the Messages

2. Why would it be the wrong season for rain before the 15th day after Sukkot?

3. What concern does this mishnah teach?

_____

_____

_____

_____

_____

A MIDRASH
[Shemot Rabbah 35:10]

THEN I WILL GIVE YOUR RAINS IN THEIR SEASON means, during the nights. In the days of King Herod the rains used to fall at night. In the morning a wind blew, the clouds were scattered, the sun shone, the earth dried up and the laborers went out and engaged in their work, conscious that their labors were agreeable to their Parent-in-heaven.

Separating the P'shat from the Drash

A. Where is the Torah found in this text?

Separating the Answers from the Messages

B. What value does this midrash teach?

C. How does this midrash change the meaning of the word z'man—which can be translated as either time or season?

_____

_____

_____

_____

_____

_____

BEYOND THIS LESSON:

[1] **Think about writing your own "Blessings and Curses" midrash**: (a) How does a curse become a blessing? (b) How does a blessing become a curse? (c) How are vows, tithes, and blessings connected?

[2] **Some other midrashim that BE-<u>H</u>UKKOTAI invites are:** (a) Why is the land punished when Israel does wrong? (b) How is Torah (Law) like rain? (c) Why does God only bless the Land of Israel when the people of Israel are good?

[3] **What other questions about parashat BE-<u>H</u>UKKOTAI would be good triggers for midrash?**

34. Be-Midbar

Numbers 1:1-4:20

Now YHWH spoke to Moshe in the Wilderness of Sinai, in the Tent of Appointment, on the first (day) after the second New-Moon, in the second year after their going-out from the land of Egypt, saying:...(Numbers 1:1).

[1] BE-MIDBAR is the first *parashah* in Numbers. It begins with Moshe and Aharon taking **a census of all the males over twenty**. According to the biblical census bureau: Reuven—46,500, Shimon—59,300, Gad—45,650, Yehudah—74,600, Yissakhar—54,400, Zevulun—57,400, Efraim—40,500, Manashe—32,200, Binyamin—35,400, Dan—62,700, Asher—41,500, and Naftali—53,400.

(We interrupt this description for a short quiz):

    a. What tribe is missing? _____

    b. Why aren't they counted? _____

    c. Yosef is not missing, why isn't he mentioned? _____

    d. In total how many are there? _____

[2] Next we are given **the locations** of the various **tribes around the Mishkan** when they are camped. (See the chart)

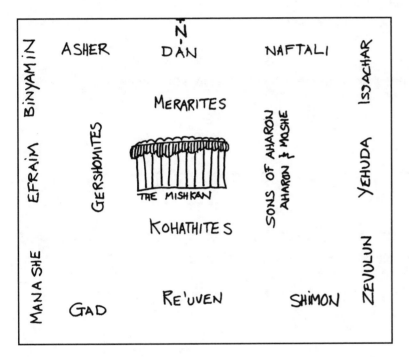

[3] Then we review **the family of Aharon and their responsibilities**, and meet a few other clans who are connected to the *kohanim*. To end the *sidrah*, Moshe is ordered to take a separate survey of the *kohanim* and then the orders for breaking camp are given.

CJ'S COMMENTS

One little, two little, three little… oh. I guess it's that time again. Here we are at Be-Midbar, the first parashah in the book of the same name.

[1] Imagine how many people there were moving on the way to Israel. These were only the men over twenty being counted! But just out of curiosity here are some questions:

a: How many men over twenty (within the tribes) were traveling?

b: Find out the number of seats which your local football stadium has.

c: How many stadiums (rounded to the nearest stadium) will it take to hold all the tribes?

Answer one: a: 603,550. b: Who cares? c. You get enough of that in math class. **[C.J.]**

[2] Were these tribes rounded off a few men over twenty? It seems highly unlikely that every tribe will have a round number of men. **[C.J.]**

Good question, but I just don't know. Here is all I can tell you. Rabbi Uri of Streslik (<u>H</u>asidic dude) said: "The number of letters in the Torah exactly equals the number of Jewish souls in the world. Every letter and every soul is critical. If one letter or one soul is missing, the Divine Presence will not stay with Israel." If you buy his mysticism—and it is a cool image—then the numbers were worked out and not rounded off. I am sure in some commentary somewhere, there is a symbolic meaning to the exact numbers, but I don't know it. **[GRIS]**

[3] Was B'nei Yisrael preparing for war? For all other practical purposes, it would make more sense to count women and children too. Weren't men over twenty eligible for combat? **[C.J.]**

You bet. There are just a few days (or weeks) between the end of the book of Numbers and the beginning of the book of Joshua. We are at the end of the 40 years. We are getting ready for the last push across Moab and Edom, and then on to the Land of Canaan. We are totally doing military prep. **[GRIS]**

CONTINUED ON PAGE **198**

THE BIBLICAL TEXT

If you read this text carefully, you will notice something funny. It introduces the children of Moshe and Aharon and then lists only Aharon's sons. See if you can read this text and then explain this problem.

Numbers 3:1-4

1. Now these are the begettings of Aharon and Moshe
   at the time YHWH spoke with Moshe on Mount Sinai:
2. These are the names of the sons of Aharon: the firstborn—Nadav,
   and Avihu,
   El'azar and Itamar;
3. these are the names of the sons of Aharon, the anointed priests,
   whom he had mandated to act-as-priests.
4. Now Nadav and Avihu died before the presence of YHWH,
   when they brought-near outside fire before the presence of YHWH
   in the Wilderness of Sinai;
   sons they did not have,
   so El'azar and Itamar were made-priest in the living-presence of Aharon their father.

1 וְאֵלֶּה תּוֹלְדֹת אַהֲרֹן וּמֹשֶׁה בְּיוֹם דִּבֶּר יְהוָה אֶת־מֹשֶׁה בְּהַר סִינָי:

2 וְאֵלֶּה שְׁמוֹת בְּנֵי־אַהֲרֹן הַבְּכוֹר נָדָב וַאֲבִיהוּא אֶלְעָזָר וְאִיתָמָר:

3 אֵלֶּה שְׁמוֹת בְּנֵי אַהֲרֹן הַכֹּהֲנִים הַמְּשֻׁחִים אֲשֶׁר־מִלֵּא יָדָם לְכַהֵן:

4 וַיָּמָת נָדָב וַאֲבִיהוּא לִפְנֵי יְהוָה בְּהַקְרִבָם אֵשׁ זָרָה לִפְנֵי יְהוָה בְּמִדְבַּר סִינַי
וּבָנִים לֹא־הָיוּ לָהֶם וַיְכַהֵן אֶלְעָזָר וְאִיתָמָר עַל־פְּנֵי אַהֲרֹן אֲבִיהֶם:

QUESTIONS ABOUT THE BIBLICAL TEXT

Write your own midrashic explanation of this:

_____

_____

_____

_____

_____

_____

_____

THE MIDRASH ANSWERS THESE SAME QUESTIONS

A MIDRASH [Sanhendrin 19b]

Even though the Torah lists only the sons of Aharon, they can be considered the children of both Moshe and Aharon. They are called the sons of Moshe because he taught them the Torah. This tells us that whoever teaches the Torah to the son of another is regarded as though he had been his father.

Separating the P'shat from the Drash

A. Find proof in the Torah that Moshe taught Torah to Aharon's sons.

Separating the Answers from the Messages

B. What Jewish value is being taught here?

_____

_____

_____

_____

_____

_____

BEYOND THIS LESSON:

[1] Think about writing your own "Moshe parents Aharon's kids" midrash: (a) Tell a story of Moshe spending quality time with Aharon's kids. (b) Tell a story of Itamar and El'azar teaching their own children. (c) How do Moshe's sons feel about not being priests and not taking over from dad?

[2] Some other midrashim that BE-MIDBAR invites are: (a) Why does God have a tribal seating plan? Is there a reason why tribes are placed in certain places? (b) Why did God want to continue rather than end tribes? What does Israel get from having tribes? (c) Look at the numbers of how many in each tribe and how many total Jews—what can we learn from this number?

[3] What other questions about parashat BE-MIDBAR would be good triggers for midrash?

35. Naso

Numbers 4:21-7:89

YHWH spoke to Moshe, saying: Take up the head-count of the Sons of Gershon...
(Numbers 4:21-22).

[1] Now we have come to *sidrah* NASO which is an odd assortment of different kinds of stuff. **Moshe is ordered to take a census of the clans of Gershonites, Merarites, and Kohatites.** All of these are from the tribe of Levi and had special duties for moving parts of the *Mishkan* when B'nai Yisrael traveled.

[2] Next we get an assortment of rules including: **removing corpses** from camp, **paying damages**, **the *sotah* test for adultery**, and **the vows of the *nazir*.**

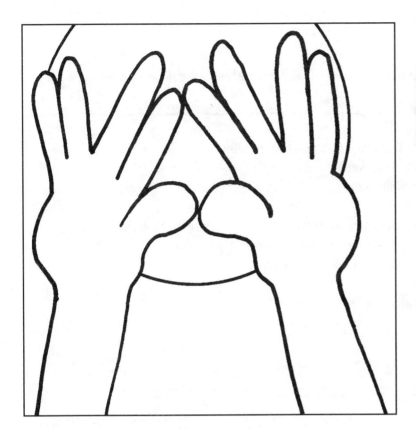

CJ'S COMMENTS

[1] Well, the summary mostly has all questions answered. I just want to clear up some things. *"Sotah"* (*samekh, vav, tet, hey*) means adulterer (in the feminine form of the word). By briefly looking up the test of the adulterer I have noticed some not-so-good things. Part of the test has to do with sacrifices and unclean water. The alleged adulterer must drink the water. If she becomes fat in the stomach and the thigh, she is a curse to her people. If not, she didn't commit adultery. The bad thing here is the drinking of the dirty water. That's not exactly the safest thing (though adultery isn't either). Another bad thing I noticed was that the woman always takes the blame. Even if he started it, he isn't guilty while she has to "face the music." Please tell me I read that wrong!

C.J., it is so nice to see that you have some feminist roots. You are of course, right (according to me). But here is a cool point. In a midrash about Ḥannah, one found in Brakhot in the Talmud, she blackmails God using the *sotah* rules. God says, "If you are found innocent, you will have children (like it won't make you sterile)." So she says to God, "I'll trap Eli alone in a tent, so there will be doubt whether or not he and I committed adultery. That will embarrass him and force my husband to demand *sotah*. One I am given the lie detector potion, you will have to make me get pregnant and have a child—just to keep your Torah true." Next, out comes Samuel. I love the idea of a feminist woman blackmailing God with a sexist piece of Torah. **[GRIS]**

[2] The *nazir* took an oath to kind of be "faithful" to God for a period of time. He had to grow his hair long, couldn't get intoxicated (drunk), and couldn't have anything from the vine (grape related). This cut him off from normal life. To find out a little more about a *nazir*, look at the story of Samson. **[C.J.]**

[3] This midrash is a good one, but I think it overlooks one way in which the word "numbers" can be used. In this sense, numbers are the numerals we count with. That inter-

CONTINUED ON PAGE **198**

[3] At this point the Torah introduces the **Birkat Kohanim** (guys named Cohen hold their hands like Mr. Spock). Then we get some special **responsibilities of the chieftains**, followed by the special gifts each of them brought. (There is a day-to-day description of their gifts in the text.)

[4] At the end of the *sidrah* we are told that Moshe could talk to God in the tent of meeting and hear God's voice coming from between the two cherubim on the *aron*.

THE BIBLICAL TEXT

Read this text carefully. See if you can figure out who these new chieftains are and why they have special offerings.

Numbers 7:1-3

1. Now it was, at the time that Moshe finished setting up the Dwelling,
   he anointed it and hallowed it, with all its implements,
   and the slaughter-site, with all its implements,
   he anointed them and he hallowed them.
2. Then brought-near the exalted-leaders of Yisrael, the heads of their Father's Houses—
3. they are the leaders of the tribes, they are those who stand over the counting—
   they brought their near-offering before the presence of YHWH:
   six litter wagons and twelve cattle,
   a wagon for (every) two leaders and an ox for (each) one.

1 וַיְהִי בְּיוֹם כַּלּוֹת מֹשֶׁה לְהָקִים אֶת־הַמִּשְׁכָּן וַיִּמְשַׁח אֹתוֹ וַיְקַדֵּשׁ אֹתוֹ וְאֶת־כָּל־כֵּלָיו
וְאֶת־הַמִּזְבֵּחַ וְאֶת־כָּל־כֵּלָיו וַיִּמְשָׁחֵם וַיְקַדֵּשׁ אֹתָם:

2 וַיַּקְרִיבוּ נְשִׂיאֵי יִשְׂרָאֵל רָאשֵׁי בֵּית אֲבֹתָם הֵם נְשִׂיאֵי הַמַּטֹּת הֵם הָעֹמְדִים עַל־הַפְּקֻדִים:

3 וַיָּבִיאוּ אֶת־קָרְבָּנָם לִפְנֵי יְהוָה שֵׁשׁ־עֶגְלֹת צָב וּשְׁנֵי עָשָׂר בָּקָר עֲגָלָה עַל־שְׁנֵי הַנְּשִׂאִים
וְשׁוֹר לְאֶחָד וַיַּקְרִיבוּ אֹתָם לִפְנֵי הַמִּשְׁכָּן:

QUESTIONS ABOUT THE BIBLICAL TEXT

Make your own best guess who these leaders who were in charge of numbers were. Why do you think they had a special privilege?

_____

_____

_____

_____

_____

_____

_____

THE MIDRASH ANSWERS THESE SAME QUESTIONS

A MIDRASH [Bamidbar Rabbah 12,20, 15,16]

The chieftains of the tribes were those who were appointed over B'nai Yisrael in Egypt. These were the men whom the Torah is talking about when it says: "And the officers of B'nai Yisrael, whom Pharaoh's taskmasters had set over them, were beaten, saying: Wherefore have you not fulfilled your appointed task in making bricks both yesterday and today…?" (Exodus 5.14). They had to stand and count the bricks which were produced each day. When Pharaoh ordered B'nai Yisrael to make the same number of bricks each day without using straw. The officers refused to tell who had not produced enough bricks. For this, the taskmasters would then beat them. These officers said: "It is better for us to be beaten rather than that the rest of the people should suffer."

Separating the P'shat from the Drash

A. How does this midrash use the word "number" to join two different stories in the Torah?

Separating the Answers from the Messages

B. According to this midrash, why were the chieftains honored?

C. What kind of role models are these chieftains? What value does the midrash teach us through their example?

_____

_____

_____

_____

BEYOND THIS LESSON:

[1] Think about writing your own "Desert Leadership" midrash: (a) Who were the leaders in the wilderness—what were their skills? (b) How did families and tribes change in the wilderness? How were they different from the way they were in Egypt? (c) What Egypt stories did they tell in the wilderness? What Egypt stories did they hide?

[2] Some other midrashim that NASO invites are: (a) How did the priestly blessing change the people? (b) Tell the story of why someone chose to be a *nazir*. (c) Why did God pick the spot between the cherubim on the ark as the spot to talk to people?

[3] What other questions about parashat NASO would be good triggers for midrash?

36. Be-Ha´alotekha

Numbers 8:1-12:16

YHWH spoke to Moshe, saying: Speak to Aharon and say to him: When you draw up the lamp-wicks...(Numbers 8:1-2).

[1] BEHA'ALOTEKHA is a *parashah* which continues and then completes the rules and statistics we have been studying and moves us back into the story of the 40 years in the wilderness. It begins with **a description of the menorah** and then moves to **the appointment of the tribe of Levi** as the assistants to the *kohanim*. This is followed by **laws about firstborn and the rules for Pesa<u>h</u>.**

[2] Next we get a description of how the *Mishkan* is taken apart and put together again. **Moshe is given an order to make two silver horns** which are to be used **to call the people** to the tent of meeting and to war. Then the order of march in the wilderness is described.

[3] And now back to our story. Moshe says good-bye to his father-in-law and **the ark is picked up and moved.**

DRAW YOUR OWN IMAGE HERE.

[4] **The people take to complaining,** and a fire breaks out. Then there is more complaining—especially about the food—in spite of the manna which fell every night. Moshe and God have a talk about how to deal with B'nai Yisrael and they appoint **a sanhedrin of 70 elders**. **Two men start prophesying on their own**. Next, a wind blows **a bunch of quail into camp** and there is meat to eat.

[5] At the end of the sidrah, **Moshe marries a Cushite woman** (a black woman) **and Miriam criticizes him**. She gets leprosy, and then Moshe prays for her and the leprosy is taken away.

CJ'S COMMENTS

[1] You say that God ordered Moshe to make two silver horns to call people to the tent of meeting and war. These are obviously *shofarot*, but I have two questions: (1) Why didn't God tell Moshe to tell Aharon, or better yet, tell Aharon, to make the *shofarot*? He is, after all, the metal worker in the family. (2) Since when are *shofarot* made of silver? My mom says these may be shofar covers. Please clear this one up. **[C.J.]**

Go and read the text carefully, and then the Rashi. From the Torah we learn that these two trumpets are made of beaten silver. These are all-metal horns, not covered *shofarot* (which are not allowed.) Rashi teaches us two clues. (a) The silver horns are made out of silver, not gold, like the rest of the Mishkan stuff, to keep them separate from the sin of the Golden Calf. We need this distinction because (a) the regular shofar (the organic one) is blown when an order comes from God. The organic shofar calls on Yom Kippur and Rosh ha-Shanah, and Rosh <u>H</u>odesh, connect us to God via the Akedah (Binding of Isaac). These silver horns are like those that precede a king. They announce orders from Moses as the head of the Bet Din. They give him authority. They are silver to show his word is important, not gold—the metal of a "wannabe god." **[GRIS]**

[2] Why doesn't Yitro stay along for the ride? Is there anything important he has to do? **[C.J.]**

There are two Yitros in the Torah—the "good" Yitro and the "evil" Yitro. They are woven into two different streams. (By the way, I don't mean evil twins, rather, two different editions of the Yitro story. In one, Yitro is a bad guy who does love his daughter, but who is a pagan. He comes from Midian, the same place as Bilaam and the daughters of Baal Peor, and is basically nice to Moses for his daughter's sake, and then goes back to his paganism. In the midrash, this Yitro was originally an advisor to Pharaoh and the one who told the New Pharaoh to beat on the Jews. "Midian" basically means "bad guy", and

CONTINUED ON PAGE **198**

THE BIBLICAL TEXT

In this *sidrah*, we again get a look at rebellion. This time, the quality of food is the major complaint. As you read this text, see if you can figure out (1) why the people are unhappy eating manna, and (2) why they considered the food they ate as slaves "free" food.

Numbers 11:1-6

1. Now the people were like those-who-grieve (over) ill-fortune, in the ears of Yʜwʜ.
   When Yʜwʜ heard, his anger flared up;
   there blazed up against them a fire of Yʜwʜ
   and ate up the edge of the camp.
2. The people cried out to Moshe
   and Moshe interceded to Yʜwʜ,
   and the fire abated.
3. So they called the name of that place Tav'era/Blaze,
   for (there) had blazed against them fire of Yʜwʜ.
4. Now the gathered-riffraff that were among them
   had a craving, hunger-craving,
   and moreover they again wept, the Children of Yisrael, and said:
   Who will give us meat to eat?
5. We recall the fish that we used to eat in Egypt for free,
   the cucumbers, the watermelons,
   the green-leeks, the onions, and the garlic!
6. But now, our throats are dry;
   there is nothing at all
   except for the *mahn* (in front of) our eyes!

1 וַיְהִי הָעָם כְּמִתְאֹנְנִים רַע בְּאָזְנֵי יְהוָה וַיִּשְׁמַע יְהוָה וַיִּחַר אַפּוֹ וַתִּבְעַר־בָּם אֵשׁ יְהוָה וַתֹּאכַל בִּקְצֵה הַמַּחֲנֶה:

2 וַיִּצְעַק הָעָם אֶל־מֹשֶׁה וַיִּתְפַּלֵּל מֹשֶׁה אֶל־יְהוָה וַתִּשְׁקַע הָאֵשׁ:

3 וַיִּקְרָא שֵׁם־הַמָּקוֹם הַהוּא תַּבְעֵרָה כִּי־בָעֲרָה בָם אֵשׁ יְהוָה:

4 וְהָאסַפְסֻף אֲשֶׁר בְּקִרְבּוֹ הִתְאַוּוּ תַּאֲוָה וַיָּשֻׁבוּ וַיִּבְכּוּ גַּם בְּנֵי יִשְׂרָאֵל וַיֹּאמְרוּ מִי יַאֲכִלֵנוּ בָּשָׂר:

5 זָכַרְנוּ אֶת־הַדָּגָה אֲשֶׁר־נֹאכַל בְּמִצְרַיִם חִנָּם אֵת הַקִּשֻּׁאִים וְאֵת הָאֲבַטִּחִים וְאֶת־הֶחָצִיר וְאֶת־הַבְּצָלִים וְאֶת־הַשּׁוּמִים:

6 וְעַתָּה נַפְשֵׁנוּ יְבֵשָׁה אֵין כֹּל בִּלְתִּי אֶל־הַמָּן עֵינֵינוּ:

QUESTIONS ABOUT THE BIBLICAL TEXT

1. Given the description of manna, why were the people unhappy with their diet?

2. Why do you think the people considered the food they ate as slaves "free" food?

_____

_____

_____

_____

THE MIDRASH ANSWERS THESE SAME QUESTIONS

A MIDRASH [Pesikta Rabbati]

As so often before, it was again the mixed multitude rebelled against God and Moshe, saying: "Who shall give us meat to eat? We remember the fish that we ate for free in Egypt; the cucumbers, and the melons, and the leeks and the onions and the garlic. Now we have shrunken stomachs. There is nothing at all! Nothing to look at except this manna " But all these murmurings and these complaints were only an excuse to move them further away from God.

First of all, they actually owned herds and cattle, so that they had plenty of meat to eat if they really wanted it. But secondly, manna had the flavor of every conceivable kind of food. All they had to do while eating it was to wish for a certain dish and they instantly tasted the food they wanted in the manna they were eating.

The truth was that they were unhappy being responsible for the yoke of the law. In Egypt, their food was no better, it was not even as good, but in Egypt their food came without responsibility. In Egypt they were slaves and they were told what to do. Their masters were responsible for their actions. Now that they were free people, they became responsible for their own actions and for following the laws of the Torah. In Egypt, the fish and other food was not free of cost, but it was free of responsibility.

Separating the P'shat from the Drash

A. Underline the "Torah-facts" in these midrashim.

B. What new information does this midrash give us about manna?

Separating the Answers from the Messages

C. How does this midrash explain the complaints about food? (Think about the meaning of "fish for free")

D. What is the message of this midrash?

_____

_____

_____

_____

_____

_____

_____

BEYOND THIS LESSON:

[1] **Think about writing your own Manna midrash:** (a) What were the things from Egypt that the people missed most? (b) Why did God give in to the complainers' demands and add quail? (c) Who "re-made" the best manna in camp? What was the awarding winning recipe at the great manna cook-off?

[2] **Some other midrashim that this _sidrah_ invites are:** (a) Why do the people keep complaining? (b) Why does God keep trying to step these rebellions when it seems to do no good? (c) What was Miriam's problem with Moshe' new wife?

[3] **What other questions about parashat BE-HA'ALOTEKHA would be good triggers for midrash?**

HAZAK, HAZAK, V'NITHAZEK

after the first havdalah. It was a real separation between holy and ordinary. [GRIS]

[4]: If Adam had NOT eaten the forbidden fruit, would God have provided a new mate for him or would he have worked it out to save Hawa from the death sentence? [Jamie Weiss]

(a) The death sentence is not a verdict but a fate. It means that once you eat from the tree of knowledge, your life is mortal—someday you will die. It is not that God would kill Hawa and let Adam start over. (b) If we played out your story, it would probably come out like a science fiction story where Adam is "cursed" to live forever, where Hawa and everyone else dies. (c) The midrash suggests something deeper. Adam had a first wife. She was Lilith. In some versons, she is the serpent's wife. After she and Adam fight and are "divorced," she becomes an eternal creature who haunts the night—eternally. She seeks out bridegrooms and male children and strangles them. (d) Adam and Hawa are bone of bone/flesh of flesh. If I was writing the story, Hawa would eat. Adam would refuse. God would punish with eventual death. Then Adam would bite the fruit out of love. The new sentence would be passed. Then as Adam and Hawa left the Garden, God would smile big time. [GRIS]

[5]: In the parashah, after the snake has given the fruit from the Tree of Knowledge to Hawa and G-d finds out, G-d begins questioning how they knew they were naked and if they ate from the Tree of Knowledge? Adam says something that makes me mad. He says the woman THAT YOU GAVE TO ME gave me the fruit and I ate. First of all, he has a brain. He could have said "No." Instead he eats and he blames his sin on Hawa. The thing that makes me even more mad is that Adam hints that it is G-d's fault, for He gave Adam this mischievous woman. Then to make the chain of blame longer, when asked what she did, Hawa says to G-d, "The serpent tricked me." Wait a second! The serpent was sly; however, there is no excuse for Adam and Hawa's behavior. They were specifically told not to eat from the tree. They decided to on their own. They should accept the blame. The good thing is that everyone got punished for their actions. [Dina Ackerman]

[6]: I was listening to talk radio last night—all this Garden of Eden and the snake is evil stuff—when one of my old questions came back to me. I would hate the Garden of Eden before the eating the fruit. Having no job. Having life that lasted forever. Having nothing that needed to be accomplished would drive me crazy. I think that God wanted us to eat the fruit. Otherwise, life would have been boring for us and for God. What do you think? [GRIS]

I disagree with Joel on the "Garden" thing. I think that maybe it might have been better in the Garden of Eden before we ate the fruit. Sure, maybe we wouldn't be so smart, but then we couldn't harm others either. That would take the knowledge of evil, and we don't have knowledge, remember? People in this day and age say that ignorance can kill you, but that wouldn't be true in the Garden. We'd live in peace with the animals and with each other. And how would we even know that we were missing out on things we have now? You only say that you couldn't live in the Garden because you've become too modernized. You've never lived there before. Personally, I think it would be a great experience. Sometimes you just wish that you could be innocent again. [C.J.]

C.J., you said: People in this day and age say that ignorance can kill you, but that wouldn't be true in the Garden. We'd live in peace with the animals and with each other. And how would we even know that we were missing out on things we have now? … You've never lived there before. Personally, I think it would be a great experience. That reminds me of Invasion of the Body Snatchers. The aliens take over our bodies, and every time, the host experiences ecstatic pleasure. All problems drop away. Yet the hero struggles against them, tries to defeat them, attempts to retain his identity, together with all of its problems—even its pain. Why? When I was in Hebrew School I learned a proverb, "You have to squeeze the olive to get the oil." Maybe part of what makes us what we are is that we have to struggle to survive. And the difficulty of the achievement heightens that achievement for us. Sure, it would be easier if things were handed to us on a silver platter. (For that matter, it would have been a lot easier for the Israelites if they hadn't had to spend 40 years in the desert.) But then the things we cherish wouldn't be ours, and we wouldn't get the same satisfaction from them. [David Parker]

[7]: Why do we want to do tikkun olam if the Garden was such a bad place? I thought that fixing the world will put us back into the "Garden". I do agree though that we were supposed to eat the apple (piece of fruit). Maybe we did not taste the apple, as much as we tasted the Garden. The apple gave us all this "knowledge" but we are all missing the taste of the Garden. I have another question to pose. Adam, people, were given the job of protecting (shomer) the things (trees and animals) in the Garden. How can we get back to the Garden if we have already destroyed so many of the species that were originally in the Garden? Have a wonderful Shabbat! [Arye Berk]

To semi-answer your questions: By protecting and sharing the earth with what few animals we have left, we may "redeem" ourselves. As for Adam and Hawa, this was probably one of those times when our villain uses the familiar phrase "If only you knew. Taste the fruit and you may experience the pleasures of life." Then he lost his legs and his descendants built a cigarette company. Call it strange. [C.J.]

[8]: When I met you today at Temple Shalom you got me thinking, which I actually don't normally do unless I have to. But don't feel badly, it's quite an interesting concept, thinking, I mean. Well my favorite passage isn't totally Noah. I like Bereshit, too. But I also absolutely HATE both of them. Noah I hate because of all the needless death. Like sure, maybe the people needed to die. But all those animals! I started thinking that when you talked about the boy who wondered about the horses. Second, I loathe Bereshit because it made it seem like women totally depend on men. Like, Eve was made from ADAM, ADAM named the beasts, and I'm sure there's more in there about ADAM, ADAM, ADAM. It's really quite annoying. [Rachel Aberle]

I know what my friend and teacher, Yosi Gordon, has taught me about creation: In the beginning there is one only person, ADAM (the Earthling). ADONAI, the God, said: "IT IS NOT GOOD THAT ADAM BE ALONE." To solve the problem, God has a plan. God says: "I WILL MAKE A COMPANION STRENGTH WHO FITS WITH ADAM." Now watch the action closely. ADONAI, THE GOD, FORMED FROM THE SOIL ALL THE WILD BEASTS AND ALL THE BIRDS. AND BROUGHT EACH TO THE EARTHLING TO SEE WHAT THE EARTHLING WOULD CALL IT. WHATEVER THE EARTHLING CALLED THE ANIMAL, THAT BECAME ITS NAME… So God, with Adam's help, paired *Kelev* (dog) with *Kalbah* (female dog), *Hatul* (cat) the *Hatulah* (female cat). Male was matched with female. BUT FOR ADAM, NO HELPER WHO FIT COULD BE FOUND. Adam (person) should have been matched with *Adamah*—but that word already had been used up; it was already the name for Mother Earth. For the first person, God needed a different solution. So here is what happened: ADONAI, the God, made ADAM sleep a deep sleep and took one side and then closed in the flesh. We'll talk about it more later, but the Hebrew makes it clear that God took a side, an aspect of the first person, not just a bone. ADONAI, the God, built that side into an *ishah* (woman), and brought her to ADAM. ADAM said: "THIS IS THE ONE, BONE FROM MY BONE, FLESH FROM MY FLESH. SHE SHALL BE CALLED ISHAH (WO-MAN). BECAUSE SHE WAS TAKEN FROM ISH (MAN)." If you listen closely, first there was an Earthling, one lonely person, whom God splits into two. By creating woman out of Earthling, Ishah out of Adam, Ish (man), also out of Adam, comes into being. And then the Torah continues: SO AN ISH WILL LEAVE HIS FATHER AND HIS MOTHER, HE WILL CLING TO HIS ISHAH—AND THEY WILL BECOME ONE FLESH. People become whole in finding their other half (Genesis 2.18ff). [GRIS]

[9]: Here is what I heard in shul this week. My rabbi, Mordecai Finley, quoted the Sefat Emet (a famous commentator) in saying: "The sukkah is the portal to the Garden of Eden." I like that image, not only because it is sort of like the sukkah being the "stargate," but because Sukkot does always come the week before Parashat Bereshit, which makes it the doorway to the Garden of Eden (story). Does this image work for you—and what do you think it means? [GRIS]

[10]: Why does the first *sidrah* start with creation but almost end with destruction? [GRIS]

Maybe it was because they raised evil to an art form. The people at the end of the ten generations were being creative too. [Shaye Horwitz]

C.J. COMMENTS
Noah continued from page 13

continued from page 13

Yes. Yes it is. [GRIS]

[3]: God says, "COME-NOW! LET US GO DOWN AND THERE LET US BAFFLE THEIR LANGUAGE, SO THAT NO MAN WILL UNDERSTAND THE LANGUAGE OF HIS NEIGHBOR." Notice the word "US." It never explains who God is talking to. Is God talking to the angels? To God's self? To someone different? *Tower of Bavel is falling down, falling down, falling down…* [C.J.]

Use Bavel as a modern day metaphor: Even though there are people all over the world, it is possible that the only true thing that separates us is language… (kinda mushy nice sounding…) [Josh Barkin]

Dear Josh, Your ideas cannot possibly be left out, they're so good! It never says that humans can't destroy the earth. Don't litter! God says that *God* will never destroy the earth again. Does this include people not destroying the earth? What do you think and why? [C.J.]

A covenant normally is an agreement or a pact. It is a two-sided promise (compromise). All we ever hear, though, is that God will never destroy the earth again. What is Noah's side of the deal, and if we don't keep it, do we get punished? Keep thinking, [C.J.]

The midrash introduces a concept called "The Noahite Laws" (a.k.a *Sheva Mitzvot B'nai Noah*). They imagine that God gave humanity via Noah seven mitzvot—at Mt. Sinai the Jewish people got another 606. (I think, but can't prove, that the number seven is reflected in the fact that the word *brit* (covenant) is used seven times at the end of the Noah story.) In any case, the actual list can only be found in the midrash, not the actual Torah text (though some of them are stated and others are implied). They are: (1) Have courts. (2) Do not abuse God's name. (3) Do not worship idols. (4) Do not rape, molest, sexually harass. (5) Do not murder. (6) Do not steal. (7) Do not cut a limb off a living animal. [GRIS]

a LITTLE bit sick here! You think Avram, Sarai, and Pharaoh were working out some prostitution deal? To tell you the truth, that could very well be! Without the Torah clarifying exactly what is going on in this portion, we can easily believe things along the lines of which you are thinking. Maybe I've listened to that *Salt N' Pepa* song a little too much. **[C.J.]**

Close but no prize, guys. Sex is involved, but it isn't prostitution. We have three interrelated possibilities. [1] The official midrashic version was that Pharaoh had the hots for Sarai and would have killed Avram to get her. Thus, by saying Sarai is his sister, Avram is offering to "sell" her to Pharaoh as a concubine or wife (not a one-night stand)— and save his own life. If that is the case, the money which would have originally been a dowry becomes the "pay-off" for a deal gone bad. It is hush money/guilt money. That is the way the midrash reads the story. It suggests that Pharaoh wants Sarai, but gets nightmares when he tries to spend the night with her. (Imagine the *Goosebumps* version.) Pharaoh then figures out that she is married—and uses a bribe to send her and Avram packing. [2] In Sumer and Arkad (the places that Avram and Sarai orignally called home)—brother-sister marriages were not uncommon— especially with priestesses. A woman named Savina Teubal has written a book to try to prove that this is the story. Pharoahs of Egypt also had a pattern of marrying family—so Avram might have been telling Pharaoh that she was a "sister-wife" (and so leave her alone). [3] This story may be a cover-up and Pharaoh didn't figure out the truth till the morning after. If Sarai is a "rape" victim, then this story is very powerful and unfortunately very modern. **[GRIS]**

It seems that we've gotten into some very interesting situations here. They both deal with the power of love, but to what extent? How far will the people in the Torah go to be with each other? How far should we go? Till death do us part? I hate to be annoying, but it can get habit-forming. I'll try not to make this painful. When discussing Adam and Eve, we see that Life and Death play some parts (or would-be parts) in the conclusion of our story. We know that, scientifically, people thousands of years ago had normal life spans of 20-30 years. We can see how this has increased drastically over time. How bad would it be to add another decade or two to our lifespans? What I'm getting at is this: What are the good and bad consequences of having the power to live forever? And would life SEEM as long to those who lived thousands of years ago as it does to us now? When I went to camp this year, I went for two months. I'd always gone for one month before. But it SEEMED like I'd been gone as long as I had been when I used to go one month. As for Sarai and Abram, were the measures he went to to protect his life and his love too large?

It seems to me like God didn't approve of the situation. He knew that Abram needed to do this to survive, that's why no one "important to the story" was killed. But God sent plagues until Pharaoh figured it out. This must mean that SOMETHING wasn't right. What do you think NOW, **[C.J.]**

You write: Now friends—I want some answers. I find the Abram/Sarai/Pharaoh story very real. We are seeing Abram as a real person with real fears—not as the superhuman hero who can do no wrong. The whole thing doesn't fit: This is the Abram who supposedly trusts in G-d and has faith that he will be protected. Yet on this occasion, he's not so sure. He hedges his bet and tries not to get killed, rather than just trusting G-d to make it all right. I'm also puzzled by what Abram thought he was accomplishing: If he said Sarai was his wife, he'd be killed, and Pharaoh would take Sarai into his house. By saying she was his sister, he didn't get killed, but she still got taken into Pharaoh's house. Nor can we say it's just G-d's way of not intervening so we can express our free will. After all, G-d sure intervened a few chapters ago with the flood. And G-d will surely do so again soon at Sodom and Gemorrah. (Plus G-d may have even intervened here by causing the sickness in Pharaoh's house.) I like this, because it shows Abram to be a person just like us who puts his pants on one leg at a time, who has fears (or are they ambitions?) and who isn't so certain that things will come out the way he wants them to do — who isn't like the person described in so many of the other stories. Maybe each of *us* also has the capacity to "be a blessing" too? **[David Parker <Parques@aol.com>]**

Dear David and the list, I think the easiest way to respond to your ideas is summed up in the common phrase "God helps those who help themselves." Who knows? Maybe God wouldn't have saved Abram had he sat around and done nothing. Of course we need to have faith in God. But if all we have is faith, nothing will get done. Without the will to start, why should God help us along the way? Hope that helps. **[C.J.]**

[2]: What is the War of the Kings? Why would a King praise someone who had just freed one of his own captives? **[C.J.]**

The War of the Kings is a "gang war" between 9 Canaanite city-states. Consider it a kind of rumble free-for-all. In the mess of fighting, Lot, Avram's nephew whom he had adopted like his own son, is captured. To free him, he has to help Malki-Tzedek win the whole war. He gets praised, not for freeing the captives—but for doing an "Arnold" and being a regular fighting machine, action adventure hero (and then refusing to take any of the booty). To check it out—read Genesis 14. **[GRIS]**

[3]: Presently, many Jews and Muslims feel the same way as Sarai and Hagar. Yet we should all realize that we are children of the same father. We have started realizing this, fortunately, and Yisrael has made peace with some countries now. We must hope that these promises are kept, and that they lead to more promises in the future. **[C.J.]**

saw the son of Hagar the Egyptian whom she had born unto Abraham, making sport." Then I looked solely at the making sport part of it. By the commentary, it says that making sport either means: shooting at Isaac's head with an arrow or threatening his life in some way. Now, are these signs of a great leader-to-be? I personally don't think so. In my opinion G-d wanted a better leader for the Israelites than Ishmael. Then, G-d had Sarah get him kicked out and Abraham made Isaac the next great leader. But, Ishmael IS Abraham's son, and is a pretty important guy. G-d makes him a great nation anyway even though he's not the best leader. So, we should learn from this: Even the smallest thing you do, says something about who you are and who you're going to become. [Ben Kort]

Ben basically asks the question: (1) Did Ishmael get kicked out because he was a bad person? or (2) Because he was not a good enough leader—and so space was left for Isaac who would do a better job? This is a deep question. Is Genesis more about "doing the right thing" or more about "how to build a nation?" And then, can you do both at the same time? Do you have to be a hard-ass to build a family into a nation? [GRIS]

[3]: I noticed that at the end of the excerpt from the Torah Avraham is giving his guests cream, milk, and the ox itself. This meal is not kosher. It may be before kashrut comes into the picture, but if these guys were angels like some people think, I'm sure they would have said something. [C.J.]

The midrash saw the same things and notes: First he served them curds. (The milk). Then they waited. Then, later, he served the meat. Kashrut is protected. [GRIS]

[4]: I like the two midrashim about Avraham. They show what a nice guy he is. Even if Avraham was supposed to be really rich, it kinda makes you wonder how he had all those clothes and food to give away. He may have had servants to make him things like that, but people must come at such a fast rate, that clothes get given quickly. I guess that's it [C.J.]

I like CJ's comments… I just have one thing to add… Rabbi Schulweis at Valley Beth Shalom (it's a shul in LA) says that one of the greatest things about people in the Torah is their imperfection. Avraham's timidness reflected in his willingness to sacrifice Yitzhak illustrates this. A stronger-willed person might have said… "G-d… I am as faithful as it gets to you, but geez! I won't sacrifice my son for you!" Avraham had already picked up his life and moved for G-d… now G-d tells him to sacrifice Yitzhak… THAT's where Avraham should have drawn the line… I think the midrashim talking about Avraham passing a test are a false attempt to over "saintize" Avraham… Let's face it: he was rather timid. I like to think that Avraham

"learned" from this timidness in the whole arguing with G-d thing (if there are righteous people, save the city) and finally stood up to G-d. So what if it's a midrash… [Josh Barkin]

[5] Va-Yera is such a great parashah. It is full of great stories and conflicts. One thing that bothers me, though, is Avraham's contradictory actions. Avraham, like a true tzaddik, argues with G-d over Sodom and Gemorrah, trying to save as many people as possible. However, when G-d tells Abraham to sacrifice Yitzhak, he is willing to do so without putting up a fight and G-d voluntarily stops him. Why does Avraham fight for the people of Sodom and Gemorrah and not for his own son? Why does G-d need convincing not to destroy whole cities and doesn't need persuasion to call off the killing of one person? [Dina Ackerman]

It is funny that you should mention this because we asked this exact question in Torah study group and got a lot of different answers. This answer is the one that the whole group came up with: The Akedah was just another test of faith, in that you sometimes have to sacrifice with and for your children. For example, you know that it may be good for them to go to Jewish schools not in your immediate area, but you send them anyway. You know it isn't easy for a child to go around with a tallit katan or yarmulke, but the child may feel that this is a sacrifice of being Jewish, and he knows that in the outcome, he will be better off because this is what God wants him to do. [Sharon Davis <mdavis@infi.net>]

When my ex-wife asked for a divorce, the most painful thing she said to me was. "You have time for everyone else, everyone at the synagogue where you work, but not for me. With all your students you are patient, but you have no patience for me." What hurt was that she was right. Home is where you run around in your underwear with the ugly parts of your body sticking out. You hide and fake much less than you do in public. One lesson of this story is that sometimes we will do things for strangers that we will not do for family. I may break or bend a rule for someone else that I will not do for my own child. That is family backlash. I have said cruel things to my sister and my parents in my life that I would have never said to any stranger. That, too, is part of family—and that may be one of the messages in the fact that Abraham will beg for Sodom but not for Isaac. Closeness also creates its own distance. I think that is a painful truth. [GRIS]

C.J. COMMENTS
Hayei Sarah continued from page 31

our relationships by interaction and by watching behavior. We choose our fantasies by the "pin-up" but, if we are smart, we choose our signficiant others by who they are—and that we learn from watching and interacting. BUT, I just love the image of Rivkah at Starbucks drawing enough Grande Lattes until all ten camels are satisfied. [GRIS]

because it is the midrash that makes it clear that Esav is evil—not the Torah.

[b] How did Esav become a bad guy—and is it biblical?

[c] What's wrong with locals—when the family at home worships idols, too? Remember, when Yaakov leaves—Rahel hoists the family idols!

We've all been raised—as non-Orthodox Jews—to think that midrashim are just "stories" that the Rabbis added to the biblical text. We think that they are quick and easy opinions, like the kind of thing we do in class when the teacher asks a question and we raise our hands with a pretty good instant answer. The truth is, most midrash is much more careful than that—it is carefully crafted to flow with the ecology of the whole Torah, and not just to respond to one problem in one verse. If you fit midrashim together, they tell a wonderfully expansive and different version of the Torah's story. So, let's take Esav:

He is a hunter. The first hunter was Nimrod. Nimrod ruled a land called Shinar. A little while later we learn that the Tower of Babel is built in Shinar. The midrash makes the connection—"Shinar" and "Shinar" and thereby makes him the bad guy (midrashically) of the Tower of Babel story. The midrash tells this great story that when Adam left the garden, God made Adam and Eve snakeskin suits with animal charms. This is why all the animals obey him. The snakeskin suits are passed down until they are stolen on the ark and wind up in Nimrod's hands. He uses them first to kill animals and then to enslave people into building the tower. A similar connection makes him the bad guy (midrashically) who killed Abraham's brother Haran, and tried to burn Abraham in a fire. He is the reason (midrashically) the family leaves Ur and heads to Haran (the city, not the brother). So, by being a hunter, Esav falls "prey" to some bad—I'm going to kill for my own pleasure—values, according to the way the rabbis read Torah.

To rub this in there is a midrash that Esav "hunted down" Nimrod and stole his "power suit." This, according to a midrash, is the clothing Esav kept in Rivka's tent. So via Torah word links, the midrash believes that the "snake" part of evil in the garden is passed on to Nimrod, who is the first "Hitler," and then is stolen by Esav.

Second, he sells his birthright. The rabbis figured that anyone who would give up his claim to leading God's family (forget the wealth) didn't have great values. In the midrash, they make it seem clever, not stupid. He thinks he is out-conning Yaakov. He says to himself, "Birthrights can't be sold—no deal can make him the elder child. And if he thinks it can, I'll kill him (later)—so I'll steal the porridge now, and 'cheat' him when he tries to collect."

Third, the fear with which Yaakov reacts when he returns has to come from somewhere. Yaakov believes that Esav might kill him—the rabbis credit Yaakov with knowing his brother's potential. In the end, Esav does get all of Dad's stuff, and keeps the birthright—despite the deal (Yaakov has his own hard-won fortune). The blessing says that the elder will serve the younger, but Esav never bows down, Yaakov does. The elder never does serve the younger in their lifetime, so this is a fantasy too. Esav should have just laughed off his younger brother's pranks, unless he was a bad guy, and Yaakov indeed reacts as if he is (even though he doesn't seem bad in the text). The rabbis note that after the big hugs and the family thanksgiving dinner, Yaakov and the kids split as fast as possible—something still has them freaked—and it is probably not guilt about the "nice guy" older brother.

Fourth, look at who Esav fathers—Edom. Edom is two things. First, they become Moab and Edom, they are the Bilam—Balak folks who are Yisrael's second worst enemy after Amalek. Second, for the Rabbis, Edom is a biblical clue to the coming of Rome. They make an obvious connction between Edom = Red, and the red uniforms of the Roman legions. They also find a deeper connection. Wherever they see Esav struggle with his younger brother Yaakov, they see Israel stuggling with Rome as to which culture—gladiators or Torah, the Senate or the Yeshiva—will determine the future of the world. At the moment, Rome is still in charge. Conquest values, legions, rule the world. You see it in Bosnia. You see it in America. You even see it in some of Israel's "military" moments. Jews live with the fantasy that one day, Yaakov will come out on top—with birthright and blessing. Even in our own hearts Rome/Esav wins a lot. That is the deep secret of these midrashim (their spiritual truth)—the hope that rather than Power Rangers (Romans), someday kids will collect Power Rabbis (Yaakov) who teach them how to do a whole different kind of (soulful) transformer trick.

Now back to the original question. Most people think that midrashim came after the Torah. The Talmud teaches that they came at the same time. (They were the oral Torah—the systems manual—that came along with the Torah software which God gave to Yisrael. YOU KNOW, click on the hug between Esav and Yisrael which seems friendly, and watch Esav try to pick Yaakov's pocket.) I personally believe, and have been trying to "prove" for a while, that midrashim are the tracings of the older Torah, the original campfire Torah which Yisrael remembered, before they later wrote it down and claimed that every word actually came from Sinai. Thanks for the comment, because I learned a lot writing this answer…. **[GRIS]**

[3]: I think the question of tricking Yitzhak was good to throw in there. Personally, I think Yitzhak wasn't so dumb

and probably knew he was being tricked. Why didn't he stop Yaakov from stealing the blessing? It is said that G-d told Rivka that her second son would be great. Maybe Rivka told Yitzhak this and he decided that Yaakov deserved the birthright. Maybe he favored Yaakov, because like himself, Yaakov was the second son. Who knows? The first midrash is okay. As usual, it makes Esav look bad. The second took longer for me to understand. Once I saw the words 'Esav is your firstborn,' it ocurred to me how Yaakov was not lying. I like the second midrash. **[C.J.]**

C.J. COMMENTS
Va-Yishlah continued from page 49

Yaakov the victory he needed to gain the courage to face his brother the next morning. The midrash suggests that it was an angel. If it was an angel, then the fight was "God's work." My question is, what were the angel's orders? What did God have in mind? **[GRIS]**

There is a midrash which says the order to the angel was not to wrestle—but to wake Yaakov up. But Yaakov fought and started it. **[Elliott Kleinman]**

[3]: Was it right for Simeon and Levi to destroy Shechem just because their sister was in love with a man (who just happened to not be Jewish)? Did they really destroy the city, or just vandalize it? **[C.J.]**

The tradition calls this "The Rape of Dinah." If you buy that it was rape, not seduction, not "true romance," then there is a problem here, just not as big a problem. (It would be just to kill Shekhem, but the not others in the city.) If you agree that the people were a city of rapists—all like Shekhem—then there is "a kind of understanding" to the story. Remember, Yaakov is none to pleased at the action. He complains to them, "YOU'VE MADE ME STINK." And his anger keeps showing up in the blessings Shimon and Levi get, first from Yaakov and then from Moshe. **[GRIS]**

Maybe it started as a Navy Seal mission to just get Shekhem (the ass), but wound up in a fire fight that went out of control. **[Elliott Kleinman]**

[QUESTION 4]: Why was Rahel buried on the side of the road instead of being brought to the Cave of Makhpela? What is she, gefilte fish? The midrashim don't give the best examples of why Rahel was not buried at Makhpela (in my opinion). But they are ideas so you can leave them if you want. Maybe we could find some better ones if you're not too crazy about them either. I'd better go now. **[C.J.]**

Maybe this is a hard question (if you don't buy the "future history" thing in the midrashim)—with no good or obvious answers. I keep thinking about Rahel's bitterness. Maybe it was the same voice which wanted to name her son "Son of my Misery" who said, "Leave me here—I want to be alone."

Yaakov could have made a deathbed promise to obey this wish—especially if he wasn't going to leave her name for Binyamin in place. Also, remember, Rahel has just stolen the idols and had her life poisoned by sitting on them (the midrash blames them for the early breaking of the water)—maybe she felt too guilty to be buried alongside Avraham the idol smasher. But, I like the answer the midrash gives—the one you rejected—that she chose to rest in Efrat because she had other, different, holy work to do. **[GRIS]**

C.J. COMMENTS
Miketz continued from page 61

[3]: The Torah section shows us that Yosef was a good record keeper; he also was probably a good mathematician. The midrash tries to argue otherwise, that the use of records had another purpose. Even if the records were kept for more than one reason, it was important that Yosef keep track of who got what, in the case of swindlers and thieves. **[C.J.]**

C.J. COMMENTS
Va-Yehi continued from page 69

The idea is—it is a just a cave. The burials make it holy, not the fact that it is a hole in the ground. History makes a place holy—not its natural form. I'll bet that you can find both usages though. **[GRIS]**

[3]: Also, what then does Makhpela mean? I looked up the answer: all words with the *shoresh* (root letters) XXX (*Khaf Pe Lamed)* have something to do with double, duplicate, multiple, etc. The word Makhpela itself means product (*arith*.); stencilling; (duplicating; mimeographing) machine. This came from *The Complete Hebrew English Dictionary* by Reuben Alcalay. Since I started writing the review of this before Shabbat, I had time to talk with my dad about it yesterday (Saturday), and he had some really interesting thoughts. He said that since the patriarchs and matriarchs were buried there (except for Rahel), it makes sense that the name of the cave where the "couples" were buried had a logical name which used the *shoresh* meaning double, etc. I realized that this could be a mystical reason why Rahel wasn't buried there. If the cave were for couples, she broke the pattern. Leah married Yaakov first and therefore got the burial spot. My dad also said that the *shoresh khaf pe lammed* (KPL) could sound a lot like the English word "couple." Linguistics make it possible that this was how the word "couple" came into the English language. Pretty cool, huh? **[C.J.]**

Rashi gives two choices: (1) That it was a duplex cave (two floors) and (2) that your father is right—the Makhpela is a couples club. (And don't forget that Adam and Eve were the

185

founders—according to the midrash.) There is, however, the hint of a third answer in the midrash. The Zohar tells that Avraham found the cave when he chased a calf there to serve to the three visitors. In the cave he found a secret passage back to the Garden of Eden (like the goat in the Agnon story, *the Fable of the Goat*). That is how he found Adam's and Eve's graves—and chose the spot. Therefore the cave is a tunnel between two worlds, "Our World" and "The World to Come—Gan Eden." **[GRIS]**

[PROBLEM 3]: Why did the brothers delay keeping the promise they had made to bury Yosef in Yisrael? Why didn't they bury him in the cave of the Makhpela with the rest of the family? Now when we see that Yosef made his brothers swear he would be buried in Canaan, we notice a few possiblities as to why they disobeyed him: 1) Yosef had always annoyed them and they wanted the last laugh, 2) Yosef was of high rank in Egypt and it was demanded against the brothers' will that he be buried there. 3) the brothers were too lazy to schlep another dead guy back to Canaan, or 4) as I hope you might have guessed, since Yosef married a non-Jew (foreigner if you'd rather, as my mom said), whereas his ancestors had married family making them automatically Jewish (or at least acceptable), he was denied a spot in the cave, and finally, 5) maybe there wasn't any room left for him. **[C.J.]**

The midrash likes both of your questions. Let's take the second one first. (a) Yosef asked to be buried in Shekhem because he said he didn't fit into the couples club—his wife was not a matriarch. (b) This was the place where the brothers had originally kidnapped him, and bringing him there closed the circle. (c) Yaakov bought this site just for his burial—that way the Jews owned two plots in the Land of Yisrael (Gen. 33.19). Hevron, where everyone else is buried, is in the tribe of Judah. Shekhem, where Yosef is buried, is in his son's tribe's space—Manashe. Later, when Yisrael and Judah split, everyone else will be in Judah, and his son's country (Efraim and Manashe) Yisrael will have their patriarch, too. To your first question, the Talmud, *Sotah* 13 says, "The Egyptians wanted to keep Yosef's magic protection so they stole the body, loaded the coffin with lead, and sank it into the bottom of the Nile. Only Moshe had the "magic" powers to raise it so that the promise could be kept. **[GRIS]**

[4]: Before I go on to review the excerpt from the Torah, I really need to ask you a question, Joel. How different is the Everett Fox translation from the translations in the original book? When school kids see these blessings their childish reactions come alive. How do you think a kid of any age would react when they saw "YISSACHAR- A BONY ASS-..."? **[C.J.]**

Probably with same laugh that God had when those words were written into the Torah. God knew about 12-year-olds, too. The original translation in *T-Toons* was written fast (just about as fast as I could type it). Everett Fox was my inspiration, back when he was my friend and his translation was all but unpublished. He has spent more than 20 years perfecting his rendition of the Biblical text—and it reveals much about the Torah's meaning. **[GRIS]**

[5]: Now: With Reuven, the best I can make out from the translation is that he basically was trying to take over as leader for his father and was doing a bad job. Maybe a better translation would say "MOUNTING MY THRONE."

Shimon and Levi who raided a city deserve their punishment, but doesn't Gad's seem like a more just punishment?

Yehuda has a good blessing because of the good transition he made. Zevulun, Yissachar, and Dan are simply predictions of the future. I guess this goes for Gad too. Asher might become a farmer. I don't understand Naftali's blessing.

Yosef was his father's favorite and therefore got the best blessing. Binyamin's blessing makes little sense to me aside from the interpretation that he'll probably become a warrior.

Yaakov is telling his sons what will happen to them, and telling them that they should prepare for the future. **[C.J.]**

For an R-rated Reuben story see Genesis 35.33. This will explain "MOUNTING MY THRONE/BED." For a clue to Binyamin, remember that Saul, the first King of Yisrael, came from the tribe of Binyamin. Saul was a great warrior—just not as good as David (from Judah). Later, when Efraim and Manashe (the full siblings) split and become Yisrael, he stays with his half-brother tribe Judah. These blessings play out in the history of the tribes once they are in Eretz Yisrael. **[GRIS]**

[6]: I know I haven't written for a few days, I'll try to do more. I must remind both myself and you that I have thank-you notes to write. **[C.J.]**

C.J. COMMENTS
Shemot continued from page 75

[4]: Poor slaves of Yisrael, G-d tells Moshe he will harden Pharaoh's heart; meanwhile, they are still hardening bricks (sigh). [C.J.] A real punishment. [GRIS]

[5]: It was a good thing that Moshe spent his time as a shepherd. Three things ultimately came out of it: (1) Moshe is left alone for a while and once God sends him back to Egypt people might not recognize him. (2) Moshe gets to relax and not worry so much about the things ahead, he'll need his worrying ability later. (3) God has time to observe Moshe and see if he is "worthy." The first midrash (Moshe takes care of lost lambs) shows two things. The first has to do with being honest. The other shows that Moshe is willing to listen to each individual and try to do what's best for everybody. The second midrash (David and Moshe work with sheep) seems a little strange to me. Of course since God is God, we can expect God to know what happens in the future. The question is how and why would God test Moshe and David at the same time? Or, more specifically, why David first? I don't particularly like this midrash. It is kind of confusing time-wise and just isn't that great in general. [C.J.]

You don't get it! God already knows that David and Moshe will be good leaders. When the Dodgers hired Jackie Robinson they knew he was a great ballplayer. They still sent him to spring training and to training camp. For God, shepherding is a leadership training program. If you learn to lead sheep the right way, then you will also be good at leading people. Moshe and David (at different points in history) and Aharon, Yosef, Yitzhak, and Yaakov—all of whom have their own shepherding midrashim (remember Lot and the muzzles)—learn how to lead from working with sheep. [GRIS]

C.J. COMMENTS
Va-Era continued from page 81

Moshe: Aharon, quick, do that yawn-arm-stretch-thing.

Aharon: Wha… okay.

Moshe: Check it out, kingy-boy, this is what my G-d sends upon you because you won't let us be free of you.

Pharaoh: My gods!

Moshe: Eeeeh, wrong! MY G-d, and unless you let us go, all I can say is…

Frog: Riiiiiibit!

Pharaoh: No! Not more animal sounds! You can go! You can go!

Frog: Bye now!

Pharaoh: Ha, ha! Now that the frogs are gone I can keep my slaves. Ahahahahahaha!

Aharon: Why you….. (*Bangs staff on the ground. Lice pop up from the ground and into Pharaoh's hair.*)

Pharaoh: Scratch, scratch.

Moshe: Lucky for you these animals don't make sounds, Pharaoh. And how unfortunate that I happen to be the last person in Egypt with a bottle of lice shampoo.

Pharaoh: Grrrr.

Moshe: Aharon, what's next on our list?

Aharon: Umm…blood… frogs… lice…here we go! Insects.

Moshe: You hear that, Pharaoh?

Pharaoh: Ahh… No itchy feeling. What was that? (*Insects swarm around and run on Pharaoh.*) Eeuuuu!

Moshe: Oh, look. I also happen to be the last person left in Egypt with a can of insect repellent.

Pharaoh: Oooooh…three days in the wilderness for a spray!

Moshe: What was that?

Pharaoh: You heard me, come on! (*Insects are whisked off Pharaoh.*)

Pharaoh: (*Leaning on a cow.*) Now, I can easily say, no way!

Moshe: Oh, well.

Cow: Mooo! (*Topples over.*)

Pharaoh: You ruined my new clothes. You idiots!

Moshe: I wouldn't be too worried about the way you look now, Pharaoh, it can only get worse. You know the drill Aharon.

Aharon: Right! (Moshe and Aharon scoop up handfuls of soot and throw it in the air.)

Pharaoh: My face may break out, but my heart remains hard!

Moshe: Your face is not the only thing that will break in the destruction. You have been warned, Pharaoh, hail will sweep the land.

(*Moshe raises his staff to the sky.*)

Pharaoh: My heart is harder than your rocks…begone!

As for my answer to the question: Moshe warned of the plagues to give himself practice for later. It was his own version of "voice lessons." [C.J.]

[2]: So why couldn't God show might in different ways? Why so much killing? [Rabbi Kerry Olitzky]

Kerry is anticipating the next couple of *parshiot* with his question, but here is a good place to ask it. God is very manipulative in the Exodus. God makes plagues so that the Egyptians will let the Families-of-Yisrael go, then hardens Pharaoh's heart so that he can't change his mind. I've always seen one of those Warner Brother cartoon images here where someone steps on someone's big feet and then punches them. They bounce to the ground and then come back up (like one of those punching bags when you were a kid). That is what God seems to be doing to the Egyptians, punching them, stepping on Pharaoh's heart, then hitting them each time they come up.

The tradition has a lot of explanations of why: (1) *Midah k'neged Midah*—a rabbinic version of making the punishment fit the crime: Pharaoh drowned all the Jewish boys in the Nile and was then drowned in the Reed Sea. (2) The second idea is that this was a "Public Service Announcement." God used the events of the Exodus to show that there was only one real God—and so the rest of the nations learned by example. As modern (liberal) post-Vietnam kids, revenge is bothersome and power isn't that impressive. Understanding why that much Egyptian suffering was necessary is still hard. We still ask, like the famous midrash we'll see later on "How can you sing when My children are drowning?" I'm open to good whys. **[GRIS]**

[3]: The second midrash for this *parasha* is very meaningful. It shows that he didn't want to ruin part of what saved himself. He felt a certain loyalty to the Nile, it is suggested by this midrash that perhaps he had such a loyalty that he wondered which he owed more, the Nile, or his people?

And now—Presenting all of our favorite pastimes, homework and thank-you-notes! **[C.J.]**

C.J. COMMENTS
Bo continued from page 85

[3]: The next two midrashim are decent, but they aren't that great. The first hardly seems to go with the story of Bo. The second one seems to say that Moshe was like God's son, not a very good picture. I'm also wondering if it is written anywhere that "God informed Moshe: "For 2,448 years I have proclaimed every new month in heaven,..." by this time, would the existence of the Earth be accurate, at least to the Jews? **[C.J.]**

C.J., you review midrashim the way that Siskel and Ebert review films. You seem to assume that most are "not good" and a few are blockbusters. Midrash, like and unlike

movies, are capsules of truth. Rather than judging them "good or bad" you could also be asking "what truth do they contain?" But you are right that some sing to each of us more than others. I just find your harsh language of evaluation sort of funny.

You are misreading the "you" in the second midrash. The "you" is for Yisrael, not Moshe. Here is the idea. Jewish time takes Jews. We begin Shabbat by lighting candles—sundown does not begin Shabbat. We end Shabbat by making havdalah, three stars do not end Shabbat. Two witnesses used to have to see the new moon before the month could begin. The shofar ends Yom Kippur, etc. To make time holy—we have to notice and separate it out in our lives with a ritual. That is the notion that, from now on, Jews control the calendar and make Jewish holidays happen in their hearts, in their souls, and in their lives. **[GRIS]**

[4]: My family and our guests had been discussing the use of "YHWH" in the new book over Shabbat/Shavuot. Here were some of our opinions: [1] One view was that using the letters YHWH to represent God sounded too much like Jehovah, because that was what the transliteration would be of *Yud Hey Vav Hey* and all of the appropriate vowels; and Jehovah is used in a different religion. This view also (I think) thought that using YHWH was somewhat disrespectful. The other views were basically the same: YHWH is perfectly respectful. A question was, why wasn't God, ha-Shem, or Adonai used instead? The answer was guessed that you wanted some sort of gender neutrality. I just wanted to let you know that your use of YHWH has become an issue of debate. **[C.J.]**

This is the easiest answer—'cause Everett Fox uses it in his translation, we are using his translation, and we are trying to be consistent. Everett says: "This is pretty standard scholarly practice, but does not indicate how the name should be pronounced. I would recommend the use of the traditional "the Lord" in reading aloud, but others may wish to follow their own custom..." **[GRIS]**

YHWH. What does it mean?!? I've been thinkin', and it might be (no offense to anyone reading this, I'm not sure if it's offensive at all) Yahovah (or Jehovah (eg. Jehovah's Witness)). I'm sorry again if I've offended anyone. Is there anyone else who has an idea? **[Ben Kort]**

YHWH is an approximation of God's name (Like Fred or Harriet). In Exodus 3:14 God sort of explains the Name by saying: "EHYEH ASHER EHYEH/I will be there howsoever I will be there" (Fox), "I am that I am" (SJV), etc. In other words, YHWH says that God is the ultimate "is"—the eternal "to be" (all built out of the root HVH). The issue on what we write and how we pronounce "G-d," "ha-Shem," etc. all has to do with the commandment "You shall not take up the name of YHWH your God for emptiness." Protecting the name of God (a la Rumplestiltskin) becomes a big deal in Jewish tradition—because misuse of the name is at least disrespect and maybe an abuse of power. [GRIS]

I realize that some use YHWH to make The Name correct in terms of transliteration and such. I realize that some use G-d without the "o" because they are trying to respect G-d's Name. I realize that some write God, with an "o," because this is the spelling of the English word for Adonai. All of these different versions of the same thing lead me to believe that G-d is a Being...not a Word. If we take things like "You shall not use the Lord's Name in vain" to mean just as it says; we see that we only have to respect G-d. To me, it's not the literal Name we worry about, it's the Being. The only reason we concentrate on the Name is because that is the only physical thing we have of G-d's (aside from the Commandments and such). The only things we're not supposed to do are say "G-d is bad," and other stuff. Some people take this really literally and focus on the Name. So you ask why and how do I write G-d? I write how I want, or I'll follow anybody else's lead to make them feel comfortable. This is all a matter of opinion. [C.J.]

I write G-d not because I don't believe in Him, but because I believe in Him so strongly that I fear, G-d forbid, that His name should be used in vain or erased; it is by no means a statement of my belief in Him. That's my two cents...
[Rena Bunder]

That's a hard one. But it depends where you're writing it. Say you're writing on a blackboard in Hebrew school, and you write God. Sooner or later your teacher will make you erase the word. Mrs. Dank says you should never write God, but I don't really know her reasons. Some people believe God's name in English is too holy to write "God." So I would say it's a hard call. But by a hair, I would say that God is okay to write. In other religions it's okay to write God. So for me, it's God, not G-d. [Sam Salkin]

I don't think that God is in the o, because I don't think anything as vast and important as God could possibly be kept in the o. My friend here reading the letter says God is in the o, but not contained by it, because he thinks God is everywhere. I don't believe in God because I'm lonely, I just believe that God is always—has been here and will be here. I don't know if it's just because I was taught that, but because I can... "feel" His presence. [Ben Kort]

I leave the "o" out of G-d (and write Ad"o"shem and stuff) because I figure there may be people reading it for whom the other ways would be offensive. I probably won't agree with them, but I want to engage them in a dialogue of respect. So I try not to say things that will unnecessarily offend them. Just like I don't put profanity on e-mail to lists. Just like I don't want them to use words that offend me— like "religious" or "observant" or "traditional" when they're talking about their brand of Judaism in implicit contradistinction to mine. [David Parker]

C.J. COMMENTS
Beshallah continued from page 89

Sea. Wouldn't one think that the Pharaoh of Egypt was too dignified to chase them? If I were Pharaoh I wouldn't go to the trouble of chasing them myself, I'd send my generals and other officers. Maybe he wanted things done right, and realized he was the only person who could do things his way. How unfortunate that he realized too late that chasing after them was a mistake. [C.J.]

I am not going to respond to your cheap political shot. But there is a great point to be made here. The rabbis compare Pharaoh to Avraham. On the day of the Akedah, he saddles his own ass (12-year-olds snicker here, please) and chopped his own wood. Likewise, Pharaoh rigged his own chariot. (See Genesis 14.6 in a translation other than Fox.) The idea is that, like the Blues Brothers, both are obsessed with "being on a mission from God." Remember, Pharaoh's heart is still hardened. He is under mind control. And, his actions manifest his craziness. We, unfortunately, can point to a number of religious sickos who take God's actions into their own hands. The problem is, we can also point to a number of heroes who do the same thing. That is why religion can be both powerful and dangerous. That is why passion is good—and passion is dangerous. [GRIS]

[3]: What we're never told is how the next Egyptian Pharaoh is chosen. Pharaoh's firstborn is killed, and he dies in the Red Sea, so who is next? [C.J.]

Here is the easy answer. If the firstborn dies, the second born takes over. It would be a great midrashic question to try to figure out if we've seen the new Pharaoh previously in the Torah. [GRIS]

[4]: People often wonder what was wrong with manna that the Yisraelites hated it so much. Doesn't it say somewhere that manna would taste like whatever one wanted it to? I guess the problem is one of two things. (1) The Children were stubborn and complained a lot. (2) Notice that it says that manna *falls from the sky daily.* Am I correct in saying that people only got a certain amount? If this is the case, if the manna falls when the people aren't able to get it, it hits the ground and gets squashed. That was their only manna and they don't want it because it's bad now. It's a good thing that they can catch quail easily. [C.J.]

Have I got good manna stuff. Let's start with the Torah facts. (1) Enter manna (Exodus 13.11 ff) YHWH SPOKE TO MOSHE, SAYING: I HAVE HEARKENED TO THE GRUMBLINGS OF THE CHILDREN OF YISRAEL—AND AT DAYBREAK THERE WAS A LAYER OF DEW AROUND THE CAMP; AND WHEN THE LAYER OF DEW WENT UP, HERE, UPON THE SURFACE OF THE WILDERNESS WAS SOMETHING FINE, SCALY, FINE AS HOARFROST. WHEN THE CHILDREN OF YISRAEL SAW IT THEY SAID EACH-MAN TO HIS BROTHER; MAH HU/WHAT IS IT? MOSHE SAID TO THEM: IT IS THE

BREAD THAT YHWH HAS GIVEN YOU FOR EATING. The Torah goes on to tell us that (1) it was white, like coriander seed and that it tasted like a honey wafer, and (2) except for Shabbat, it would spoil if you tried to store it overnight.

The idea that manna adjusted to an individuals palette—and tasted like any fantasy food you wanted—is midrash. The midrashim also have fun with the meat rebellion. First they point out that the Yisraelites had herds and flocks. If they wanted meat, they were driving meat. So—clearly the rebellion was about more than meat. I know two great, and different answers. (1) That "flesh" was a hint that what they really wanted was "skin." They were missing the nightlife and the pleasures of Egypt—and meat was only the example. It was "Take us back to the sin capital—to the flesh-pots." (2) Manna was angel food. It was perfect nutrition—no waste—no byproducts—no excrement. You ate manna and never had do to number 2. This freaked some Yisraelites out. They said, "I am no angel, I need my excrement." The deep psychological point was, offer people a life without the need to get into deep do-do, and some people can't take it. Some people need to make messes to survive. **[GRIS]**

[5]: I know who Yehoshua is: the future leader of the Yisraelites. Amalek was the evil tribe which attacked those who were unable to fight back. Aharon was obviously Moshe's brother; but who was <u>H</u>ur? **[C.J.]**

<u>H</u>ur was the father of Uri who was the father of Betzalel. He came from the tribe of Judah. If you play the midrashic game well, you learn that Kalev (Caleb) and his second wife (Miriam, Moshe's sister) were <u>H</u>ur's parents. He was one of Moshe's helpers. His son was ben <u>H</u>ur, but not the famous Ben Hur. But the big midrash is that he lost his cool at the Golden Calf and got killed by the mob trying to stop it. **[GRIS]**

[6]: When you say "*As long as Moshe can keep his arms in the air…B'nai Yisrael wins the battle…*" Is that just an expression, or did Moshe literally have to hold up his arms? If he did, that must have been pretty painful. I hope that battle was short, for Moshe's sake. **[C.J.]**

Yes, it is usually taken literally. But here are two great comments. The <u>H</u>ofetz <u>H</u>ayyim noticed that the Torah actually says, "WHEN MOSHE HOLDS UP HIS HANDS…" It doesn't say, "WHEN MOSHE HELD UP HIS HANDS." In every generation, we still need Moshe to hold up his hands to defeat evil. But here is the big deal (comment two). Aharon, the peacemaker holds up one hand—<u>H</u>ur, the passionate fighter holds up the other. To lead Yisrael, to succeed, you always need an Aharon holding one hand and a <u>H</u>ur holding the other. **[GRIS]**

[7]: As far as the Song of the Sea being a bad thing, it is bad. It is not right to celebrate someone else's death. It was okay in some ways, though, because B'nai Yisrael celebrated God's triumph. These two midrashim are great. The second continues what the first started. It makes sense that the angels couldn't sing the Song of the Sea because they weren't the ones who experienced the miracle, as the second midrash states. That's all for this *parasha,* stay tuned next week for the continuation of the story of B'nai Yisrael. **[C.J.]**

He put it in his back yard and it grew like a tree. Whenever someone wanted to marry his daughter, he would tell them (as Merlin did) that if you can pull the staff out of the ground, you can marry her. Every time someone tried, the staff became a snake and ate them. Finally Moshe does the deed. Why did Yitro let a non-pagan marry his daughter? The midrashic answer is that they made a deal that half the children would be pagans and half Jews. This is why we have the "bridegroom of blood" scene we talked about when Tzipora had to circumcise Gershom who was the "pagan" son. (*Pirke de Rabbi Eliezer* 40)

Most midrashim have Yitro convert at Exodus 18.9 where the Torah says: "AND YITRO WAS JUBILANT BECAUSE OF ALL THE GOOD THAT YHWH HAD DONE FOR ISRAEL, THAT HE HAD RESCUED HIM FROM THE LAND OF EGYPT." Others say that he is still trying to get to manipulate God's power through his closeness to Israel. (*Sanhedrin* 94a). He fades off into history two ways: One version says that he abandoned Midian and went on as a preacher of monotheism to the masses of non-Jews, the other that he founded the Kenites, idolaters who continue to give trouble to Yisrael (like Amalek). Confusing! **[GRIS]**

[2]: The use of new laws was also important. The use of no idols makes sense. Why would God want people to worship others after all that God had done? What I don't understand is why stones cut with metal tools can't be used in an altar. Maybe it would have made more sense had I lived back then. **[C.J.]**

Let's look at the verse in question (Exodus 20:22): BUT IF A SLAUGHTER-SITE OF STONES YOU MAKE FOR ME, YOU ARE NOT TO BUILD IT SMOOTH-HEWN, FOR IF YOU HOLD-HIGH YOUR IRON-TOOL (*HAR-B-KHA*) OVER IT, YOU HAVE PROFANED IT. Rashi says, "<u>H</u>AR-B-KHA is a sword. The altar was designed to extend people's lives by allowing them to repent. A sword is designed to shorten a person's life. One force cancels out the other when they are brought together." Does that help—or do we still need to use the "way-back machine?" **[GRIS]**

[3]: I can't be sure why exactly Mount Sinai was chosen over other mountains. Here is my guess though: Maybe Mount Sinai is the same mountain where Noah landed after the flood. The point is not because it is the same mountain physically, but the same mountain spiritually. This was the mountain God saved Noah on and also the one He saved B'nai Yisrael on. God didn't really save the people until He gave them the Ten Commandments. This would lead to their rescue from life's evils and problems. This place would also, therefore, mark the location of two covenants. This shows trust between two sides. Now I'll see what the midrash says. **[C.J.]**

A quick one. Here is a case of your being wrong—but doing so brilliantly. You make a wonderful midrash. It even has the rhythm and insight of classical midrash. Your mistake, not looking in the Torah. Mount Ararat is given as the ark's landing point (Gen 7.4) It is more or less a known location in Turkey. Wrong geography which we get from a Jeremiah quote. But, really good thinking and a nice lesson! **[GRIS]**

[4]: The midrashim focus on a similar, but different topic from the one I focus on. They really say why the other mountains were not chosen. I said why I thought Mount Sinai was chosen. The difference being process of elimination or right-out choosing. **[C.J.]**

Until next week, **[C.J.]**

and both are probably related to the Babylonian full moon holiday *shab/pattu.* **[GRIS]**

[5]: We are given all of these different laws and then warned not to follow pagan customs. A pagan in this usage of the word is someone who is not Jewish. It makes sense that G-d instructs us not to become pagans in this place, because after all G-d has done for us, giving us these laws, everything is in vain if a Jew converts. Luckily, everybody accepts the laws, and Moshe goes back up for round two of the Ten Commandments. **[C.J.]**

Pagan does not equal non-Jew. There are non-Jews who are not considered pagans. Noah was one. Yitro is another. The deal is basically this. God gave Noah seven laws: (1) Have fair courts. (2) No swearing with God's name. (3) No idols. (4) No sexual misconduct. (5) No murder. (6) No stealing. (7) No cutting legs off living animals and eating them (cruelty to animals). Non-Jews who conform to these are considered to be "righteous gentiles." They get a place in the world to come. A pagan is someone who does any of those seven things (and thus breaks the rules). Generally, Jews think of pagans as people who worship more than one god, and thereby reject the Torah's central truth. **[GRIS]**

[6]: Got to go. I hope it's dinner time. **[C.J.]**

C.J. COMMENTS
Mishpatim continued from page 101

That isn't exactly true. As the Talmud reads the text (and you look more carefully) there are a lot of restitution rules (you gotta pay for what you broke, stole, or lost) and some crimes with lashes. You do know that "AN EYE FOR AN EYE" always means the *price of an eye* for an eye. We never actually harm someone else's body to get even. That, too, is Jewish law. **[GRIS]**

[4]: Notice that when referring to laws, we see rules of the "sabbatical year." Sometimes you might hear about people who take a year off from their job: this is their sabbatical year. Why am I mentioning seemingly meaningless information? Notice the similarity between the words "sabbatical" and "Sabbath." Where does Sabbath come from? Shabbat! Shabbat refers to the day of rest G-d took on the seventh day and the day we rest each week. Coincidentally, the Sabbath takes place every seven days whereas the sabbatical year takes place every seven years. **[C.J.]**

The introduction of Shabbat is in the second chapter of Genesis, the story of creation. Genesis 2.2 says: "GOD HAD FINISHED, ON THE SEVENTH DAY, HIS WORK THAT HE HAD MADE AND THEN (VA-YISHBOT) HE CEASED FROM ALL HIS WORK, THAT BY CREATING, GOD HAD MADE." Shabbat comes from the root ShVT "to rest" or "to cease." And Sabbatical does come from Sabbath—

C.J. COMMENTS
Terumah continued from page 105

long did the candles burn? Were they supposed to burn eternally like the *Ner Tamid* (Eternal Light)? I think that it's kind of sad that we don't use the original type of Menorah any more. It's just a symbol. **[C.J.]**

Actually, we do use the menorah. Almost every single synagogue has a menorah in its sanctuary. In one way, this is a *zekher*, a remembrance of the original menorah in the *mishkan*. But like the original, ours still has seven lights for the seven days of creation. Ours still looks like a tree of life and a burning bush. All of the stories and lessons learned from the original (and there are deep lessons in the detailed descriptions of the design) are still experienced when we go to shul. In that sense the menorah is far more than memory. **[GRIS]**

[3]: The first midrash is a hopeful one. God says that the Jews possess the materials and that each Jew could provide everything for the *mishkan*. I don't take this midrash literally. To me, it means that each person has the will to do good (in this case: building the *mishkan*). It also shows that God has hopes and expectations for each and every one of us. **[C.J.]**

C.J. COMMENTS
Terumah continued from page 191

You are on the right track here. But it goes deeper. I could give you a million verses which are used to prove this—but the big idea is that the *mishkan*, which is the place where God is our neighbor, is a model of the universe. Yisrael creates the *mishkan* with the same words and clauses that God creates the cosmos. So, the deal is, in ourselves, we have the opportunity to build a meeting place with God, and that meeting place is a replication of the whole creation. You have a whole universe in you. It is there, ready for you to do your own creative work. **[GRIS]**

[4]: The second one gives the reason for so many materials that each material helps atone for a sin. I think that it could go far enough to say that each material represents a sin of each of the twelve sons of Yisrael plus either Dinah or Yisrael himself. **[C.J.]**

I like your commentary a lot. Let me add to it. In Midrash *Tanhuma* there is a passage which lists 13 blessings (acts of *hesed*) which God did in exchange for the Tabernacle gifts. It is a complicated passage (built on word-plays) but it boils down to saying everything the Families-of-Israel did in building the *mishkan* came back as a gift to themselves—through the effort and then through God's appreciation. **[GRIS**

C.J. COMMENTS
Tetzaveh continued from page 109

midrash. It explains that the Jews are pure like olive oil, and rise above others like oil and water. This midrash does brag and disrespect others in a way, but it builds our self-esteem. **[C.J.]**

I'm sorry that the first midrash didn't sing to you. I like it. Here is why. Too many Jews I know think that the rabbi owns the bima. It is his pulpit. That is a lesson we have learned from Christianity. It is one of those things that happened when rabbis stopped being primarily educators and became clergy. Jews gave up taking responsibility for their own Jewishness. I don't really need to know how to *daven* if I can read responsively. I don't have to know how to study Torah if I can listen to a sermon. This midrash warned that people could make the same mistake with the *Kohanim*. They could have believed that they did all the holy work to connect the Jewish people to God—and individual Jews had no responsibility. This midrash says holiness is based on olive oil. It is the tree every Jew has in their back yard. The oil, the

foundation of the holy connection belongs to and comes from every Jew, not just people on the bima. **[GRIS]**

And then there was the joke about Popeye and Olive Oyl… **[C.J.]**

C.J. COMMENTS
Ki Tissa continued from page 113

Wouldn't one think he'd have a little more sense than that? He's been working hard for these mitzvot and now he destroys them? Maybe he knew that after something like this had happened he would need new rules anyway. **[C.J.]**

Here we have one of my own mistakes coming back to haunt me. In the Cecil B. DeMille film *The Ten Commandments,* Moshe hurls the tablets at the calf and the two explode with the contact. My Sunday school teachers saw that film and told me the story that way. That's the version I wrote in the original *Torah Toons,* because that's the way I remembered the text. Later in life I know the mistake I made. (One you didn't pick up.) The actual text (the way Fox translates it) is "MOSHE'S ANGER FLARED UP, HE THREW THE TABLETS FROM HIS HAND AND SMASHED THEM BENEATH THE MOUNTAIN. HE TOOK THE CALF THAT THEY HAD MADE, AND BURNED IT WITH FIRE, GROUND IT UP UNTIL IT WAS THIN-POWDER, STREWED IT ON THE SURFACE OF THE WATER AND MADE THE CHILDREN OF ISRAEL DRINK IT. (Exodus 32.19-20) In one midrashic version, Moshe doesn't even intentionally smash the Tablets, but rather lets them fall. The explanation: The letters which God carved personally into the tablets made the stones light, but when they saw the sin, they fled, and the stones became too heavy to carry. (*Shemot Rabbah,* 46.1) Cecil B. DeMille has made his own midrashic contributions to the Jewish tradition which will probably last forever. Green smog to represent the angel of death is another one of his innovations. **[GRIS]**

[4]: Does everybody have to drink the gold/water? Weren't there any people who didn't party with the calf? Or were they all killed like Hur (in the midrash)? **[C.J.]**

The deal is actually more complicated. The midrash blames the *eruv rav,* the mixed multitude (the non-Jews who went with the Families-of-Yisrael) for the whole thing. They lead the idolatry. Here is the expanded version of the scene. Idolatry is like adultery. It is cheating on the One with whom you have an exclusive relationship. There is a strange ceremony later in the Torah called *Sotah.* The deal is, if they think a woman committed adultery (and it is sexist in my opinion that it is only women) they give her this drink. If she is innocent—she lives. If not—her belly swells. Moshe makes a *sotah* mix for all of Yisrael. Every single person had to drink. The next morning all of the sinners—those who actually believed in and worshipped the calf—had swelling stomachs. They were taken to the *Bet Din* and later executed if they had been warned by at least two witnesses and were then observed breaking the commandment. Three thousand were killed. Later God sent a plague that killed all those who had sinned, but for whom the *Bet Din* had too little evidence. The survivors repented. The answer to your question is, yes, all of the people had to drink, 'cause it was a way of proving they were innocent. But, the much harder question in our age is—why is idolatry—incorrect belief—a capital offense? It is not very tolerant! [**GRIS**]

[**5**]: I have two answers to the question of why God only gave Moshe ten commandments. The first is that maybe they were only ten of the many commandments, but some of these commandments were pretty long. Remember, this is Moshe with the speech impediment who has to learn this. Maybe he feels that he can only relay so much, that he'll have to memorize more later. The other answer is that Moshe might be ready, but B'nai Yisrael are not. First, he needs to give them the basics; then they can get into the more specific laws. The midrash teaches two important lessons. The first is that things should be taken slowly, one step at a time. The second is that there is always more to learn. [**C.J.**]

C.J. COMMENTS
Va-Yakhel continued from page 117

appearance in order to work on their spiritual health was a big deal. [**GRIS**]

[**3**]: It is obvious that since this is to be God's dwelling place, it should be described in detail. But the major question is not why the *mishkan* gets so much attention, but why other events and places get less. I'd say that the Torah often leaves out what would seem to be key details for three reasons. The first reason is that the Torah would eventually become (how do I say this without becoming rude?) too long. There are even rules regarding the rolling of the Torah which have to do with the patience of the congregation. The second is because the purpose is to teach and to educate. By telling you everything, the Torah won't educate you. It will become a dull, droll, meaningless double scroll. By letting your imagination have some freedom, the Torah allows you to make some decisions for yourself. The purpose of this is to help you make decisions later on in life as well. My last reason is that the Torah needs to be somewhat mystical. To make you at least partially believe what is going on, some of the key details are left out. Will a true magician show you

all of the steps to his magic trick? Of course not! The same principle is used in the writing of the Torah. [**C.J.**]

Actually, there is a slightly different solution in the Rabbinic tradition. Remember, God taught two Torahs on Mt. Sinai. One was written, one was oral. Basically, the oral is hidden in the written. Think of it like being a CD-ROM game where, when you click on the right icon, new layers open up. So that the final Torah, the Torah we get to learn, is much, much larger than then actual words which are on the page. *Torah Toons* and this kind of midrash are part of the magic, regrowing the much larger story hidden in the visible (written) Torah. [**GRIS**]

[**4**]: I definitely agree with the midrash you use for this *parashah*, Joel. I feel that by learning about the past we can figure out what to do for the present and the future. That doesn't mean that we should dwell in the past, but that we need to know about it. Since we don't use sacrifices any more, we should make up for it. That is why the study of discontinued practices and ritual objects is important. The study helps us to atone and to learn to do so. Tomorrow is the last full day of school, then less than half a day Thursday! [**C.J.**]

C.J. COMMENTS
Pekudei continued from page 123

live. The deeper truth is that the "cloud" is the symbol of the *Shekhinah* which is the part of God which gets up close and personal, the neighborly part of God. Yisrael is protected by the wings and shadow of the *Shekhinah*—both of which are cloud images. Fire is the Torah symbol. When God teaches Torah, there is fire. Put the two together, and God protects like a parent (with a cloud) and teaches with fire (like a superstar ruler). It is an *Avinu Malkeinu* thing. [**GRIS**]

[**3**]: The midrash shows that the more we do good deeds, the closer we will be to God, and the closer God will WANT to be to us. At the time of Moshe, God felt close to the people. I don't agree with the midrash in this sense. At first, Moshe doubted his ability and did not want to lead the Jewish people. The people themselves became real kvetches once in the wilderness. If anything, God came among the people because of pity. [**C.J.**]

I disagree. I think God saw potential. I think pity was the last thing on God's mind. God is a great talent scout—after all, God chose you. [**GRIS**]

[**4**]: As for the "design your own video game" idea, I remember trying to do this and having a real hard time. It took me a while. Keep it or leave it—it's your call. Goodnight! (Oops, sorry, did I wake you?)! [**C.J.**]

people to move from the kind of worship they already knew to acquire a true knowledge of God. Sacrifices are not the real goal, because prayer and similar kinds of worship bring us closer to God's true intent. ...That was the message of the prophets." Maimonides is saying that sacrifice was a "primitive" Jewish form and the prayer service which evolved from it was a "higher" form. He roots himself in prophets like Amos who said, "I HATE, I DESPISE YOUR FEASTS, AND I TAKE NO DELIGHT IN YOUR SOLEMN ASSEMBLIES. EVEN THOUGH YOU OFFER ME BURNT-OFFERINGS, AND MEAL OFFERINGS—I WILL NOT ACCEPT THEM. NOR WILL I CONSIDER THE PEACE-OFFERINGS OF YOUR FAT BEASTS. TAKE AWAY FROM ME THE NOISE OF YOUR SINGING AND DO NOT LET ME HEAR THE MELODY OF YOUR PSALMS. INSTEAD, LET JUSTICE WELL UP AS WATERS AND RIGHTEOUSNESS LIKE A MIGHTY STREAM." Amos is saying sacrifices can't atone for you—if your actions are corrupt. Rambam says, "It is true knowledge of God that teaches you how to get close." For Rambam, knowing God is always the goal—because once you do, it is easy to do what God wants. Remember, the sacrifices in Hebrew are called *korbanot*. The root of "sacrifices" is *KRV* which means "close." For us, somehow in the blood and guts of Leviticus we need to discover ways to get close to God. That is an interesting challenge. **[GRIS]**

[2]: *Olah* is a really interesting title for this sacrifice. First, note the fact that this is a freewill offering. Also, remember that by making sacrifices, the Jews felt and became closer to God. The root which *Olah* comes from, *ayin, lamed, hey*, means to ascend. Making an offering, especially if it is of one's own free will, helps them ascend in holiness. **[C.J.]**

For the record, here is the way an Olah worked. (1) **Hava'ah/Bringing:** The owner of the sacrifice personally brings the animal to the courtyard and tells the Bet Din, "I want to offer this *korban*." (2) **S'miḥah/Placing Hands:** The owner puts his hands on the head of the animal. (3) **Vidui/Confession:** The owner confesses his sins and states that he has made *t'shuvah*. (4) **Shehitah/Slaughtering:** The animal is killed. (5) **Kabalat ha-Dam/The Collecting of the Blood:** The blood is collected in a special pan. (6) **Halkhah/Walking:** The blood is carried to the altar. **Zerika/Sprinkling:** The blood is sprinkled on the altar. (7) **Shefikhat Sherayim/Pouring the Leftover:** The extra blood is spilled into a special drain. (8) **Hafshait ve'Nitu'akh/Skinning and piecing.** Just like it says. (9) **Hadakhah/Rinsing:** The meat is rinsed. (10) **Meliḥah ve'Hatarah/Salting and Burning:** The meat is salted, the sciatic nerve is cut out, and then the parts which are to be cooked are cooked and the parts which are to be totally burned so that they go "up" to God are burnt "up." An *olah*

is to be burnt-"up" entirely—that is why it is called an "*olah*" a "going-up." (Maimonides, *The Doing of the Sacrifices*)

If you look carefully at these 10 steps, they divide into two categories. Many of the steps are the same as the preparation of any kosher meat. Four of the steps are specifically connected to *t'shuvah*. The **S'miḥah/Placing Hands** focuses on the sins of action—done with the hand. The **Vidui/Confession** focuses on speech sins. **Zerika/Sprinkling** focuses on the spilling of blood. **Hakravat ha'Aimurim/The burning of the guts** (which are the parts burned up when the rest is eaten during the *Shlamim*) focuses on sins which come through thought—inner-sins of passion. (Ibid)

An *Olah* is "a freewill offering." It pardons 3 kinds of sins: (a) not doing positive mitzvot, (b) doing a negative mitzvah, and (c) thought-sins. It is sort of a "spiritual-laxative," an all-purpose cleanser. Other sacrifices are responses to specific incidents—this is a spontaneous offering—a kind of cure for the blahs, rather than the response to a particular moment of guilt over a given action.

[3]: For *Minhah*, think about the times of day. The *Minhah* service takes place during the afternoon. Also, remember that *Minhah* is the "meal" offering. Long ago, the main meal took place during the afternoon (lunch was then called dinner, whereas dinner is now the same as supper). For someone living in the desert, meals would consist of dairy products and "meal" (grains) mostly. If *Minhah* is an offering of flour (a type of meal) and oil, and meal would make up the main meal, that doesn't change the fact that I am being confusing and you should try figuring this out from what I've given you. **[C.J.]**

Minhah is the poor man's *Olah*. It was designed to be offered if you could not afford to offer an animal. Philo says that the grain replaces the blood. Just for the record, there were five different *minhah* recipies: plain baked, deep-molded and fried, shallow-molded and fried, ḥallah, and the wafer. By the way, the best guess is that the word *Minhah* actually means "gift" and that first this sacrifice was called "a gift", then *Minhah* offerings got identified with a time of day—afternoon. You are probably wrong about the grain/lunch connections, because while the *kohanim* got to eat some *Minhah* offerings, the bringer never did. **[GRIS]**

[4]: *Shlamim* is simple enough. *Shin, Lamed, Mem* are the root letters meaning peace (like Shalom). This is the peace offering. **[C.J.]**

This is the "Bar Mitzvah/Bat Mitzvah sacrifice. It is the offering which (a) just says "Thank You—Give Peace a Chance" and then (b) everyone gets to join the banquet, including God, the *kohanim*, and those bringing the offering. This is the sacrifice which is a big communal meal—with only the stuff that people wouldn't eat being "burnt up" for God. **[GRIS]**

[5]: *Hatat* is the sin offering. This I needed some help for, so I looked in a High Holidays Ma*h*zor. I was flipping through the pages when I noticed *Al Het*, a repentance prayer listing our sins. Each new line begins (V) *Al Het sheHatanu l' fanecha b....* This means (I'm trying my best to translate it myself): "For the sin we have sinned the sin before You of..." This is proof that the root *het, tet, alef* means sin. Hence, *Hatat* is an appropriate name for this offering. **[C.J.]**

Our big question is—what is the difference between the *Hatat* and the *Asham*? First we look at *Hatat*. This is the "whoops" offering... Officially, these are for unintentional sins, the ones we didn't know we were doing at the time—and only figured out were wrong later. The classic example is eating non-kosher food by mistake. The classic expansion: having "unkosher" feelings invade our heart. **[GRIS]**

[6]: *Asham*. This is the guilt offering, and again I looked at this *Mahzor* (I used *Mahzor Hadash, The New Mahzor*) as a reference. This time, I found what I had been looking for: the repentance prayer *Ashamnu*. This is the first word in another alphabetical list of sins. The first: *Ashamnu*. This book translates it to "We have trespassed". *Asham* is an offering made when someone trespasses into the area of doing evil; it is a guilt offering. **[C.J.]**

There are (once again) five kinds of *Asham* offering: theft, using Temple stuff for personal gain, misusing a female slave, breaking a Nazirite vow, and being a leper. They don't make my top five list, but this is what the Gemara says the Torah means. **[GRIS]**

[7]: When I answered the question "Why do you think these three animals were chosen?", here was the answer I came up with. They could either be characteristics of Jews or of God, whichever you like better. The ox symbolizes strength because of the work it has to do. Oxen would do work such as pulling carts and carrying loads. The ram symbolizes leadership. Its horns are used as the shofar which gathers people together at its call. The goat symbolizes giving because of the milk it gives.

The first midrash is okay. I would say that it shows God's flexibility for not making us hunt in the hills, but what's wrong with the fields? The second midrash is similar to my own. The difference is that this one symbolizes different acts of different people, whereas mine symbolizes the different characteristics of a Single Being. **[C.J.]**

Good stuff—say, "Goodnight C.J." **[GRIS]**

C.J. COMMENTS
Tzav continued from page 131

In that day "He shall turn the heart of the fathers to their children, and the heart of the children to their fathers, lest I come and smite the earth with a curse."

In my mind this means: The parents will teach their children, and the children will remember, and learn of their ancestors, and pray instead of sacrifice. That day they will be accepted again; that day we will earn our blessing. You will find the Haftarah for *Shabbat Ha-Gadol* on page one thousand five of the Hertz Bible.**[C.J.]**

Mazal Tov. Now duck 'cause we're going to throw candy. **[GRIS]**

C.J. COMMENTS
Shmini continued from page 135

Judaism. I studied and studied and studied the passage. Here are a collection of answers:

They did four things wrong: [1] they came close to God without permission, [2] they did the sacrifice wrong, [3] they brought kitchen fire into the sanctuary, and [4] they didn't communicate or cooperate. Some of these explanations suggest (in my mother's words when I climbed up to steal a cookie and fell and hurt myself) "God is punishing them." Some of them suggest that they did the pyrotechnics wrong and got burnt the way that kids do when they use fireworks in a unsafe way. **[Va-Yikra Rabbah 20]**

Suggests a holy accident. They were very holy children but got so carried away getting close to God in a special way that they got careless and mixed the incense wrong. **[Biur]**

Closeness to God takes discipline and control (or else you can get burned). From their death we are not to learn that our personal expressions are not what God wants, but rather to pay careful attention to the official rituals. **[Samson Raphael Hirsch]**

They were drunk from the celebrations. They got careless. They got themselves fried. **[Rashi]**

The are basically two explanations: (1) God was punishing them for doing something wrong. (2) They suffered the natural consequences of burning their incense in the wrong way. One way is a punishment, the other is an accident. The bottom line—as to which explanation is right—you mix your incense and you take your chances. **[GRIS]**

[2]: The translation of the text seems to imply that Nadav and Avihu went to make a Sacrifice While Intoxicated (SWI). God decided to kill them because it wasn't right for them to sacrifice when they had no idea what they were doing, weren't in control, and were therefore treating a holy thing with disrespect. I am able to see the comparison in the midrash, but some people might not like this one because of "political correctness." Maybe a different midrash would be better. **[C.J.]**

Back to Aharon, Nadav, and Abihu. All through the Torah we see people getting what they deserve, God getting even. One great example of this is when Lavan tricks Yaakov into marrying Leah instead of Rahel. Wasn't it Yaakov who had tricked his father, Yitzhak into giving him the birthright instead of Esau? So here God shows us that what goes around comes around. This has to do with Shmini because I think God was punishing Aharon for making the golden calf and betraying him in the wilderness. Aharon's punishment was the death of his sons. **[Dina Ackermann]**

Dina, your answer here really scares me. I don't want to think that God kills children because of something their parents have done in the past. That is cruel. That is unjust. That is not a God I want to worship or in whose image I want to be created. All of the other indications in this *sidrah* are that God has forgiven Aharon, that once again, God is allowing him to come close. If God was "fooling Aharon," setting a trap so that his sons would come close so that God could zap them in order to get revenge for last week's news, I would turn Buddhist at once. Traditionally, there are three possibilities: [1] God killed them because they broke the rules. [2] They got themselves killed by doing the sacrifice wrong. [3] God gifted them with an opportunity for *Kiddush ha-Shem*, coming close to God while teaching Israel an important lesson. They became a sacrifice—a closeness offering. Pick your poison. [GRIS]

[3]: The next section of the *parashah* deals with *kashrut*. I've heard that a famous rabbi (who was also a doctor) once said that pigs aren't healthy to eat, so it's good they're not kosher. Are any of the other non-kosher animals unhealthy to eat? Are there any other reasons why these animals shouldn't be eaten anyway? **[C.J.]**

What is the reason for keeping kosher? Is it for health? Or respect of living animals? **[Noah Cohen]**

The "kosher is healthy" thing misses the whole point. *Kashrut* is a spiritual lesson about discipline and knowing our place in the eco-system. Here is the piece I've found really interesting this year. ANY ISRAELITE WHO SLAUGHTERS AN OX OR A SHEEP OR A GOAT IN THE CAMP OR WHO SLAYS IT... OUTSIDE OF THE TENT OF MEETING AND DOES NOT BRING IT NEAR AS A OFFERING TO THE ETERNAL.... THAT PERSON HAS BLOODGUILT... AND HE SHALL BE CUT OFF... WHEN THEY WANT SOMETHING SLAUGHTERED...THEY ARE TO BRING THEM TO THE PRIEST AT THE TENT OF MEETING... [Lev. 17.3-

5]. The original idea that seems to be expressed here is that the only way that the Families-of-Israel were allowed to eat meat was when it was done in the context of worship. It seems to say "Go to a *kohein* to get a hamburger." That is to be contrasted with YOU MAY SLAUGHTER ANY OF YOUR CATTLE OR SHEEP AS I COMMANDED YOU... [DEUT. 12.15] AND YOU MAY EAT IN YOUR SETTLEMENTS, [DEUT. 12.21] which seems to say, "Anyone can kill and eat meat anywhere—as long as it follows the laws of *kashrut* and *shehitah* (the kosher kill). Rashi resolves the contradiction by saying that the first text—the one from Leviticus—only applies to animals which were already set aside to be sacrifices. I think that you are probably looking at a change in Jewish life as *kashrut* moved out of the Temple and became for everyone. [GRIS]

On the *kashrut* thing—It has nothing to do with health or respect for living animals (though these are two important lessons Judaism emphasizes)—it is spiritual purity. It is respect for God. Also, this is just one more thing that Jews have to separate them. During havdalah we say, "...Hamavdil bein kodesh le-hol, bein or le-hoshekh, bein Yisrael le-amim..." ("Blessed are you Lord our God, King of the universe,) Who separates between holy and profane, between light and darkness, between Israel and other nations..." Again with *kashrut* we separate meat and milk but on a greater level we separate ourselves from others and therefore become holier and closer to God. **[Dina Ackermann]**

I think the point you are making about *kashrut* and spiritual purity is a piece of true Torah. But, it doesn't deny the other truth of *kashrut*. The process of *shehita* (ritual slaughter) is clearly related to *Tzar l'Ba'alei Hayyim* (not being cruel to animals). *Kashrut* is clearly also about limiting hunting and limiting the pain that eating meat could cause. **[GRIS]**

That's it for SHMINI **[C.J.]**

C.J. COMMENTS
Tazria continued from page 139

Tazria continued from page 139

been 14 days for both, but the circumcision needed to take place on the eighth day. Shortening the period of isolation allows the mother to attend." [GRIS]

[2]: Does the *kohein* have to offer sacrifices in both circumstances, or does the *brit milah* automatically make her pure if she had a son? **[C.J.]**

The Torah makes it clear that the same sacrifice is offered in both cases—son or daughter. The fun part is that this is a sin offering. So you ask: "What is the sin in having a child—I thought this was a miracle"? Rabbi Simeon says this in *Niddah* 31b: "She offers a sin offering not for the act of intercourse which produced the child, not for the act of giving birth, but to apologize for anything rude she might have said during labor." It is like the Bill Cosby routine where he says, "In the middle of labor my wife stood up in the stirrups and said that my father wasn't married to my mother." [GRIS]

[3]: Why does the leper have to shave his head and does that include shaving his beard? If the leper is a woman, do the same rules apply? What exactly does the leper cover his mouth with? And if they cover their lips with anything, doesn't that make it a lot harder to shout "Unclean, Unclean?" Just another reason not to take modern medicine for granted. [C.J.]

The head shaving is part of the cleansing ritual, not part of the cure. It is the transition from the end of the leprosy back to society. The Talmud asks the same sort of question you do: "All his hair?" And then it answers, "Every bit of hair—everywhere (except for the eyebrows). *Sefer ha-Hinukh* says, "All hair is shaved, so that the end of the disease feels like a rebirth, and he or she is now as naked as a newborn." The covering of the lip, the Talmud suggests is clothing up to the lip. Imagine walking around with a turtle neck turned up and over your mouth. This is sort of a biblical surgical mask. [GRIS]

[4]: Comparing sins to leprosy makes sense. Once one starts sinning, it can be a downhill path from there. The consequences aren't good. If leprosy spreads, those consequences aren't good either. You could almost picture one who sins getting this disease as a way of showing them the paths they took. The midrash better explains my opinion. [C.J.]

More later, [C.J.]

C.J. COMMENTS
Metzora continued from page 143

MISHKAN; AND BEHOLD, MIRIAM WAS LEPROUS, SHE WAS WHITE AS SNOW:... AND AARON SAID UNTO MOSES, MY LORD, I BEG YOU, LAY NOT THE SIN UPON US, ...WE HAVE DONE FOOLISHLY.. LET HER NOT BE AS ONE DEAD, OF WHOM THE FLESH IS HALF EATEN WHEN SHE COMES OUT OF HER MOTHER'S WOMB. AND MOSES CRIED UNTO YHWH, SAYING, HEAL HER NOW, O GOD, I BEG YOU. AND YHWH SAID TO MOSES, IF HER FATHER HAD BUT SPIT IN HER FACE, SHOULD SHE NOT BE ASHAMED SEVEN DAYS? LET HER BE SHUT OUT FROM THE CAMP SEVEN DAYS, AND AFTER THAT LET HER BE RECEIVED IN AGAIN. AND MIRIAM WAS SHUT OUT FROM THE CAMP SEVEN DAYS: AND THE PEOPLE JOURNEYED NOT 'TIL MIRIAM WAS BROUGHT IN AGAIN. From this story, the rabbis conclude that *metzora* and *tzara'at* comes from "speaking against." And they conclude that isolation

C.J. COMMENTS
Be-Har continued from page 161

[2] I don't really understand the property rules. How can property go back to the family of the original owner? So, in the time of the *Mashiah*, people will get the lands of their ancestors in Israel? How will people know which properties belong to whom? [C.J.]

The Hebrew word for tie is TEYKU. It is an abreviation of the words *Tishbi Ya'aneh al ha-She-elot uT'Shuvot*. It means that when the Messiah comes, Elijah the Prophet will return ('cause he didn't die but went up to heaven alive in the pyrotechnic chariot miracle) and answer all the unanswered questions. Elijah will tell us who gets Boardwalk and who gets to build a hotel on Park Place. [GRIS]

[3] What's wrong with lending money for interest? It isn't always a nice thing to do, but if you know somebody has the money they owe you and they just don't give it back, it's something you should do. It's not fair that you should be taken! Are you not allowed to lend money BEGINNING with interest, or not allowed to add interest as well? [C.J.]

Think Willie Nelson, John Cougar Mellencamp and *Farm Aid*. If farmers borrow money at interest, they always lose the farm. Farming isn't a steady thing. There are always bad years. Money at interest really hurts farming families. It could cause them to lose their farms and then starve. Later, when Jews went into business, they needed to borrow money. You can't grow a trading business without investments and futures. (The Stock Exchange is all about betting against interest that business will grow.) The farming rule, no interest, didn't work anymore. Jews needed to borrow money in order to make money. Just like the *Prozbul*, they needed a work-around. They needed a way to get around the Torah without breaking it. This time the solution was called an *iska*. It was a fancy kind of partnership. While Jews couldn't lend money to another Jew at interest, they could pay themselves back at interest. The *iska* was a way that a partner could invest money in a partnership, the other partner could use it, and then pay the partnership back with interest. To borrow money you became a partner and paid yourself interest that your partner could take. The *iska* was created with a kind of protection which said that some of the loan was always to be forgiven.

The laws of *ribbit* (interest) are intense. You were allowed no benefit from a loan. The person who borrowed money was prevented from saying a more intense "good morning" than usual to the loaner, from lending the loaner his or her car, or doing any other favor or act which was considered a "benefit" from giving the loan. [GRIS]

[4] The text and the midrash say that making one who needs money pay interest is like enslaving them, which is

C.J. COMMENTS
Be-Har continued from page 197
Be-Har continued from page 197

very true. But if somebody is just borrowing money for something they don't "need," you should be allowed to charge interest after they don't pay you back for some time. I'm not sure if I'd do that in real life, but I'm sticking by that point. [C.J.]

See? Even a short *parashah* can bring out feeling! [C.J.] P.S. Any reason why idolatry is mentioned right after interest?

C.J. COMMENTS
Be-Hukkotai continued from page 165
Be-Hukkotai continued from page 165

posed to (which can often be a very nice blessing). If rain fell in the summer (I am referring to a large amount of rain) crops which had been growing would die, and the land would flood. When everything happens normally, the crops have already been harvested and people are ready when the rains come. [C.J.]

Remember, Israel has three growing seasons and three harvests. The rains come after the summer harvest and before the winter wheat crop. [GRIS]

C.J. COMMENTS
Be-Midbar continued from page 169
Be-Midbar continued from page 169

[4] It seems to me that there could be many explanations for why Moshe's sons are excluded. Here are some of mine:

1) Moshe was not married to a Jew, therefore, God counted the sons as belonging to his wife Tzippora (if a Jew marries a non-Jew, the mother's religion determines the child's religion).

2) The objects of discussion were the biological sons of Aharon, but Moshe acted as another paternal (fatherly) figure (My Two Dads). [C.J.]

You are wrong about the non-Jew thing. Moses' kids were circumcised and converted in the midrash back when they were infants. So, they were always Jewish (according to the midrash). Second, the notion of Jewish mother and not Jewish father, according to the Talmud, starts at Sinai. That is why Isaac, Jacob, Joseph, etc. are Jewish—'cause they each had a Jewish dad. Third, Moses' kids were at Sinai. Everyone who was at the giving of the Torah, and who said *"Na'aseh v'Nishmah,"* "I do" to God's wedding contract, became a Jew. At Mt. Sinai, every Jew became a "Jew-by-Choice." So you've

got to find another reason. They could have rejected Judaism and their father and fled with Yitro when he left. They could have just been ordinary kids. They could have been rejected by the rest of the Jews, just because they had a non-Jewish mother—we need midrash to answer this one—but we have a clear tradition that they are Jewish. [GRIS]

Hey, by the midrash, I was close. To dream the impossible dream... [C.J.]

C.J. COMMENTS
Naso continued from page 173
Naso continued from page 173

pretation of the text makes understanding it harder. But if you think of the chieftains as the heads of numbers, it may come to mind that they were the leaders of the population: those numbers. Going back to the midrash, the last line ("It is better for us to be beaten rather than for the rest of the people to suffer.") shows the ones who counted numbers also saving the numbers. Their children would become the chieftains of the tribes. That was a fun one. [C.J.]

C.J. COMMENTS
Be-Ha'alotekha continued from page 177
Be-Ha'alotekha continued from page 177

Yitro is the Big Kahuna of Midian. The other Yitro is a Baal T'shuvah (a Jew by choice.) Take the gematria of Yitro which is 606, add the 7 mitzvot of a Noahite, and Yitro comes out a 613—a kosher deal. Through Moses and through Mt. Sinai, this Yitro converts and then heads out to teach the truth of the One God to the masses. This is his mission, while Israel heads for the Promised Land. Pay your money. Take your chances. Choose. [GRIS]

[3] Now, I've got a lot dealing with Cushite/Tzippora/Moshe: First, Cushite means that the woman Moshe married was presumably from the land of Cush, an ancient land which was made of the modern countries of Sudan and Egypt. We know little about this land, but it is also mentioned as one of the lands owned by King Achashverosh in the Megillah. Even though as a woman from Cush she would be black, so would the Israelites, seeing as they had lived in Egypt so long. If they weren't "black" they were only shades lighter, therefore we can't really define Cushite as "black." Second, what happens to Tzippora? In a book I have they say she was often called a Cushite. Are they simply mentioning her? Is she dead? Did Moshe marry someone else while still married to her? What is it with Moshe marrying non-Jews?

Okay, this can be partially self-answered. Seeing as there is no "conversion" in the Torah, the only true Jew was Avraham. If all mothers determine the sons' religion, there are no "Jewish" men and no "Jewish" women for them to marry. Technically, they all marry non-Jews. But does this mean we aren't "True Jews." Help, I'm confusing myself! **[C.J.]**

All that in one question. And it is very convoluted. Think midrash and here are some answers.

[a] In one midrashic path, Moses moves out on his wife (because he can't lead the people and play favorites. She is alone. She acts like a widow. She dresses in black. Miriam is really angry for her. She yells at Moses. God gives her leprosy. Moses realizes she is right. He gets God to heal her. He goes back to his black wife. They live sort of happily ever after. And the text is safe.

[b] Path two: Wife and kids walk out with Yitro. Moses suffers the burden of leadership—and takes a new wife—an outsider. Miriam runs the same "How dare you?" routine and we go in and out of leprosy. Loose lips causes rashes…

[c] Just because conversion is not in the written Torah, doesn't mean it isn't there. Conversion is part of the Oral Law, therefore, buried in the Torah and revealed through Moses' oral teaching which later gets written down as the Talmud. Conversion is no problem—just snip and dip.

[d] Yes, you are still a Jew. (See the patrilineal/matrilineal shift at Mount Sinai comment above). You can't get out of that easily. **[GRIS]**

[4] The food the Israelites ate in Egypt was food for free, not "free food." They only remembered it as good food once they started getting sick of manna. They looked back on it as part of the "Good Ol' Days." At the time they had it, the taste was probably made worse by the moods of slaves. Think about this: Chocolate is good, but what if we had to eat it all the time? Some might say "Hey, I could do that!" but after a while, the chocolate wouldn't taste as good as it used to, when it was still a treat. People would complain that there was no more variety in their diets. This is the same situation. The Midrash does not focus on the same points as I do, but still has a meaningful lesson. **[C.J.]**

See you next time! In the words of you know who: "Ḥazak, Ḥazak, V'nitḤazek."

CJ' S LAST WORD

Truthfully, there is another book and a half to the Torah (the rest of BE-MIDBAR and DEVARIM). The idea of this book is not to give you extra work. It is not to give you homework (even if your teacher gives it that way). Torah Toons was made to guide you on the right path. From what you have learned in reading our text and following our conversation, try to interpret the rest of the Torah on your own.

Since the beginning of time, teaching was meant so that a person could learn to do things by oneself. Don't give the poor man the fish, give him the fishing pole. Here, we have given you the tools to learn. Now, maybe you can study Torah by yourself. And maybe, you will be able to learn about life.

You should also remember that there are always new things to learn in the Torah. For this reason, there is no real "end" to the Torah. Every year we begin again. Torah has no ending. It is the beginning.

I'm fine. I'm just about done writing "Homework Blues." I simply have to put it in order and write it down. I'd better go. Today we must party because on this day in 1960 *The Flintstones* premiered. **[C.J.]**

Well, without three-toed Fred, there would have been no *Torah Toons*. **[GRIS]**